"In these days when human wickedness has been manifested on such a vast scale it is consoling to read a story of human holiness, or rather of the superhuman holiness conferred by God on a faithful recipient. . . . His life from his conversion onward was a fulfilment, as perfect as is possible, short of complete sinlessness, of the twofold commandment of charity. This biography depicts Father Sullivan as the living victim of his love for God and for his poor and suffering neighbour.

"Both alive and after death he effected many cures. The admirable caution of his biographer leaves open the question whether these were miracles in the strict sense — i.e., beyond the capacity of natural causes — or simply answers to prayer in which God's instrument was wholly natural. Does it, we may ask, really matter? God's work is God's work, whatever its instrument. This is one of those biographies which must leave the reader with Jacob's words on his lips, 'Truly God is in this place.'"

FATHER JOHN SULLIVAN, S.J.

Father John Sullivan, S.J.

FATHER JOHN SULLIVAN, S.J.

By

FERGAL McGRATH, S.J.

With Illustrations

LONGMANS GREEN AND CO.

LONDON ◇ NEW YORK ◇ TORONTO

LONGMANS, GREEN AND CO.
55 FIFTH AVENUE, NEW YORK
221 EAST 20TH STREET, CHICAGO

LONGMANS, GREEN AND CO. LTD.
OF PATERNOSTER ROW
43, ALBERT DRIVE, LONDON, S.W. 19
17, CHITTARANJAN AVENUE, CALCUTTA
NICOL ROAD, BOMBAY
36A, MOUNT ROAD, MADRAS

LONGMANS, GREEN AND CO.
215 VICTORIA STREET, TORONTO

DE LICENTIA SUPERIORUM ORDINIS

Nihil obstat : REGINALDUS PHILLIPS, S.T.L.
Censor deputatus

Imprimatur : E. MORROGH BERNARD
Vic. Gen.

Westmonasterii, die 28a Junii 1941.

PRINTED IN THE UNITED STATES OF AMERICA

LIST OF ILLUSTRATIONS

Father John Sullivan, S.J. . . . *Frontispiece*

Lady Sullivan . . . . *Facing page* 16

The Sullivan Children about 1866 „ 16

John Sullivan about the age of Sixteen . . . . „ 17

John Sullivan as a Young Man . „ 17

PREFACE

THE writing of this Life was attended by peculiar difficulties. To begin with, as will appear abundantly throughout the work, Father Sullivan gave during his lifetime the least possible encouragement to a future biographer. He left practically no writings that reveal anything of his interior life. Many of his letters have been preserved, but they are, with few exceptions, brief and impersonal, valuable only as unconscious records of constant acts of charity. The matter of his sermons and exhortations was largely borrowed from the great spiritual writers, and, though when actually delivered they were alive with his own personality, they reveal little of him when written down. Again, Father Sullivan was seventy-one at the time of his death, and, for various reasons, it was not found possible to commence serious work on the Life until six years later. The large majority of those who knew him in youth were then dead, and not a few of his later intimates also.

The reader, therefore, must bear with patience the excuses frequently offered for the paucity or absence of information concerning certain periods of the Life. The author's task has seemed to him to resemble that of an archæological expert faced by the task of reconstructing the civilization of some ancient city from the fragments found in one of its long-buried refuse-heaps. If this comparison seems exaggerated, let it be considered what a wealth of matter would have been available if, for instance, Father Sullivan had left a diary of his stay in the monastery of Mount Athos, or if the Life had been undertaken when the memories of his sister and of such friends as Herbert Wilson, K.C., and Dr. Louis C. Purser were still available.

Perhaps the Providence of God has ordained that the Life of Father John Sullivan should be composed in this painful and unsatisfactory way, so that thereby stress might be laid on what was possibly his most striking virtue, contempt of self. With all its defects, the work is offered as a humble and sincere tribute to the memory of a man whom from boyhood the author learned to love and revere.

Further recollections of Father Sullivan, letters written by him, or details of favours alleged to have been granted through his intercession will be gladly received.

I am indebted to the courtesy of Messrs. Burns Oates & Washbourne for permission to quote from the Introduction contributed by Father Sullivan to *The Dilemma of John Haughton Steele*, by Father Joseph Darlington, S.J., and from an article by Abbot Hunter Blair, O.S.B., published in the *Dublin Review* for July, 1938.

DECLARATION

Conformably to the Decrees of Pope Urban VIII, the writer declares that in the following pages the words Saint, Miracle, etc., are employed in a purely historical sense, and without any intention whatever of anticipating the judgment of the Apostolic See.

CONTENTS

I. FORBEARS 1

II. FAMILY AND CHILDHOOD . . . 12

III. THE SCHOOLBOY 24

IV. THE UNDERGRADUATE . . . 33

V. THE YOUNG BARRISTER . . . 41

VI. CONVERSION AND VOCATION . . 63

VII. THE NOVICE 76

VIII. EARLY YEARS AS A JESUIT . . 84

IX. THE SCHOOLMASTER . . . 94

X. THE FRIEND OF THE AFFLICTED (I) . 118

XI. THE FRIEND OF THE AFFLICTED (II) 148

XII. THE ASCETIC 156

XIII. THE DIRECTOR (I) 164

XIV. THE DIRECTOR (II) 177

XV. INNER VISION 189

XVI. TEACHINGS (I) 199

XVII. TEACHINGS (II) 212

XVIII. THE SUPERIOR 234

XIX. THE END 246

XX. RETROSPECT 253

APPENDIX. FAVOURS AFTER DEATH . 264

CHAPTER I

FOREBEARS

JOHN SULLIVAN was a Dubliner born and bred, but his family on both sides came from Co. Cork. Social habits are sometimes oddly crystallized in the speech of a people, and the above statement, if made in recent times in almost any company in Dublin, would not fail to raise a laugh. There has sprung up in the new Ireland a humorous tradition, now almost as well-worn as that prevailing across the water about the thriftiness of the Aberdonians, that Cork men in large numbers are constantly coming to seek their fortunes in the metropolis. Cork men will tell you—and perhaps they are not far wrong—that the joke is a grudging tribute to the preponderance of brains in the South. Be that as it may, Dublin in every age has been the richer for this soft-toned inflow, and it certainly did not lose when, in the 'forties of the last century, Edward Sullivan, the future Lord Chancellor of Ireland and father of Father John Sullivan, left his native Mallow to commence in Dublin his legal career.

His father, Edward Sullivan, was a wealthy provision and wine merchant in the main street of Mallow. He was a Protestant, and it requires little knowledge of Irish history to be aware that this was a fact requiring some explanation in the case of a Cork Sullivan. There were, in point of fact, two very strange religious *causes célèbres* in the history of Edward Sullivan's family. It was the more recent of them that explained his protestantism, but it will be clearer to narrate the earlier event first.

For this incident, the main source is a series of articles in the *Journal of the Cork Historical and Archæological Society,* by Dr. Henry F. Twiss.[1] Dr. Twiss had drawn the matter for his articles from public records in the Co. Cork Record Tower Collection.[2] These documents were at one time in the Record Tower of Dublin Castle, but were transferred to the Four Courts, and perished in the fighting of 1922.

The date of the incident is 1749, and it may be recalled that at that time Mallow was at the height of its fame as a fashionable health resort. The medicinal properties of its springs had been discovered in 1724, and the town rapidly became a centre of gaiety. *Pue's Occurrences,* a Dublin bi-weekly journal, under the date 18th April 1738, has the following announcement:

"This is to give notice that there is a spacious Long Room at Mallow, near the City of Cork, lately built to

[1] Henry Fitzpatrick Twiss (formerly Berry), M.R.I.A., F.R.S.A.I., D.Litt., I.S.O. (1847–1932), was Assistant Deputy Keeper of the Public Records of Ireland from 1868 to his retirement in 1912. He was a well-known contributor to historical and archæological journals, and wrote a history of the Royal Dublin Society, which is a valuable guide to Irish economic problems in the eighteenth and nineteenth centuries.

He was the son of Dr. Parsons Berry, of Mallow, and, as will be seen later, was connected with the Sullivan family. He took his wife's name of Twiss on her inheriting her family property in Co. Tipperary.

The references to his articles are:

"The Kells and Philpotts in Mallow," Vol. XV, April–June, 1909.
"Mallow and some Mallow Men," Vol. XXIX, No. 130, July–December, 1924. Continued to Vol. XXXII, No. 137, January–June, 1928, inclusive.

[2] Carton 60, No. 256. *P.R.O.I.*

entertain the nobility and gentry, who are minded to divert themselves during the season of the Spaw: there will be Balls, Ridottos, musick meetings and all other diversions as are at Bath, Tunbridge, Scarborough, Aix-la-Chapelle and the German Spaw, etc., with good musick; and that Mr. Mort. Murphy, who has taken the Long Room, with other conveniences from Hon. Colonel Jephson, of Mallow, above mentioned, will take care to be provided with the best teas, coffee, chocolate and other things necessary, with good attendance, as also with some of the best Dublin newspapers twice a week.

"N.B.—The said Mr. Murphy will make a new Minuet for every Ball night, if required."

On July 17th, 1739, *Pue* quotes a "private letter from Mallow" to the effect that "Much gaiety is expected here in this season; a great deal of good company has arrived. There are Balls and Publick Breakfasts twice a week. The ladies and gentlemen dine together as at Scarborough; the ordinary 1*s.* a head: the publick breakfast fixed at 6*d.* and the Lodgings a crown a week each chamber."

As time went on, the recreative side of Mallow life tended to overshadow the therapeutic. There was a popular saying:

> "Whiskey mixed with Mallow Spa
> Makes the finest drink you ever saw"

and there seem to have been an ever larger number of the *habitués* of Mallow who ceased to bother about the mixing. Towards the end of the century the "Rakes of Mallow" were immortalized by "pleasant Ned Lysaght," a legal light of the Munster circuit. Lysaght was himself a Clareman but, by all accounts, was well able to compete in joviality with the Mallow associates whose exploits he celebrated.

> "Spending faster than it comes,
> Beating waiters, bailiffs, duns,
> Bacchus' true begotten sons,
> Live the rakes of Mallow."

In this gay, noisy Mallow of the middle of the eighteenth century, there lived a prosperous apothecary named Robert Philpot, who had a daughter Elizabeth. She had long been receiving the attentions of a young man named Randal Kell, son of Randal or Randolph Kell, a wealthy merchant also resident in Mallow. Robert Philpot had forbidden the marriage, and the young couple, who were both Protestants, conceived the extraordinary plan of going to a Catholic priest who was living in the town, Father John Everard, or Ilard, and asking him to marry them. More extraordinary still, Father Everard agreed to perform the ceremony, though no conceivable canonical grounds can be suggested to justify his action. On the night of Sunday, April 9th, 1749, Robert Philpot missed his daughter, and traced her to the house of a Mrs. Mary Brereton, where he found her with Randal Kell, whom she declared to be her lawful husband.

If Robert Philpot was the typical father of the eighteenth-century novel, it is a pity that his remarks about the Reverend Father Everard have not been recorded. For that matter, the comments of Father Everard's bishop would have been worth hearing. But further details of the extraordinary story are scanty. At the General Assizes held at King's Old Castle, Cork, on August 5th, 1751,[1] a presentment was made by the Grand Jury against Father Everard "in that he had celebrated Mass contrary to law and had married Randal Kell and Elizabeth Philpot, two protestants of the Church of Ireland as by law established." Informations were sworn by many witnesses, but, even in the documents available to Dr. Twiss, there was no further information about the case to be found.

However, it appears that Robert Philpot soon forgave his erring daughter, for on May 6th Randal Kell of Mallow and Belcher Pedder of Cork became sureties in a bond preparatory to the marriage of Randal Kell and Elizabeth Philpot. This marriage, according to the rites of the Church of Ireland, probably took place in the old church of Mallow, but there is no mention of it in the records. In his will, Randal Kell the elder mentions Elizabeth and Randal Kell and their children, Robert Philpott, Pedder, William, Mary and Ann.

Ann Kell married in 1777 John Lynch, and their daughter, Anne, by her second marriage, became the wife of Edward Sullivan.[2] Some information about the Lynch family is given in a note contributed by Canon J. F. Lynch to *Historical and Topographical Notes on Buttevant, Castletownroche, Doneraile, Mallow, and Places in their Vicinity*, collected by Colonel James Grove White (Vol. III, p. 156). The note is on the district of Gortnacross.

"1713 Gortnagross (sic) was demised to Edward Hawkins by Benjamin Lawton. In 1754 Edward Hawkins was succeeded by his son-in-law, John Lynch

[1] There is no explanation of why the case was not brought against Father Everard until over two years after the event.

[2] Her first husband was a purser in the Royal Navy, named John Surflen.

of Mallow, who had two sons; the elder, William, was my great-grandfather; the younger, John, was father of Robert Lynch of Mallow and of Anne Lynch, whose second husband was Edward Sullivan of Mallow, by whom his eldest son was the late Sir Edward Sullivan."

Some sixty years after the extraordinary marriage of Randal Kell and Elizabeth Philpot, there occurred in the town of Mallow an equally extraordinary funeral. Again, the only available record of this event is the series of articles of Dr. Twiss already alluded to, the relevant State Papers having perished in 1922.

The funeral was that of James Sullivan, father of Edward Sullivan, and grandfather of the Lord Chancellor. This James Sullivan had spent his life in the employment of the Jephson Norreys family, owners of Mallow Castle. According to local tradition, he had risen from comparatively humble origins, but eventually seems to have held some position of trust. Dr. Twiss describes him as a sub-agent, and some MSS. memoranda in the Ulster Office of Arms, Dublin Castle, state that, at the time of his death, he was steward to Sir Denham Jephson Norreys. He had been baptized and brought up a Catholic, but, on his marriage to a Protestant, Mary Fitzgerald, in 1782, he either formally became a Protestant, or at any rate allowed all his children to be brought up Protestants. His defection cost the Church dear, for in the twelve years between 1785 and 1797, he had twelve children, of whom ten survived. He was evidently in a position to give his family a good education. His second son, James Sullivan, M.D., attained eminence as a physician in Dublin, where he resided in Lower Gardiner Street. He married, in 1824, Hon. Eliza Maria Smythe, daughter of Lionel, fifth Viscount Strangford. She was a sister of the poet Lord, translator of Camoens, and friend of Byron, who knew him as "Hibernian Strangford." Edward, who was James Sullivan's eighth son, was a good classical scholar, and conducted the early classical education of his son Edward, the future Lord Chancellor. He was intended for the law, but circumstances led him to enter on a business career. Mary, the eldest daughter, married in 1806 Henry Berry of Mallow, and was the grandmother of Dr. H. F. Berry (afterwards Twiss), whose writings have been so largely drawn on for the history of the Sullivan family.

It is not improbable that James Sullivan's connection with the influential Protestant owners of Mallow Castle played a part in his change of religion. That it was not a conscientious conversion but due to some material motive, would seem to be indicated by the fact that on his deathbed, in January 1814, he was reconciled to the Church by his parish priest, Father Thomas Barry.

This Father Barry is a well-known figure in the history of Ireland at the close of the eighteenth century. His story is told by D. Owen Madden,[1] W. J. Fitzpatrick,[2] Dr. R. R. Madden[3] and many other historians. After the rising of 1798, the Royal Meath Militia were quartered on Mallow, and shortly before May 4th, 1798, some of them conspired with certain townsmen to blow up the Protestant Church when the Yeomanry would be at service there. Father Barry heard of the plot and informed the commander of the Yeomanry. For this service he received a pension of £100 a year

[1] *Revelations of Ireland*, Ch. 5, p. 130. [2] *The Sham Squire*, p. 324.
[3] *The United Irishmen, Their Lives and Times*, Vol. 1, p. 395.

from the Secret Service funds, and earned the sobriquet of "the Protestant priest."

His conduct on the death of James Sullivan, however, was militantly Catholic. Although, as has been said, the official records were destroyed in 1922, the index to them escaped, and it contains the following précis. (State Papers, Series 1. 1790–1831, Sub-heading "Catholic Clergy.") "Funeral, complaints of priests' conduct at, corpse carried away by a mob at Mallow, Mass said and harangue delivered at Cove churchyard, letter (3 and encl*res*) Revs. J. Kingston,[1] J. R. Cotter, T. G. Trench, date Jan.–Oct. 1814." (Carton 408. No. 1568.)

Dr. Twiss, who had access to the complete records, states that "In the State Paper collection, *P.R.O.I.*, are to be found informations sworn by Rev. John Rogerson Cotter, Curate and Rev. James Kingston,[1] V.G., under the heading "Riotous conduct at James Sullivan's funeral, 1814." The conduct of the priests was said to be in violation of the Statute 27, Geo. III, c. 15, against disturbing clergy in the discharge of their duty in church, and 21 and 22, Geo. III, c. 24, prohibiting Romish priests from performing divine offices in churches or churchyards."

The exact date of this ecclesiastical fracas is given by an entry in the parochial register of the old church of Mallow for January 19th, 1814, stating that James Sullivan was "buried in part. Priests interfered and finished the Service." As a result of his action, Father Barry lost his secret service pension. On the other hand,

[1] This appears to be a copyist's error, *The Almanack and Directory* for 1814 and 1815 gives among the list of Vicars-General, late Established Church of Ireland, the Rev. James Hingston, LL.D., Vicar-General of Cloyne.

though nothing is known on the point, it would be surprising if the title of "the Protestant priest" did not die a natural death.

As has been said already, Edward Sullivan, the eighth son of James Sullivan, devoted himself to business in the town of Mallow. Dr. Twiss says that he amassed a considerable fortune, which on his retirement, he expended in purchasing portions of the Castle Hyde estate near Fermoy, and property in West Cork, when in 1853 they were sold in the Incumbered Estates Court. Whether he ever lived on these estates is not known, but in 1861, having retired from business, he went to live in Dublin at No. 4 Regina Terrace, Raglan Road (afterwards No. 11 Raglan Road). He remained there until shortly before his death in 1867, but there is reason to think that he actually died in No. 32 Fitzwilliam Place, the residence of his son Edward, then Solicitor-General.

The *Dictionary of National Biography* makes the interesting but unsupported statement that Edward Sullivan was a friend of Thomas Moore. In Moore's Diary[1] two Sullivans are mentioned. The first "Mr. Sullivan" is referred to on a couple of occasions in the entries dealing with a visit of Moore to Paris in June 1820. The references are casual, but imply that this Sullivan was a friend and travelling companion of the poet. Beyond this, nothing is known of him.

The second Sullivan is mentioned in August 1823, when Moore had come over to Ireland with Lord Lansdowne to make a tour of the country.

"Aug. 4th. After breakfasting with Kate and John,

[1] *Memoirs, Journal and Correspondence of Thomas Moore,* edited by the Right Honourable Lord John Russell, M.P., 1853.

set off in the steamboat[1] for Cork. . . . An intelligent young man aboard the steamboat, who went also up the Carrigaline river with us yesterday, on my mentioning my intention of setting off for Beecher's[2] to-day, said he was going to Mallow too, and would, if I chose, secure a place for me in the coach when he took his own. . . . Walked a little about Cork; visit from the French Consul. Off in a sort of diligence to Mallow at half-past-two; went outside with my boat friend, whose name I find to be Sullivan."

It seems highly probable that this second Sullivan referred to by Moore was Edward. He was certainly living in Mallow at that date, his son Edward, the future Lord Chancellor, having been born there in the preceding year.

On August 6th, two days after his meeting with Edward Sullivan, Tom Moore visited Lohort Castle, the residence of Lord Arden, and met with a Rev. Mr. Cotter, who appears to have been a first cousin of the Rev. John Rogerson Cotter who, in 1814, had sworn informations against Father Barry on the occasion of the burial of Edward Sullivan's father.[3] The interview that followed is too entertaining to be passed over.

"I was introduced to Mr. Cotter, the clergyman of the place, who has invented a new musical instrument which he calls the Basso Hibernicon, of the *serpent* family. Walked over to his house with him to hear it; a dreary spot called Castlemagner from a ruin (named after one

[1] From Cove.

[2] Later passages refer to Rev. Nicholas Beecher, of Ballygiblin.

[3] The Rev. John Rogerson Cotter was the son of Sir James Laurence Cotter, of Rockforest, Mallow. The Rev. Joseph Rogerson Cotter, Vicar of Castlemagner, 1816–1834, was the son of the Rev. G. S. Cotter, Rector of Ightermurragh, a brother of Sir James Laurence Cotter. (Brady's *Records*.)

of Cromwell's generals) which stands on a bank above the stream. . . . The parson's own house, a waste and ruinous concern; and the embrasure in the hall door, to fire through, speaking volumes for the comfort of his neighbourhood. Had his wife down to accompany the display of his Basso, upon a wretched little old pianoforte. The instrument very sweet and powerful, and will be, I have no doubt, an acquisition to bands and orchestras; it is seventeen feet long. Told me he took it over to London, and played on it before the officers of the First Life Guards, taking the precaution of covering it with cambric muslin lest the invention should be borrowed. What a treat for Francis Conyngham etc.! A parson from the Co. Cork with his huge Hibernicon wrapped up in cambric muslin."

Though several more pages are devoted to the poet's experiences in Mallow, there is no further mention of the intelligent young man named Sullivan. It is, however, possible, as the *Dictionary of National Biography* suggests, that this chance meeting ripened into friendship.

CHAPTER II

FAMILY AND CHILDHOOD

EDWARD and Anne Sullivan had four children, Edward, born in 1822, James born in 1824, who died when a boy of thirteen, Anne born in 1826, who was married to Arthur Stanley Jackson, Q.C., and William, born in 1828, who became a solicitor, and was Clerk of the Records in the Supreme Court, Dublin. According to Dr. Twiss, Edward, the future Lord Chancellor, was born in the house which is now No. 130 Main Street, Mallow, a quaint old house with a projecting bow window, standing on the west of the entrance gate to the church grounds. He was educated at the endowed school at Midleton, which had numbered amongst its pupils John Philpot Curran and Barry Yelverton. In 1839 he entered Trinity College, where in 1843 he obtained First Classical Scholarship and graduated in 1845. He won the gold medal of the College Historical Society, of which he was auditor in 1845.

In 1848 he was called to the Irish Bar and in 1858 took silk. In tracing his career in Dublin, one interesting proof of his shrewd business sense comes to light. His first permanent address was No. 41 Eccles Street, where he lived from 1851 to 1861. For the first two years he and his brother, William Sullivan, Solicitor, were, according to *Thom's Directory*, the sole occupiers of the house. In 1854 two other solicitors, Edward Farmer and John Moriarity, shared that address and in 1855 still another legal luminary joined the band, in the person of Robert Mayne, Solicitor. One cannot help guessing that it was not sheer philanthropy that led the future Chancellor to offer the hospitality of his roof to these satellites. Farmer left the little band in 1856, Mayne and Moriarity disappeared in 1857, and from that year until 1861 the Sullivans had the house to themselves. It may be noted that Isaac Butt lived near them in No. 64, and that in his house was the organ played at the first performance of *The Messiah*, which took place at the Fishamble Street Theatre in Dublin in 1741.

Edward Sullivan's rise to the top of his profession was remarkable. It must be recalled, too, that it was a period of great brilliancy at the Irish Bar. Amongst his contemporaries were Francis McDonagh, O'Connell's counsel in 1844, Isaac Butt, Serjeant Armstrong, Jonathan Christian, Lord O'Hagan, John Naish, Baron Dowse, and Chief Baron Palles. In 1860 Sullivan became Third Serjeant, in 1861 Bencher of the King's Inns and Second Sergeant, in 1865 Solicitor-General, in 1868 Attorney-General, and later in the same year Master of the Rolls, which position he retained until his elevation to the Lord Chancellorship in 1883. In 1881 he received a baronetcy.

He is recalled as an able and firm judge, though never a very profound lawyer, rather a terror to those practising before him, especially solicitors. The *Dictionary of National Biography* gives as his outstanding characteristics his well-stored mind, his readiness, tenacity and eloquence. On his death in 1885 Chief Baron Palles spoke of him as "the Bayard of the Bar."

He was a Liberal in politics, and was returned to Parliament for his native Mallow in 1865 and 1868, when his appointments as Solicitor-General and Attorney-General forced him to seek a seat. In *Studies*, for September 1917, Father George O'Neill, S.J. published a number of extracts from an autobiographical sketch by Canon Sheehan entitled "The Moonlight of Memory." This sketch was afterwards printed in full by Dr. Twiss, and published with a collection of his articles on Mallow in 1928. Canon Sheehan, who was then a boy in his 'teens, recalls Mr. Serjeant Sullivan's election campaigns: ". . . the elections were hotly contested; and party feeling ran very high. He was a good popular speaker; and he had some clever tricks in catching the popular imagination. The ballad-singers sang:

> "Hurrah for Sullivan. He's the man
> That will chase the fox through Duhallow
> He's now come forth to lead the Van—
> He's one of the Rakes of Mallow!"

Canon Sheehan adds a detail that recalls vividly the depths to which Parliamentary elections had sunk before the Reform Bills: "Small boys wrote orders (unlimited) for porter on copy-book leaves, which orders were honoured by every publican."

Sir Edward Sullivan took a prominent part in many of the leading political and legal issues of his day. As Solicitor-General he appeared for the Crown in the trials of the Fenians in Cork in '67, and had the name "Scorpion Sullivan" hissed after him in the streets. He supported ardently Gladstone's campaign for Disestablishment, and Morley attributes largely to his guidance and influence the Irish Land Act of 1870. It was mainly at his instance that the step was taken in 1881 of arresting Parnell, and during Lord Spencer's second vice-royalty, he was the mainspring of the Government in suppressing the Invincibles. R. Barry O'Brien, in his *Dublin Castle and the Irish People*, says of Sullivan: "No person exercised more authority in the Administration of Ireland, in his day, than this able lawyer."

He was a man of considerable learning, and was familiar with German, French, Italian and Spanish literature. At his death he had a very valuable library, part of which, sold in 1890, realized £11,000. He published a number of volumes of essays, written in a curiously combative, yet effective style, dealing with an amazing variety of subjects, from military reform to the proper use of farmyard manure.

No writer who deals with his career makes any reference to a breach with Gladstone. It is curious, therefore, to find in what appears to be his last volume of essays, *Stray Shots*, published in 1884, a series of violent attacks on his former leader. The book begins with an Introduction, which is a kind of political and economic profession of faith, and contains the following articles:

"I believe that Gladstoneism is the national enemy:

"I believe that Gladstoneism has made the Repeal of the Irish Union inevitable:

"That it has ruined Egypt:

"That it has unsettled India:

"That it has fanned class antipathies to a heat never before seen in this country:

"That it has everywhere brought the honour of England into contempt:

"That it is a policy of 'cant and re-cant':

"That it will ruin the Empire:"

Many of the succeeding essays develop these theses. It is remarkable that a number of the other articles of this creed have a surprisingly modern sound, thus, "I am in favour of female suffrage," and "I believe that the distribution of wealth is of more importance than its accumulation."

The Chancellor was a small man, though powerfully built and vigorous in his demeanour. At one of his election meetings in Mallow, when he was addressing his constituents, Christopher Wallis, a solicitor, a large and powerful man, raised him up in his arms and exclaimed, "*Multum in Parvo.*" In the days when he was Serjeant-at-Law, this smallness of stature earned him the name of "The Little Serjeant" in contradistinction to "The Big Serjeant," Serjeant Richard Armstrong, a Co. Armagh man, who at one time was a M.P. for Sligo borough.

In 1850, when he had been practising at the Bar for only two years, Edward Sullivan married Elizabeth Josephine Baily, the eldest daughter of Robert Baily, a wealthy land agent and property owner, living at Ringview, Passage West, Co. Cork. The Bailys were Catholics, and the future Lady Sullivan's only brother, Robert Francis, was a man of deep religious feeling and a great friend of Father Mathew, the apostle of temperance. She had three sisters, of whom the eldest, Margaret, became the wife of John Francis Maguire, the well-known leader of the industrial revival of Cork, a Member of Parliament, and founder of the *Cork Examiner*.

Lady Sullivan

The Sullivan Children about 1866
In front from left: Edward, John, William
Behind: Robert and Annie

John Sullivan about the age of Sixteen

John Sullivan as a Young Man

Edward and Bessie Sullivan had five children, of whom John was the youngest. As was common in the case of mixed marriages before the *Ne Temere* decree, it had been agreed that, in the event of there being a family, the boys should be brought up Protestants and the girls Catholics. The eldest child was the only daughter, Annie, who was born in 1851. Annie Sullivan inherited the sincerely religious and charitable character of her mother. She was a prominent member of the ladies' sodality at the convent of the Sacred Heart, Lower Leeson Street, Dublin, from 1886 almost up to her death. She devoted much time to charitable work, conducted a Registry Office for domestic servants (a work which in those days had a large element of philanthropy in it), and, in conjunction with other members of the sodality, started the first scheme known in Dublin for providing poor children with fresh-air holidays. Annie Sullivan was greatly attached to her youngest brother, and her name will recur frequently in the history of his conversion. She died in 1918.

The eldest son, Edward, afterwards Sir Edward, who was born in 1852, was called to both the Irish and English Bars, but devoted his life to literature and a remarkable hobby, the study and practice of book binding. He was regarded as one of the greatest authorities of his day on the subject. A work of his which is of particular value in tracing the history of art in Ireland is the collection of rubbings which he made of the bindings of the Parliamentary records in the Four Courts, Dublin. These records perished when the Four Courts was burnt during the fighting of 1922. They were MS. journals of both houses of the Irish Parliament from 1613–1800. From 1707 on, they were triumphs of the bookbinder's art, of great size, about twenty-one inches tall, full-bound in crimson morocco with vellum inlays and green title-pieces. A few reproductions, on a very small scale, were published by Sir Edward Sullivan in art periodicals, and he made a complete set of rubbings, which were sold at Sotheby's in 1926 and are now in the National Museum, Dublin.

The loss of the originals would have been less grievous had it been possible for Sir Edward to carry out a project of publishing fifty large-scale plates of these splendid books, probably the most majestic series of bindings in the world. A prospectus was issued by Quaritch in 1905, accompanied by a superb reproduction in gold and colours of the *Commons Journal* for 1747, but support was lacking and the book was never published (though recorded by Wolfgang Meyer in his *Bibliographie der Buchbindereiliteratur*).[1]

Sir Edward also published a study of the *Book of Kells*, with twenty-four magnificent coloured reproductions of its pages, and a variety of other works of a somewhat dilettante type, including a translation into English prose of the first book of the *Divina Commedia*, and an edition of the *Memoirs* of Buck Whaley, that fantastic figure of eighteenth-century Dublin.

Specimens of Sir Edward Sullivan's own work as a bookbinder are treasured by connoisseurs, and there are some of them preserved in the National Museum, Dublin.

The second brother, Robert, born in 1853, met with

[1] For the details of Sir Edward Sullivan's work on the Irish Parliamentary Records, I am indebted to Mr. Colm O'Lochlainn, of the Three Candles Press, Dublin, and to Mr. G. D. Hobson, Director of Messrs Sotheby's.

a tragic end at an early age. His death will be described later.

The third brother, William, was born in 1860, and succeeded to the baronetcy on the death of his brother, Sir Edward, in 1928. He held for a time a commission in the Royal Inniskilling Fusiliers, was later called to the Irish Bar, and acted as Resident Magistrate in various parts of the country. His first wife, who died in 1934, was the daughter of Baron Dowse, a well-known legal figure at the end of the last century. Sir William was deeply devoted to his youngest brother, John, and was present at his death-bed, surviving him by only four years.

Just three months before the birth of his youngest son, Serjeant Sullivan had gained one of his most brilliant victories in the first trial of the famous Yelverton case. For some reason or other, legal encounters of the present day seldom take on the dramatic aspects of the great trials of the last century. The Yelverton trial presented all the traditional ingredients of drama, a young and beautiful plaintiff, formerly a Sister of Charity in the Crimean hospitals, a dashing young artillery officer, heir to a peerage, as defendant, the romance of a secret marriage, the pleasant spectacle of injured innocence seeking the paternal protection of the majesty of the law. The issue was the validity of a Catholic marriage solemnized between the Honourable Major Yelverton, a Protestant, heir of Viscount Avonmore, and the Catholic Miss Theresa Longworth, the daughter of a prosperous silk manufacturer in Manchester. For his own reasons, the Honourable Major wished to repudiate the sacred contract, but in the witness-box, before a packed and excited court, he had to submit to a castigation from the Little Serjeant as severe as any ever administered in a court of law. Beginning with the famous question, "Major Yelverton, did you ever love Theresa Longworth?" the Serjeant dragged the witness through every phrase of the marriage service, "for better, for worse, for richer, for poorer," and then made him acknowledge that, if he were to win his case, it must be by proving that his every word, uttered before the altar, had been a cruel lie.

As a result, the Dublin jury gave an unhesitating verdict for Miss Longworth. It was a great triumph for the Little Serjeant. The case, however, was reopened in Scotland and finally carried to the House of Lords, who decided for Major Yelverton, and the unhappy Miss Longworth lapsed into obscurity.

It was on May 8th, 1861, when the echoes of the Yelverton case had hardly died away, that John Sullivan, the youngest of the family, was born at No. 41 Eccles Street. In accordance with the agreement made between his parents, he was baptized on July 15th in St. George's Protestant Church, George's Place, which adjoins Eccles Street. The late Mother Dunne, of the Sacred Heart Convent, Armagh, whose family was united with that of the Sullivans by the closest bonds of friendship, remembered how she saw Lady Sullivan weeping after the birth of John, wishing that God had sent her a girl instead, whom she would have been able to bring up in the Catholic faith.

Lady Sullivan had a much-valued companion, Miss Eliza O'Neill, who used to recall that John received private baptism shortly after his birth, owing to his delicacy. Possibly the ceremony on July 15th was an iteration of the sacrament, or it may have been the private baptism alluded to, in the sense that few were present. In this connection it may be of some interest to note that the nurse who had charge of John's brother, William, as a baby, disclosed many years later that she had baptized him surreptitiously. It is well-known that such a zealous, though irregular procedure was not at all uncommon amongst the older generation of Catholic nurses in Irish Protestant families, their affection for their heretical little charges prompting them to run no risks about their eternal salvation.

The part of Dublin around Mountjoy Square, which included Eccles Street, had long been the Mayfair of Dublin. But already in the 'sixties, the city's centre of gentility had begun to shift southwards. In the year of John's birth, the Sullivan family moved to No. 30 Fitzwilliam Place, which had only just been built, and in 1863 they transferred to No. 32. Sir Edward died in this house in 1885, and Lady Sullivan in 1898. As far as can be ascertained, John Sullivan lived there, except when away studying or travelling, until he entered the Society of Jesus in 1900. His brother, the second Sir Edward, certainly occupied the house after his father's death, at first with his mother and sister, and then with his sister alone, until 1910.

We have only a few fragmentary recollections of John Sullivan's childhood. Mother Dunne recalled playing with the Sullivan children in Fitzwilliam Square, and how great a joy it was to her, then a little girl of about nine, when the nurse would entrust her with the perambulator of little John, who was a most winning child, always content and smiling.

The late Mother Stanislaus Joseph, of the Mercy Convent, Baggot Street, Dublin, whose name will occur again in this narrative, remembered hearing from his sister, how, as a very small boy, John used to be brought down to the dining-room for dessert, and how his first remark on entering the room always was, "I want my twaret (claret)." This reminiscence will be read with amusement by those who knew Father John in later years as a teetotaller of the most uncompromising type.

A relative of Father Sullivan heard from two Little Sisters of the Poor who visited her, the following incident which gives another glimpse of his childhood. The date when it occurred cannot be fixed, except that it was prior to 1924, nor could the Sisters who related it be traced, but there are reasonable grounds for thinking it to be authentic.

The Little Sisters have at Kilmainham, in the suburbs of Dublin, a well-known home for aged men and women, St. Patrick's House. An old woman died there who had been an inmate for many years, and on the morning of the funeral, the Sisters saw a very shabbily-dressed priest coming into the Church and kneeling down at the Mass. They were very curious to know who he was and afterwards asked his name. He told them that he was Father John Sullivan, and that the old woman had been his nurse when he was a child. He added that, when taking him out for a walk, she always brought him into a Catholic Church to say a prayer, and that this had no doubt played a part in his conversion.

There is preserved at Clongowes Wood College a curious relic of Father Sullivan's childhood, a little bracelet, which one would at first sight take to be crochet-work made with light brown silk. One end terminates in a cluster of artificial berries made out of the same material. Actually the bracelet was made from John Sullivan's hair when his progress towards man's estate was marked by the cutting off of his ringlets. It was made in Paris for Lady Sullivan, and given many years later by Annie Sullivan as a keepsake to Mother Stanislaus Joseph. I have never seen mentioned elsewhere this curious method of preserving a baby's hair, and it would be interesting to know if it were a recognized Victorian custom. Possibly it was peculiar to France.

CHAPTER III

THE SCHOOLBOY

IN 1873 John Sullivan entered Portora Royal School, Enniskillen, where his brothers had all been educated. He remained at Portora for six years, and gave ample proof of more than usual ability. There is in the museum library at Clongowes College a set of his school prize-books and medals, and it is noteworthy that in 1875, 1876 and 1877 he was awarded prizes for Holy Scripture. As might be expected, there are many prizes for Classics. All during his life Father Sullivan preserved a taste for the Classical authors, especially the Latins. In the Senior Grade examination of the Intermediate Education Board in 1879 he came third in Greek, and had high, though not remarkable marks in Latin. Many years afterwards, when Father Sullivan was at Clongowes, one of the community brought down the old Results Book to recreation, and jokingly read out these marks. Father John rose and left the room, and it was one of the rare occasions in his life when he was seen to be thoroughly put out. Those who knew him will have no doubt that this was due not to affectation, but to a genuine dislike of hearing anything said to his credit.

It is only to be expected that, after a lapse of sixty-seven years, but a handful of John Sullivan's contemporaries at Portora still survive, and that only scanty memories of his schooldays can be recalled. The headmaster of Portora at the time was the well-known Dr. William Steele, whose son, John Haughton Steele, was to enter the Catholic Church in 1910, after a lifetime of devoted work as a clergyman of the Church of Ireland. A younger son of Dr. Steele, Rev. William B. Steele, now living near Portora, entered the school just as John was leaving, and recalled him as "a very quiet, gentle-mannered boy and a favourite of my mother and her sister, Miss Haughton." Rev. Canon C. M. Stack, of Carrickmacross, added these details:

"I entered Portora in August 1878, and was consequently only a schoolfellow of John Sullivan for a year, until October 1879. He was at the top and myself at the bottom of the school, and there was little acquaintance or association between us. However, my recollection of him is that he was tall, with a good, light figure and fair hair—I should say a handsome boy.

"I remember that in October 1878 when the boys who were his seniors entered Trinity College, he was made monitor of the Junior Dormitory, and introduced a more severe discipline than his predecessor. I was not in this dormitory, but I got a pretty severe thrashing, well deserved, from him for 'cheek.' He was a quiet, studious fellow and popular with the seniors."

John Sullivan was a man of sincere loyalties, and, in after life, he always spoke of his old school with esteem and affection. In 1933, the Life of Father Steele was published under the title *The Dilemma of John Haughton Steele*, by Father Joseph Darlington, S.J., himself a convert clergyman. Father Sullivan contributed a Preface, which must have been written very shortly before his death. It may be quoted fittingly here, almost in its entirety, as it gives some interesting glimpses of his schooldays.[1]

"The youngest of four brothers, all educated at Portora Royal School, and where I myself spent almost six years, when John Steele's father was headmaster, and afterwards a resident student in Trinity College, Dublin, for over four years, I was intimately acquainted with most of the scenes and persons mentioned in this biography, and so I have been asked to write a preface.

"At the extreme end of the grounds of Portora, where the path that runs along the narrow Channel of Lough Erne, at some elevation, comes to an abrupt termination, stands the ruin of an old plantation castle, overlooking the lake. At the foot of this castle was the place of departure for the boats carrying the dead to their last resting-place in the holy island of Devenish, a little lower down in the Lough.

"As all were not privileged to accompany the dead on their last voyage, scenes of weeping and wailing were frequently witnessed there, hence the name Portora, 'the Harbour of Tears,' or 'Tearful Bank.'

> "Stabant orantes primi transmittere cursum,
> Tendebantque manus ripae ulterioris amore,"
>
> *Aeneid* VI, 313–314.

The Rev. E. Hogan, S.J., in his work, *Onomasticon Goedelicum*, suggests a derivation that would mean 'The bank of the creek of the seagull,' but 'The Harbour of Tears' was the derivation the writer of this preface heard as a boy in Portora.

"Into this 'Harbour of Tears' he came, bathed in

[1] Amongst Father Sullivan's papers was found a typescript of this preface differing somewhat from the published version. A few paragraphs from this have been included, as adding some interesting details.

tears, as a boy of eleven years, in the January of 1873, but it was with more plentiful tears he left it in the October of 1879. . . .

"There were many reasons for this attachment to Portora. The boys enjoyed much liberty in the midst of beautiful scenery. Especially attractive and never to be forgotten were the various excursions on the waters of Lough Erne. The school possessed several excellent four-oared boats, and sometimes the boys could remain out the whole day, encamping on one of the many beautifully wooded islands of the Upper or Southern Lough, where they made a fire and cooked their meals. Excursions on the Lower or Northern Lough were not allowed, as being too dangerous, but report told of wonderful rocky islands covered with wild birds' eggs, notably Gull Island, on which one could not set foot without walking on some kind of gulls' eggs.

"But there was another attraction nearer home, the noble person of the headmaster, Dr. William Steele, father of the subject of this biography. He was a great Christian divine, an excellent administrator, just and fearless in his dealings, an admirable teacher of many subjects, but especially of the Greek and Latin languages. To his inspiration many a distinguished scholar in Trinity College, Dublin, owed his great love and appreciation of the Classics. Whenever he came among the boys, which was frequently, his approach was heralded by the vigorous shaking of a large bunch of keys, which he held in outstretched hand, so that all had timely warning of the approach of the headmaster. He was almost always present at the boys' dinner, which he himself carved.

"On Sunday mornings, Dr. Steele used to take the

boys of the highest class in the Library, where he expounded to them the Epistle of the Sunday. I can never forget his masterful exposition of the famous Epistle of the Sunday taken from the Second Chapter of St. Paul's Epistle to the Philippians. 'For let this mind be in you, which was also in Christ Jesus; Who being in the form of God thought it not robbery to be equal with God; but emptied Himself, etc.' He had the Greek Testament before him, and I well remember how he dwelt on what he called the remarkable expression τὸ εἶναι ἶσα θεῷ, 'the being equal with God,' and on the phrase ἑαυτὸν εκένωσε, 'He emptied Himself' and especially the phrase ἁρπαγμὸν, which he translated 'a thing to be clutched at.'

"In my first year at Portora, John Steele was appointed curate-in-charge of his father's benefice of Devenish, close by, where he remained for nine years, so that I saw him frequently, heard him preach to us boys, and was examined by him in one of our most important examinations.

"Dr. Steele, on his appointment, at once opened the classes of Portora to the sons of Catholic parents, and in my own class there were several Catholic day boys, and one of these was first in the class in Latin and Greek. John Steele tells in his autobiography how amongst the Catholic boys there came a very talented young mathematician, who afterwards became a distinguished professor at Maynooth.[1] Dr. Steele, he tells

[1] This would appear to have been John O'Doherty, whose father was Head Constable of the Royal Irish Constabulary in Enniskillen. He was a brilliant mathematician, was certainly at Portora as a boy, and is recalled to have been a great favourite of Dr. Steele. He matriculated in Maynooth in 1874 as a Second Divinity student, having probably done his previous studies at St. Macartan's seminary, Monaghan. As well as being a mathematician, he was apparently an excellent theolo-

us, taught this young student almost entirely himself, and always regarded his success with great satisfaction.

"But his best scholar was his own eldest son Frederick, John's brother; shortly after obtaining first place at the October Entrance Examination in T.C.D. in 1866, he was drowned in Lough Erne near Devenish Island. His sad death excited much sympathy, which showed itself in the institution at Portora, in 1868, of the Frederick Steele Memorial Prize, for Latin and Greek Prose composition and verse. The prize consisted of a large silver medal and twelve sovereigns in gold.[1]

"I write so much here of Dr. Steele, because the unworldly and heroic act at the close of John's life was largely due to his father's noble virtues implanted in him, which in due course enabled the son, like Abraham, when called to leave home and kindred for conscience' sake, as we shall see, 'obey to go out, . . . not knowing whither he went.'

"John inherited also the piety of his mother, a cousin of the Rev. Samuel Haughton, S.F.T.C.D. She taught him to regard St. Patrick as the founder of his and her religion. From childhood she turned his mind towards the Christian priesthood, as she understood the term. 'My mother,' he used to say in later years, 'brought me up to be a priest as St. Patrick was, and I can never be anything less than that.'

"One of the most distinguished pupils of Dr. Steele

---

gian, as the prize lists at Maynooth show. Immediately after his ordination, he was appointed professor, not at Maynooth, but at St. Macartan's, and died three or four years afterwards. His three brothers were also priests, and were all Canons of the diocesan chapter of Clogher, whilst his only sister was a nun in the Convent of Mercy, Ardee.

[1] This prize was won by John Sullivan himself in 1879. The medal, which bears a fine head in relief of Frederick Steele, is preserved in the Clongowes Museum.

was the late Dr. Louis Claude Purser, for some years Vice-Provost of Trinity College, and at the time of his death President of the Old Portora Union.

"In a letter to me just six months before his death on Easter Sunday, March 27th, 1932, he alludes to Portora with great affection and to the family of Dr. Steele: incidentally he adds that of John he knew nothing except of his death. Hence it was, that a few days before his death, I put into the hands of Dr. Purser, at his residence, Waterloo Road, the life of John Haughton Steele, as this account appeared in the *Irish Monthly* ten years ago. He was delighted to have it, and promised to read it. I was to see him in the following week. Is it too much to hope that probably the last, or one of the last books that Dr. Purser read, before going into eternity, was this very life of the second son of Dr. Steele?

"In the same letter Dr. Purser wrote: 'I often thought of you, but did not know clearly about yourself, except I heard you had joined the Jesuit Order.' And he continues: 'There is no question that you are happy and with the very purest form of happiness: you are to be envied in attaining to the happiness that is laid up in heaven.'

"This present biography tells of the heroic sacrifice made by John Steele and how he attained to 'the Treasure laid up in Heaven' by his own unassisted efforts. Dom Bede Camm, O.S.B., writing of his Reception, says: 'I never saw in my life a more wonderful conversion.' . . .

"This life of ours has been called a 'Valley of Tears,' and so we must expect at times the tears will flow—and even sometimes flow plentifully—but leaving this life we leave all our tears behind us. In Heaven, thank God, there are no tears.

"So leaving the shores of Portora on his last voyage for interment in his beloved Island of Devenish, we can well believe that John Steele had left all his tears behind in that 'Harbour of Tears,' and so he now rests in peace under the shadow of St. Mary and under the protection of St. Molaise."

During the course of John Sullivan's schooldays at Portora, there occurred the tragic death of his second brother, Robert. The Sullivans had, in addition to their town house at Fitzwilliam Place, a villa, Undercliffe, at Killiney, on Dublin Bay. Father Sullivan's niece, Mrs. Wilmot Lloyd, recalled hearing him relate how Gladstone stopped with them there on one of his unofficial visits to Ireland and unbent so far as to take John and his brother William, both then small boys, on his knee.

In 1877, the Sullivans were, as usual, spending the summer and autumn at Undercliffe. They were very intimate with the family of William Exham, an eminent Q.C., who also had a villa at Killiney, Court-na-Farraga, now a well-known guest-house. At that time Robert Sullivan was aged twenty-four, handsome, talented, and a great favourite in Dublin society. On October 18th, about midday, he set out in a small sailing-boat in company with Mr. Exham's son John and his daughter Constance, young people barely grown-up. They brought a gun to amuse themselves by shooting at seagulls, and Robert had on a heavy cartridge-belt. A sudden squall capsized the boat just opposite where the Harcourt Street and Westland Row railway lines meet. The accident was witnessed from the shore, but there was no boat at hand, and the first to reach the spot were some fishermen who had to row from near Bray. They found John Exham clinging to an oar, unconscious but still alive. The dead body of his sister was lying across the other oar, but there was no trace of Robert Sullivan. When John Exham regained consciousness, he recounted how, when they were thrown into the water, he swam to recover an oar which had floated away. Meanwhile Robert Sullivan had seized the other oar, and swimming over to Miss Exham, gave it to her, begging her not to be frightened but to bear up and they would all be saved. Almost immediately he sank himself, probably weighed down by the cartridge-belt. The body was never found, though the Sullivan family even employed the services of a diver to search for it.

The tragedy caused a painful sensation in Dublin, where the two young victims were well known. It has been described at some length, as, on John Sullivan's own testimony, it had considerable spiritual significance in his after life.

CHAPTER IV

THE UNDERGRADUATE

IN 1879 John Sullivan won a classical exhibition from Portora into Trinity College, Dublin. Twenty-one years later, when he became a Jesuit novice, he gave the following account of his University studies in the brief autobiography which it is customary to write at entrance:

"I obtained a Royal School Exhibition at Entrance (£30 a year; afterwards raised to £40) for four years. I failed to obtain a Classical Scholarship, though I tried twice. I took my degree in 1883, getting a Senior Moderatorship, and gold medal in Classics. I had a taste for Classics, but could do nothing in Mathematics, and for that reason I had considerable difficulty in getting through some very ordinary examinations."

He was apparently a painstaking as well as outstanding student of the classics. The late Henry Bowen, of Bowenscourt, Kildorrery, near Fermoy, was a close friend of his at Trinity. He used to recall the lectures of Professor Tyrrell on Cicero's letters. Tyrrell was to edit later, in collaboration with Professor Purser, the complete collection of Cicero's letters in six large volumes, an edition that is still counted a very brilliant performance. But it has always been notorious that Purser did all the spade-work, whilst Tyrrell emended the text, and turned off brilliant translations of Cicero's idiomatic phrases. Both Tyrrell and his colleague Palmer (the editor of Horace's satires) were brilliant exponents of the art of emendation—at that time considered to be the main work of a classical scholar and the final test of his mastery of grammar, idiom and literary taste. But Tyrrell hated all drudgery, and disliked all the modern development of archæology, epigraphy or the scientific study of manuscripts.

Henry Bowen's recollections give confirmation of this weakness of Tyrrell's. Whenever any knotty point of history or archæology turned up, he would appeal to John Sullivan, who had usually made up the matter in advance. Tyrrell's reliance on his conscientious student became so great that one day when John Sullivan was unexpectedly absent, he refused to go on with the class.

This incident has a further interest. It is unlikely that John Sullivan should have come so closely into contact with Tyrrell and not have been influenced by him, as were many young men of the day, for Tyrrell was astonishingly brilliant. But he was also bitterly anti-Catholic.

In November 1903, when the Robertson Commission had reported on the problems of Irish University Education, and there was much talk of a National or Catholic University, Tyrrell printed the following sonnet in the *Student's Magazine*:

> Is Erin of a truth by golden bands
> Bound to the throne of God? Yon spire elate,
> Rear'd high the squalid scene to dominate,
> Does it to Heaven beckon suppliant hands?
> Nay, rather a grim monument it stands
> Of cold observance, the incestuous mate
> Of superstition, destined of blind fate

To draw the very marrow from the land's
Poor starving delvers, and in empty air
Scatter their wasted energies. Around
Its huge ugliness scorns the common ground
And points to Heaven: but to seeing eyes
Each soaring steeple lifts its tall head and lies.

There was a storm of protest after publication, for Tyrrell was one of the leading spirits in Trinity at the time, and it was argued by Trinity supporters that Catholics were at no disadvantage if they went there for higher education. Tyrrell wrote a letter by way of explanation, in which he said that he had written the sonnet to protest against "the undoubted fact that the Catholic clergy inculcate in their flocks cold acts of observance in lieu of sincere feelings of religion"; and went on to express his indignation at "the ill-considered zeal of the rank-and-file of an unscrupulous priesthood, practising on the ignorance and superstition of an illiterate peasantry."

John Sullivan's acquaintance with the Tyrrell family may possibly have been a partial explanation of his extreme asceticism in later life, and reaction from all his earlier Trinity memories. Professor Tyrrell was a first cousin of Father George Tyrrell, who was born in February 1861, only four months before John Sullivan, in Dorset Street, a few minutes' walk from John Sullivan's birthplace. None of Father Sullivan's contemporaries can recall him speaking of any meeting with George Tyrrell, and indeed it would not have been likely that the family of the future Lord Chancellor would have had any acquaintance with the family of the struggling sub-editor of the Dublin *Evening Mail*.

There were, however, two associations with the

Sullivans in the youth of George Tyrrell, which, though remote and accidental, are interesting. In 1873 George Tyrrell was sent for a year to the endowed school at Midleton, where Sir Edward Sullivan (as also his life-long friend, Judge William O'Brien) had been educated. In his *Autobiography*, George Tyrrell gives many vivid pictures of his schooldays. Latin and Greek were splendidly taught, but the surroundings were incredibly Spartan, which is only to say that they were the normal school surroundings of eighty years ago.

The other association of the Tyrrells with the Sullivans was a local one. In 1876 George Tyrrell and his mother went to live in Eccles Street, the street where John Sullivan had been born, with a Miss Lynch, who kept lodgings at No. 4. She was no connection of the Tyrrells and had never known them until they came to lodge with her, but friendship sprang up between her and George Tyrrell, and her deep Catholic piety apparently influenced him all his life. His last letter to her in 1894 (he was still a Jesuit at the time) contains this passage, poignant in view of what was to come.

"Well, on the whole, life is a sad business, and I shall not be sorry when I have to meet Mother and Louy and Willie (his sister and brother)."

In Miss Lynch's lodgings in Eccles Street, young George Tyrrell studied for a sizarship in Trinity College, but failed both in 1877 and 1878. The following year, under the influence of old Dr. Maturin, Rector of Grangegorman, a High-Church clergyman of the earlier Tractarian school, and father of Father Maturin, he became a Catholic, and entered the English province of the Society of Jesus in 1880.

It was in 1879 that John Sullivan entered Trinity

College. It is highly probable that he heard talk of the conversion of young George Tyrrell. That a first cousin of the ultra-Protestant Regius professor of Greek should have become not only a Catholic but a Jesuit must have caused considerable stir both inside and outside the University. And without doubt John Sullivan must have heard a great deal about George Tyrrell's elder brother, Willie, who had been a favourite pupil of Professor Tyrrell, and a confirmed agnostic as an undergraduate. He was a cripple from childhood, owing to a fall, and died of hip-disease in 1876. A classical prize was founded in his memory at Trinity, and his cousin, the Professor, later published some of his Latin verses and translations in *Kottabos*, a collection of Greek, Latin and English verse by fellows and graduates of the college. In Father Tyrrell's *Autobiography* there is a good deal about Willie's agnostic views at this time.

Much later, when John Sullivan was a Jesuit scholastic, the crisis came in Father Tyrrell's life. During the three years when Mr. John Sullivan was studying theology at Milltown Park, the whole crisis of Modernism came to a head. Father Tyrrell was dismissed from the Society of Jesus by Father Martin, the General, early in 1906, and Pius X issued his *Lamentabili* in July 1907, just three weeks before Father John's ordination. Such events would have stirred any convert; but the personal link with Professor Tyrrell must have added to the emotional strain, and may well have been a lasting influence in Father John's religious life. The remarkable strain of intellectual humility that was so apparent in him was certainly the very antithesis of the root teachings of Modernism.

In passing, it may be mentioned that there was one—

and probably only one—characteristic shared in a high degree by George Tyrrell and John Sullivan. In George Tyrrell's *Autobiography* there is a very moving picture of the brave struggles of his young widowed mother against adversity. Her visits to him when he was a young Jesuit scholastic were "among the tenderest of my memories," and he records with gratitude that when she was dying, the Provincial, Father Purbrick, told him to spare no expense for her comfort. Father Sullivan's love for his mother will appear in many passages of this memoir, and it played a dominant part in his life.

Of his other professor, Palmer, Father Sullivan used to relate a good story at his own expense. During one of his lectures, Palmer had occasion to explain that the verb "to kiss" could be rendered in Latin by three different constructions, *osculari* with the accusative *osculari cum* with the ablative, or *osculari ad invicem*. Then, turning to John Sullivan, whose shyness and dread of the fair sex were proverbial amongst his acquaintances, Palmer maliciously asked, "And which construction do you usually employ, Mr. Sullivan?"

A short but interesting contribution from the pen of John Sullivan is to be found in Volume V (1884–85) of *Hermathena*, a periodical devoted to classical studies, which is still published at very irregular intervals by Trinity College. In the 'eighties and 'nineties it was famous as a very brilliant magazine, to which Tyrrell, Mahaffy, Palmer, Bury, Purser, Maguire, all contributed for almost all numbers.

The number issued in the winter of 1884–85 is remarkable for a very vicious attack by Tyrrell and Maguire on Sayce's *Empires of the East*, which had just appeared; and in which Sayce used the results of recent archæological excavation to discredit Herodotus. Tyrrell and Maguire accused Sayce of slovenly scholarship. Sayce defended himself, and was defended by Mahaffy; all in this one issue of *Hermathena*.

Immediately after this controversy, on pp. 142–5, appears a very severe review, signed by John Sullivan, of a recent edition of Aeschylus' *Agamemnon*, by D. S. Margoliouth—then a young fellow of New College, Oxford, but later an admitted master of all Arabic studies, and one of the most learned men in England (by origin a Polish Jew). Margoliouth died only in March 1940, and was given a long obituary notice in *The Times* for March 23rd.

John Sullivan was evidently asked to review this latest Oxford edition of Aeschylus by the Editor of *Hermathena*, so as to show up the carelessness of English, as compared with Trinity scholarship. Margoliouth must have done his work very carelessly, and was never counted an authority on literature of this kind.

John Sullivan (who had just won his Moderatorship with Large Gold Medal) begins his review with this paragraph:

"A cursory glance at this edition of the *Agamemnon* will clearly show that it has been produced with undue haste. Not only does it abound in misprints, careless accentuation, neglect of punctuation, and wrong references; but also many suggestions and changes have been introduced into the text as the emendations of the editor himself, though they have been proposed years ago. Most of them can be found in the well-known editions of Paley, Kennedy, and Davies."

The reviewer then justifies these charges by a long list of forty-three emendations printed by Margoliouth, for each of which he names an earlier scholar as responsible for the emendation, with (as a rule) the printed edition from which Margoliouth could easily have learned these facts. After this list, the review adds some examples of misprints, wrong references and careless accentuation. The review ends without further comment, at the end of this long list of errors.

So far as can be judged, this castigation was thoroughly well deserved; but it comes oddly from so young a scholar. John Sullivan never made any further contribution to classical scholarship, and probably thought that this type of learning was exceedingly barren and fruitless; whilst Margoliouth lived to be admittedly one of the most learned (and certainly one of the most eccentric) figures in English scholarship.

The only indication which we have of John Sullivan's religious views at this time is found in an anecdote which he related to a relative a short time before his death. He told how one of the "skips" (as the college servants, both men and women, are called), herself a Catholic, used to harangue the students on the subject of going to church on Sunday. Regularly on Sunday mornings she would urge them to go. One Sunday she attacked Mr. John Sullivan on the subject, and he replied that he was tired of going to church, since it meant nothing to him, but that if she would bring him to her church he would go. Though doubtless somewhat nonplussed by this unexpected fruit of her missionary efforts, she agreed and they went together. There is no record however, of what his impressions were, or whether he continued to go to Mass at this time. As will be seen later, he did attend Mass regularly at some period previous to his formal reception into the Catholic Church.

CHAPTER V

THE YOUNG BARRISTER

AFTER taking his degree in 1883, John Sullivan entered the Law School of Trinity College. In the account of his studies previously mentioned, he says: "After leaving college I studied for the Irish Bar, but though I completed all my studies, I was never called." This is a puzzling statement. He could not have become a member of the Irish Bar unless he had entered King's Inns as a student. Yet his name does not appear on the register, and his contemporaries never remember him as a student there. The only other meaning which the statement can have is that he completed all his studies for the LL.B. degree, with the intention of getting called to the Bar later. Yet even this interpretation is not quite satisfactory, as he does not appear in any of the records of Trinity College as having taken the LL.B. degree. On the contrary, in a printed list of graduates, published in 1895, he is entered simply as B.A. 1883.

Sir Thomas Molony, Vice-Chancellor of Dublin University, and formerly Lord Chief Justice of Ireland, was a contemporary of John Sullivan in the Law School. He remembered that in 1884 John Sullivan got first prize in Civil Law and in 1885 first prize in Feudal and English Law, he himself coming second on each occasion. But in 1886 Sir Thomas had no recollection of John Sullivan being in the School, and made the not improbable suggestion that the death of his father in 1885 so shocked his sensitive nature that he determined to leave Dublin and its associations, and read for the English Bar. Sir Thomas recalled writing to him to sympathize with him in his bereavement, and receiving a letter which showed that he was deeply affected.

John Sullivan's own account of his studies concludes thus:

"Afterwards I went to London, where I studied for the English Bar at Lincoln's Inn, and was called to the English Bar in 1888." This would necessitate his having entered Lincoln's Inn in 1885, and bears out the supposition that he abandoned his studies for the LL.B. degree.

His father's death, on April 13th, 1885, came indeed with a tragic suddenness, calculated to affect deeply his sensitive and affectionate nature. The Lord Chancellor had been in his usual vigorous health up to the previous day. The obituary notice in the *Freeman's Journal* of April 14th mentions the familiar appearance in the Dublin streets of his lithe active form with its quick step. The Prince and Princess of Wales, afterwards King Edward and Queen Alexandra, had just begun their visit to Ireland, and the Lord Chancellor had sat next to the Princess at the Royal Banquet in Dublin Castle on April 11th. On the morning of the 13th he felt a slight pain, which grew worse in the afternoon. A doctor had hardly been summoned when the Lord Chancellor died, sitting in his arm-chair, of an aneurism of the aorta. Next day his obituary notice disputed pride of place in the newspapers with the account of a great meeting in his native Mallow, summoned by one William O'Brien (not his old legal friend, but the young Nationalist who had represented the constituency since 1883) to protest against the "flunkeyism" of the conservative majority of the town commissioners, who had decided to present an address of welcome to the Prince of Wales.

Little can be learned of John Sullivan's career as a barrister.[1] He seems never to have appeared in the English Courts, but he worked in chambers with Mr. R. F. McSwinney, a well-known expert in mining law. He acted at one time as Marshal to Lord Justice Mathew when on circuit. There are various recollections of his having appeared in the Irish Courts in company with Judge William O'Brien, at Cork, Limerick, Killarney, Carlow and Naas. It seems certain that on these occasions he was merely acting as registrar, a function which required no legal qualifications at all.

It was at this period of his life that he made those extensive travels which provided him with such a fund of reminiscences in after life. He did the usual continental trips, and also made walking tours in Greece, Macedonia and Asia Minor, visiting scenes made familiar to him by his classical studies. He learned modern Greek, and became intimate with the Prime Minister of Greece, M. Tricoupis, who facilitated him on his travels, even, on at least one occasion, going as far as to provide him with an escort of soldiers. He spent several months in one of the Orthodox monasteries on Mount Athos, and even thought of entering there as a monk.

[1] According to *Debrett* for 1895, his chambers were at 9 Old Square, Lincoln's Inn, W.C., and he was a member of the Reform Club.

A brief but vivid memory of John Sullivan on his travels was recalled by Mr. A. W. Perry, of Rathdowney, Leix. Mr. Perry had first met John Sullivan in 1879 when visiting the late Herbert Wilson, K.C., then a student at Trinity, at his rooms in college, and had at once been struck by his attractive character. Later, when studying brewing at London University College in 1885, he met John Sullivan again. It was just after the death of the Lord Chancellor, and John had been left with ample means. He was noted for his generosity, and Mr. Perry recalled being frequently entertained to dinner by him, in company with other students whose allowances were on a modest scale. Many years later, in 1892, Mr. Perry had been ordered to St. Moritz to try to get rid of asthma. On his arrival, the first person he saw was John Sullivan, who had just arrived after a tremendous journey on foot, alone, as usual, and carrying with him a towel, so that he might enjoy from time to time a plunge in the icy cold Alpine lakes. The Moritz Bad Hotel had just been opened at the bottom of St. Moritz, and John Sullivan promptly invited his fellow-countryman to a dinner there worthy of the occasion.

In later years, on occasions when his reserve could be broken down, Father Sullivan would pour out a wealth of memories connected with his travels, of which only fragments can be recalled, his first impressions of Greece in springtime—valleys filled with the pink and white of peach and almond blossoms; his days in the Monastery of Mount Athos, where the pious pilgrim arrived at the door with what dignity he could muster, hauled up in a basket at the end of a rope; the bandit who accosted him in some lonely spot and whom he unromantically bought off with a packet of cigarettes; his visit to Homeric Zachynthus and the strategos or mayor bearing the Hellenic-sounding name of Morfeios, who turned out to be the descendant of a remote Irish Murphy whose wild-goose flight had led him to this unexpected haven.

One got from these travel reminiscences of his the impression of a mind keenly sensitive to all that was striking and beautiful. He was never boring, for, apart from his rare sense of humour, he was completely lacking in that fundamental qualification of a bore, the desire to have his say in spite of all discouragement. On the contrary it was noticeable that, at the least sign of anyone else taking up the conversation, Father John could pass at once from his own vein of reminiscence and become absorbed in what his companion had to say.

Several friends of Father Sullivan heard him speak of a trip to Greece taken in company with Dr. Mahaffy. The only detail of this journey recalled is that when they visited the Acropolis, Mahaffy asked his young friend to act as cicerone to the party. It is interesting to recall that in 1876, when John Sullivan was still a boy at Portora, Dr. Mahaffy made another trip to Greece, on which occasion his companion was a young Oxford undergraduate named Oscar O'Flaherty Wills Wilde. Wilde had been at Portora with John Sullivan's elder brother Edward (whose reminiscences figure largely in Frank Harris's *Life of Wilde*) and before going to Oxford, had had a brilliant career at Trinity, where he had Tyrrell and Mahaffy as professors and won the Berkeley gold medal for an essay on Greek poetry.

In the *Dublin Review* for July 1938, the late Abbot Sir

Hunter Blair, O.S.B., published some very interesting personal reminiscences of Wilde. In the course of these he describes how he induced Wilde, a fellow-undergraduate of his at Magdalen, to join him at Rome and see something of Catholicism at head-quarters. Wilde was tremendously impressed with all he saw. Together with his convert friend, he had an audience with Pius IX, who laid his hands upon his head and expressed the hope that he would soon follow his *condiscipulus* into the City of God. On their return to the *Inghilterra*, Wilde locked himself into his room and dashed off a poem with his impressions of the Vatican still fresh on his soul.

One of the fourteen stanzas ran as follows:

> Before yon field of trembling gold
> Is garnered into dusty sheaves,
> Or ere the autumn's scarlet leaves
> Flutter like birds above the wold:
> I may have run the glorious race,
> And caught the torch while yet aflame,
> And called upon the Holy Name
> Of Him who now doth hide His Face.

Abbot Blair continues: "That April day was, I think, the high-water mark of Oscar Wilde's *rapprochement* to the Catholic Church. . . . Next day he went off to continue his tour in the company of Professor Mahaffy, a delightful comrade, no doubt, but not one to encourage anyone's predilection for the Roman Church. They went to Ravenna . . . thence to Greece and the Ionian Islands. When Oscar and I met at Oxford in the ensuing summer term, I realized that he was changed. He had become Hellenized, somewhat paganized, perhaps, by the appeal of Greece to his sensitive nature; and Rome had retired into the background."

The article, which is one of extraordinary interest, concludes with an authentic account of Wilde's deathbed repentance and reception into the Catholic Church in November 1900 by one of the English Passionists in Paris. At that time Dr. Mahaffy's other travelling companion, John Sullivan, was a Jesuit novice of two months' standing. There are many mansions in our Father's house, and, mercifully, there are many roads leading to it.

Just after his return from Mount Athos, John Sullivan was stopping at the Reform Club with his brother Edward when he became seriously ill. Dr. Mapother, a well-known Dublin surgeon, who had settled in London, was summoned. He diagnosed small-pox, and had the patient removed to what was then Highgate small-pox hospital. It is an interesting commentary on the progress of medical practice in the past fifty years to note that Father Sullivan used to recall how the only precautions against infection taken by the doctor were to wear a mackintosh and to stand at the end of the bed. The illness was a light one, and had no serious after-effects.

When at home in Ireland, John Sullivan was a popular figure, with a touch of remoteness that marked him out from others, though it did not separate him from them. Those who recollect his later poverty of dress will hardly be able to repress a smile at the description given of him by the late Father Tom Finlay, S.J., as "the best-dressed young man about Dublin." Dr. Thomas Bodkin, formerly Director of the National Gallery in Dublin, and now Professor of Fine Arts at the University of Birmingham, recalled talking to Sir William Sullivan on one occasion and commenting on the holiness of Father John. "You would think it all the more extraordinary," said Sir William, "if you had known what a fine whist player he was as a young man." The recollections of Mr. A. W. Perry, whose meetings with John Sullivan have been already mentioned, bear out those of Sir William. The group of students who used to meet at Herbert Wilson's rooms in Trinity all learned their whist, and especially the art of finessing, from John Sullivan, who "knew Cavendish from cover to cover."

Cycling was all the rage in the 'nineties. The old "penny-farthing" machines had just been superseded by the "safety," which had made cycling possible for at least the more daring of the gentler sex, and the coming of the pneumatic tyre in 1888 had given the new pastime an extraordinary impetus. By 1895 the makers were unable to cope with the demand for machines. John Sullivan, like most of the young men of his acquaintance, developed a passion for cycling. A relative recalled an expedition led by him to a beauty spot in the Dublin mountains, John flying along in front, his fair hair blowing in the wind, and the three young girls who made up the party laughingly imploring him to slacken the pace.

He retained this taste for cycling all his life, but it was a very different figure that was seen years later on the roads around Clongowes, mounted on a dilapidated machine, and laboriously pedalling his way through mud and rain to bring comfort to some humble cottage.

There was great social life in Dublin at the time. Golf, motoring, bridge and the cinema were still things of the future, and, as a result, friends gathered more regularly and in larger numbers at one another's houses, whilst the art of conversation flourished.

A very popular social centre was the house of Judge James Murphy, a Limerick man, and a Judge of the Queen's Bench. He was an able lawyer, and acted as Crown Prosecutor in the trial of the Invincibles in 1883. His wife was a daughter of Mr. Justice Keogh, a stormy figure in the politico-legal history of the second half of the last century. Mrs. Murphy's only sister had been engaged to Captain Kane, R.N., of *Calliope* fame; but died before the marriage could take place.

The Murphys lived at Glencairn, a beautiful estate near Stillorgan at the foot of the Dublin mountains. It was well known to later generations of Dubliners as the residence of Richard Croker, the former Tammany Boss, and even better known as the place where Orby, Croker's Derby winner, was partly trained.

Judge Murphy liked to have clever young men around him, and he was a life-long friend of Sir Edward Sullivan. Hence it was natural that Sir Edward's three sons should be constant visitors at Glencairn. Mr. Stephen Gwynn, in his *Reminiscences of a Literary Man*, gives a pleasant picture of the gatherings there. Mrs. Murphy was a Catholic, so Catholics and Protestants mingled freely—not so common a thing in the Ireland of that day. Indeed, one of the most constant and welcome guests was the parish priest, none other than the famous Father Healy of Bray, in whose presence the conversation could never have been anything but sparkling. Mr. Gwynn gives an attractive sketch of this most lovable of priests, a strong candidate for the daring title of the wittiest Irishman who ever lived. In addition to the pleasant company, Judge Murphy's guests found at Glencairn an excellent cellar, including a quantity of "64 Lafitte," the greatest Bordeaux ever known, which had been laid down by Judge Keogh and inherited by his son-in-law.

One of Judge Murphy's sons had as his godfather Edward Sullivan, the Chancellor's eldest son, and was named after him. He is now the Right Hon. Mr. Justice Edward Sullivan Murphy, Lord Justice of Appeal in Northern Ireland. Mr. Justice Murphy recalled what a welcome guest John Sullivan was at Glencairn.

"John was rather shy and retiring. He was a great favourite with my father and mother, and all the members of my family were very fond of him. As I was following in my father's footsteps, so far as a classical education was concerned, John seemed to take a special interest in me, and often talked about passages in Greek or Roman authors with me, whilst at other times he talked of English poetry. I can recall his appreciation of 'The Bridge of Sighs' with its lovely concluding words. I would describe him as a man of great taste in English literature and the Classics, serious-minded, somewhat shy, and always most kindly, especially to young people."

A few more touches were added to this description by Judge Murphy's daughter, Jessica, now Mrs. Blagden.

"My father was devoted to John Sullivan, and enjoyed his deep classical and literary knowledge. It was generally on Sundays that he came to us, and then a thin young man would walk into our very argumentative midst. He never joined in our outdoor games —I fancy he was delicate, though a good walker. He was intensely shy and reserved, and he rarely lifted his beautiful blue eyes and looked one straight in the face, but when he began to talk he was always interesting. I remember his description of the monastery on Mount Athos which he had visited. He spoke modern Greek at the time, I think.

"Life was not so rapid and strenuous in those days as it is now, but even then one felt that John was somehow apart from it. I feel sure that even then he was living in a spiritual and contemplative world of his own, and only leaving it when he was with people like my father. Though shy and aloof from us, one felt his charm of character."

Another intimate friend of the Lord Chancellor and his family was Mr. Justice William O'Brien, P.C., also a Judge of the Queen's Bench. Like Sir Edward Sullivan, he was a County Cork man, and though a Catholic, had been educated at Midleton school where Sir Edward had received his schooling. He was a remarkable figure, a man of deep religious feeling and exemplary private life, but in his judgments unorthodox at times to a degree. Mr. Maurice Healy, K.C., in his *Old Munster Circuit* has given a picture of him which does not err on the side of flattery. He was the Judge in the trial of the Invincibles, in which James Murphy appeared as Crown prosecutor. Dubliners of that day were familiar with the sight of Sir Edward Sullivan and Judge William O'Brien walking together on the banks of the Grand Canal near Fitzwilliam Place, engrossed in conversation, and stopping occasionally when the Chancellor became emphatic in some argument he was propounding.

William O'Brien shared with his friend Edward Sullivan the taste for collecting rare books, and amassed a remarkable library, containing several early Shakespeare folios and some one hundred and fifty fine *incunabula*. These treasures he bequeathed to the library of the Jesuit theologate at Milltown Park. Like many another lawyer, he made an invalid will, naming as beneficiaries the Jesuit Order, a body which then had no legal status, but his next-of-kin confirmed the legacy by consent.

Judge William O'Brien, who was a bachelor, had two nieces who had been brought up in America, the Misses Otis-Cox. Miss Carrie Otis-Cox, now living with her sister at Le Havre,[1] in an attractive sketch of John Sullivan as a young man, gave also some pleasant glimpses of the Dublin of the 'nineties in which he was such a popular figure.

"As well as I remember, it was in 1893 that I met John Sullivan. My sister and I spent the winter of that year and the spring of the next with my uncle, Judge William O'Brien, P.C., who lived at 84 Merrion Square, Dublin. He was a life-long friend of Sir Edward Sullivan, the late Lord Chancellor of Ireland. They spent all their spare time and their vacations together, in fact, I think that my uncle, who was a bachelor, dined every Sunday evening at 32 Fitzwilliam Place, the Sullivan residence. Their friendship was such that he was looked upon as one of the family, and he in turn seemed to have as much affection for the Sullivan children as if they were his own. William Sullivan, who was my uncle's registrar, and a very charming man, was married to Charlotte, daughter of Chief Baron Dowse. She was kind enough to chaperon us to a number of entertainments in Dublin. But I think the one who was

[1] Written before the invasion of France.

nearest my uncle's heart was John, about whom he spoke continually with the greatest affection and interest. So that it seemed quite natural that, when Judge O'Brien's two American nieces landed in Dublin, the first people to call, the very morning of their arrival, were William and John Sullivan. I distinctly remember John's low voice, his blue eyes, and his strange far-away expression, albeit he was quite alive to what was going on and what was said.

"We spent much of our time in France then, and my uncle had often mentioned that John was looking worried and absent-minded. He wondered if it was his health, or if he was contemplating becoming a Catholic. My uncle's voice used to take on a tone of awe and mystery when he spoke of such an eventuality. My sister and I who were just turned twenty, and who had lived among French Catholics nearly all our youth, did not realize the significance of such a step at that period and in that milieu.

"But to come back to John, I think he took us for our first drive in Dublin on an outside car, and pointed out the different landmarks. I remember how interesting he was, and how amused he was at a remark I made. Having been brought up with the tradition of the O'Brien descent from Brian Boru and the kings of Ireland, I noticed something that was a great blow to my fairy-tale ancestral pride. 'Are all the public-houses in Dublin owned by O'Briens?' I asked, after I had seen the name a number of times over what we called in America 'beer saloons.' 'No,' answered Mr. Sullivan with a laugh, 'some are owned by Sullivans.'

"At that time John Sullivan had a great friend, a Greek, or rather a Cyprian, called Demetrius Yacovides, a young medical student at Trinity. They used to be a great deal together and came to see us at Merrion Square. The contrast was striking between John's fair hair, blue eyes, and phlegmatic manner, and the young Greek's alive, pulsing personality. Mr. Yacovides invited us to tea at his rooms. In those days young girls were not allowed the same liberty as to-day, but as John was to be there, my uncle decided it was all right. My sister and I concluded that John must be a very model of perfection, since Uncle William was all smiles in a case where he might have been very crusty. We were let go out with John whenever the occasion presented itself.

"Years have passed, but I can still see the old Merrion Square dining-room with its polished mahogany and silver, and John, quiet as the monks he was telling us about, reading extracts from the letters of his Mount Athos friends, with his friend, Demetrius Yacovides looking at him in amused and friendly admiration. Those letters were from monks John had met when staying at Mt. Athos, when he travelled through Greece and Salonika. The letters usually begin by 'My dearly beloved John,' and had a religious trend and an intellectual flavour. They were to me reminiscent of the Epistles. I hope I did not titter as I listened, especially as John seemed to derive the greatest pleasure and satisfaction from them. And, by the way, I remember once talking about John and his travels in Greece to his sister-in-law, Mrs. William Sullivan, and saying something about baggage. She exclaimed: 'Baggage, my dear! John takes a toothbrush and a couple of shirts when he travels.' But I vaguely remember hearing my uncle say that John, in relating some of his adventures, had said that a sleeping-bag was a very necessary article in some of the Greek hotels and inns, at that time! John used also to tell of the strict Lenten fast at Mt. Athos, and how, on the Easter festival, a gargantuan repast was offered to guests and visitors.

"It was during his travels in Greece that he met, in Athens, M. Tricoupis, the Prime Minister. Introducing John to some notables, M. Tricoupis informed them that this young Irishman not only could converse with them in modern Greek, but in ancient Greek as well, 'which few of us can boast of being able to do,' added the Prime Minister.

"Coming back from Greece John fell ill at Brindisi where he must have caught small-pox. When he reached London he sent for a doctor who diagnosed his case, and sent him to an isolation hospital where he was splendidly cared for. My uncle always said that it must have been during that long and lonely time that John pondered and made up his mind to join the Catholic church.

"Now I must leave Greece and come back to Dublin. We felt very much at home with John, and used to tell him just what we thought about everyone and everything. One day he took us to the Zoo, and while we wandered about looking at the animals, we amused ourselves by finding points of resemblance between them and different people we knew. We were particularly struck by the giraffe and the way it arched and craned its neck. Both my sister and I exclaimed, 'Why, Mr. Sullivan, that giraffe looks like Mr. X. He arches and moves his neck in the very same way.' Mr. X. was a young and promising barrister, whom we had met at a dinner-party some days before. Needless to say how amused John Sullivan was, especially as we went on to find further points of resemblance between the inhabitants of the Zoo and some grave and sedate Dubliners. I also remember that John, who was simplicity itself, had bought biscuits for the animals, and as they were quite good, we ate some ourselves. At that time the fashion in France was to wear veils of different colour and texture, which were gathered tightly under the chin, coiled around the neck, and tied behind. It was next to impossible to raise them to eat, without a desperate struggle, which destroyed the harmony of the whole. I remember that I often refused cakes or sweets rather than have the trouble to lift my veil. That day John watched my struggle and came to my rescue, only making matters worse, so he mumbled something about one of Cervantes's heroes whose helmet had to be raised so that he could be fed, or something to that effect.

"Another day we walked to a place called, I think, Sandymount. It was a long walk, and we were due at Lady Sullivan's for tea. Annie and John were there when we arrived and there was great discussion as to whether or not it was to Sandymount we had been, as they considered it would have taken much more time. We took some shells out of our pockets, which we had brought as a proof of our wandering. 'We picked these on the sand,' we said to the amusement of the family. Tea at Lady Sullivan's used to be great fun, and Annie was very lively and always knew the latest news or gossip. John used to sit on the sofa, his cup of tea in his hand, and listen with a bored expression, although highly amused at all our nonsense. He could not help his expression, it was natural.

"John Sullivan was a catch in the matrimonial market, and his sister, to whom he was the apple of her eye, was not slow to perceive the enemy's attack from whatsoever quarter it came. I remember a big dinner-party at which John was a guest as well as my sister and I. With veiled, but clear intention, he had been seated next to an ambitious mother, who dreamed of him for a son-in-law. Annie Sullivan came to see us the next day to talk over the dinner at which she also had been a guest. 'Did you see how nicely John was pinned?' were her very first words.

"Judge Murphy was very fond of John Sullivan and we used often to go to Glencairn, the Murphys' place at Stillorgan, if I remember rightly the name of the village. We went one afternoon with my uncle to tea, and we were told we would meet a great English beauty, over in Ireland for a visit. As we were all gathered for tea in the drawing-room, older people such as Mr. Stephen Ronan,[1] Mr. Henry,[2] and other barristers being in the garden, and John no doubt strolling in the grounds, with probably the oldest and surely the most intellectual and dry-as-dust of the visitors, the beauty entered the drawing-room, flanked by a youthful *cavalier servant* in the person of Dick, one of Judge Murphy's sons, a college youth.

"The beauty flung herself down on the carpet in an artistic attitude and smiled, ready to be worshipped. In France, where we had been brought up, no such nonsense was allowed, even from a beauty. In truth my sister and I failed to see the greatness of her beauty,

[1] Stephen Ronan, K.C., later Lord Justice of Appeal, and after 1921, Lord Justice of Appeal for Southern Ireland.

[2] Denis Henry, K.C., later Solicitor-General, Attorney-General and first Chief Justice of Northern Ireland.

and thought her eccentric. John came in to tea, stayed in a corner near Mrs. Murphy and said nothing. When the end of the afternoon drew near, we rose to go to take the train to Dublin. John made a move to accompany us, but was promptly told he must stay to dinner. He did not appear over-pleased, but was so pressed that he could not get out of it, and looked quite helpless. I remember my uncle was very struck and said, 'John did not want to stay, he wanted to come back with us.' John, who was not a lady's man, was probably supremely bored, unless he spent the evening listening to Judge Murphy, for whom he had great friendship.

"At that time John was worried about his health, in fact he seemed to brood over it, and my uncle thought he was getting slightly hypochondriac. He would eat no bread except a kind much in vogue at the time, called Hovis bread. It used to be got specially for him, in fact perhaps from London. And I know that once, when there had been a big dinner-party at the Lord Chancellor's, to which many important people had been invited, Annie had emphatically declared, that on no consideration, was the special Hovis bread to be put on the table for John, as was done when the family was alone. I wonder if John thought of all this when he became such an ascetic! At that time his complexion had a peculiar hue, which my uncle called autumn leaf, and his hands were such a deep red as to be nearly blue. One could not help noticing them, especially as he had a trick of passing his hand through his thick hair, which, added to his general expression, would have given him a bored and wearied look, were it not for the genial smile with which he greeted friends.

"I have an idea that John left on another trip to

Greece or some foreign parts, after we came back from spending Easter in Rome with my uncle, for I have no other recollection of seeing him again. I know that it was Willie Sullivan who took us down to Queenstown, where we boarded the Cunarder for New York, my uncle being too busy with the trial of the Pike card case to come to see us off.[1]

"John was received into the Church in 1896. We went to live in France in that year, and probably heard of his conversion through Uncle William, who often came over to see us. Then came my uncle's death in 1899. I remember that I was sent over to Dublin, reaching there a day or so before the end. Mass was said in the bedroom of the house in Merrion Square, where my uncle lay in the habit of the Third Order of St. Francis. I remember how much older, and especially how changed John Sullivan looked. We knelt and said the Rosary beside the bed. John answered the Mass and received Holy Communion, and I remember being struck by his fervour and saintly look and demeanour.

"After the funeral John came to see me. We sat in the same mahogany-furnished dining-room. The house had never been cheerful or comfortable, and it was ghastly that day. John was kind and thoughtful and friendly. I had never seen death before, and the loneliness of it all was a shock to me. We had had such a sheltered united life. I think I made some remark about

[1] A *cause célèbre* in which a member of a well-known Cork family was accused of cheating at cards. The case excited intense excitement in Cork, and the court was packed for the trial. An eye-witness, who was himself smuggled in disguised as a barrister in wig and gown, recalled how Judge William O'Brien made room on the Bench for his two handsome nieces, who sat there during the hearing with William Sullivan, the Judge's Registrar.

my uncle being so terribly alone, and I seem, even now, to hear John say, 'The dear Judge will be remembered where it is worth being remembered,' and I know he alluded to the Masses and prayers that would be said for him everywhere.

"I never saw John Sullivan again. I went down for a few months to Cork, and then back to France. A year later John wrote to me, enclosing two religious pictures and telling me he was entering the Society of Jesus.

"To hear that he was dead, was a shock. Years pass and we do not realize how swiftly they have gone. I think his belief that his conversion was due to his mother's tears is very touching. My sister remembers my uncle telling her than when Lady Sullivan died, John put armfuls of white lilies in her grave."

Another reminiscence of the young John Sullivan was given by Mrs. Esther O'Kiely, wife of Professor O'Kiely, of University College, Dublin. It recalls an incident, seemingly trivial, but which evidently encouraged John Sullivan on his journey towards the Catholic Church.

"I have a very pleasant memory of Mr. John Sullivan, who stayed at Glencar Hotel, Co. Kerry, which was my home at the time, in 1894 and 1895. I was then a little girl and had a governess to teach me my lessons. She and I used to sit by an open window that looked out on the front garden. On my first meeting Mr. Sullivan, he was standing outside the window. I remember that morning well. It was early summer, a bit cold, and there Mr. Sullivan stood on the gravel wearing a grey tweed suit, the trousers pulled up beyond his knees, no shoes or stockings. We were doing Catechism, and the governess stopped the catechism as she took it for granted that he was a Protestant. He asked me what I was learning. I told him it was catechism, and he asked if he might listen to the instruction. First he had a glance at the 'Butler's,' and, handing the little book back, he sat on the window-sill and I am quite sure paid more attention to the lesson than I did, as I felt naturally shy of this big man's presence.

"When the lesson was finished, he asked me if he might take the book until evening, and if he might come in next morning to hear the instruction again. I said, 'Yes, of course,' and he went off, much to my relief, because I could see myself making plenty of mistakes in my other lessons, and felt more at ease with the catechism.

"Next morning Mr. Sullivan went a bit further, for he walked right into our schoolroom. I remember the governess was teaching me something else, but he asked if she would continue the Catholic instruction. She did, of course. He listened and asked questions on the Catechism. I was doing a little Bible History, too, and Mr. Sullivan was much interested in this book, and took down the name of it, saying that he would get one for himself and also a Catechism, so that when he would come to Glencar next he would be able to follow the instructions more clearly.

"Mr. Sullivan used to go for long walks while staying in our house, generally off the road, by river, lake and mountain. He was a rather silent man, not anxious to gossip.

"The Christmas of that year, he sent me a red book called *The Catholic Rosary*. It was as large as *Chatterbox*. I remember this so well as I was disappointed it was not a *Chatterbox*. He came again the year after and this time was a most welcome guest to our schoolroom, just because I knew him better and he appeared still more friendly.

"He appeared to have carried out his intention of the summer before, as he had with him *The Lives of the Saints*, and told us some very nice stories out of it, but he would insist on hearing the Catechism lesson right through. He attended regularly, but never remained on to hear any of the other lessons. I remember that he used to inquire a good deal about Confession and the Mass. He did go to Mass while at our place, but never showed any anxiety to meet the local clergy. He only visited Glencar twice. At Christmas for many years he always sent some little remembrance, but never a *Chatterbox*, always some book with religious stories.

"I lost sight of him completely afterwards, as I went to the Ursulines in Cork to school, but when on holidays at home in 1906, I got a personal message from him. A young Jesuit student, who was visiting his family in our neighbourhood, brought me kind remembrances from Mr. Sullivan, and told me that he was going on to be a priest."

CHAPTER VI

CONVERSION AND VOCATION

OUR knowledge of John Sullivan's spiritual life before his entrance into the Church is, unfortunately, meagre. However, it is interesting to note that he had already developed a virtue which was afterwards to be one of his most striking ones, love of the poor. His father's and his own great friend, Judge Murphy, was a very charitably minded man. From him he learned the practice, when asked by a poor man for alms, of not merely assisting him financially, but of stopping on the road to talk to him, hearing his troubles, and giving him a word of sympathy. When the news of his reception into the Church reached Dublin, a Presbyterian friend accosted Judge Murphy, who was a staunch Protestant. "Did you hear," he asked, "that your friend, John Sullivan, has become a Catholic?"

"Don't worry," replied the Judge good-humouredly, "John Sullivan would go to heaven even if he became a Presbyterian."

It was on December 21st, 1896, that John Sullivan was received into the Catholic Church by Father Michael Gavin, S.J., at Farm Street, the well-known residence of the Jesuits in London.

A few incidents have been already mentioned which may have contributed in some slight degree to his conversion, but it is unfortunate that, up to the time of the writing of this Life, no information has come to light concerning the motives that led him to take the final step. It is quite likely that he spoke of them to some of his brothers in religion, but there was no common knowledge of them, not a very surprising fact to those who knew Father John's intense humility and dislike for talking about himself.

It is quite certain, however, that the prayers and example of his mother played a powerful part in his conversion. Reference has been already made to the preface which he wrote for the biography of John Haughton Steele. There is a passage in it in which, after speaking of the heroic sacrifice of John Steele, Father Sullivan goes on to say: "But the story of the conversion of the writer of this preface is more simply told, and may be summed up in the words of St. Augustine: 'Me fidelibus et quotidianis matris meae lacrimis, ne perirem, fuisse concessum.' In other words, 'I believe that to the faithful and daily tears of my mother it was granted that I should not perish.' (St. Augustine de Dono Persev., sec. 52.)"

This debt to his mother is acknowledged even more explicitly in a letter written on March 9th, 1913, to the mother of a boy of seventeen, Jack O'Riordan, who had died at Clongowes on February 23rd preceding. The letter is worth quoting almost in full. It is one of the very few in which Father Sullivan showed anything like self-revelation.

"I cannot tell you how much we miss your dear Jack. His memory is still fresh here, the boys frequently speak of him, and I was told that several boys were seen saying the Rosary at his grave last Sunday. His simple and innocent life always impressed the boys, but his beautiful death has produced a wonderful effect upon them, better than any sermon, or even Retreat. I told them in the chapel how grateful you were to them for all they had done for your dear boy, and how much consolation they had given you in the midst of your great sorrow.

"I was very sorry that I had to leave you that Saturday you were here. I would have liked to have heard more about Jack. I owe everything in the world to my mother's prayers, and so know the power of a mother's prayer, especially in the hour of sorrow. I can form some idea of your anguish from what I saw of my own dear mother when her best-loved son and the one whom she almost idolized was taken from her at the age of twenty-four without a moment's warning. She never saw his face again, and never even had the satisfaction of weeping at his grave, for his remains were never found. I cannot tell you what agony she endured during the days after his loss, hoping against hope that his remains might be recovered. I believe that only for her passionate love for Our Lord and for her boundless faith, she would have lost her reason. To her prayers at that time and to her resignation to God's will I believe I owe everything, and God alone knows how much that means.

"Please forgive me for these personal details, but your sorrow has brought everything back to me again."

Father Sullivan had taught this gifted and holy boy, and wrote a very beautiful obituary notice of him in the school magazine, *The Clongownian*, beginning with a quotation which I have been unable to trace, "The less of this cold world, the more of heaven." His affection was evidently returned, for the boy's mother recalled how, on the eve of her son's last return to Clongowes, he was speaking of Father Sullivan and said, "Perhaps you don't know, Mother, that Father Sullivan is a saint." In after years Father Sullivan continued to correspond with Mrs. O'Riordan, and there are many references in his letters to "our little cemetery where everything is very peaceful." His own mortal remains rest there now, a few feet from those of the boy he loved.

That a man of the strong character and fine intellect of John Sullivan must have trodden a well-reasoned and firmly determined path towards the light of faith goes without saying. But it would indeed have been strange if his mother's prayers and example and not influenced him. He loved her deeply—the filling of her grave with lilies was no mere precious affectation—and she was a woman of great and sincere piety. Father John once mentioned to a friend that she went to Holy Communion every day of her life—a much rarer practice in those days than now—and in another passage (which was never printed) of the preface to John Steele's life he spoke of her goodness to the poor and of the influence it had on him in his youth.

All his life he had a remarkable devotion to St. Augustine and St. Monica. No doubt this was largely due to the similarity which he perceived between St. Augustine's conversion and his own. He could quote long passages from the saint's works, and hardly ever preached without making some reference to him. I remember him pointing out to me, as a boy, with what beautiful appropriateness the Gospel of the raising of the widow's son was appointed for the feast of St. Monica.

John Sullivan's life as a Catholic was marked by unusual fervour even while he remained in the world. Miss O'Neill, his mother's companion, recalled how, on returning home after his reception into the Church, he went straight up to his room and stripped it himself of everything that might appear luxurious, contenting himself with the plainest furniture and a carpetless floor. As has been already mentioned, he had been fastidious to a degree in his dress. Now his silk underwear was replaced by ordinary linen, and his supply of ties, in the choice of which he had been inordinately particular, was reduced from a couple of dozen to a few of the plainest pattern.

In a letter written on January 1st, 1899, by Judge William O'Brien to his sister, Mrs. John Otis-Cox, at that time residing in France, there occurs the following sentence: "Mr. John Sullivan is in the country. He is become quite a saint, and is an example to all people of religion and grace in conduct and manners." He was a great friend of Mother Leontia Callan, the then Mother Abbess of the Poor Clare convent, Ballyjamesduff, Co. Cavan, which he visited frequently while staying in Park, Virginia, with his brother Sir William, who was Resident Magistrate for Cavan at the time. His visits are still recalled by members of that community. He told Mother Leontia that he intended joining a religious Order. She assured him that his vocation was for the Society of Jesus, and she was not mistaken, as the sequel showed. When there was no Mass in the Parish Church, owing to the absence of the local priests on retreat, he cycled to Mass in the convent every morning. He never used the prie-dieu left for him, but always knelt on the floor. His appearance, even at that time, was edifying and austere. One day at recreation, a Sister remarked that Mr. Sullivan was very holy looking. "Holy," exclaimed an old lay-sister—herself most saintly. "Why, you could light a lamp before him!"

He gave many spiritual books as presents to the Community. *The Liturgical Year*, by Dom Guéranger, O.S.B., is still read daily in the convent refectory.

From the beginning of his life as a Catholic, John Sullivan seems to have felt himself to be called to the priesthood. There is no record of how the interior call came to him, but he spoke openly of his leanings to friends of his. Amongst these friends were some well-known members of the Jesuit Order, who were constant visitors at his father's house, Father James Cullen, the founder of the Pioneer Total Abstinence Association, and Fathers Edward, Tom, and William Kelly. The three Fathers Kelly were brothers, and Dublin born. They did not leave behind them any such permanent achievement as did Father Cullen, but they were men of remarkable ability and amiable character. Father Edward was at various times Rector of Clongowes and Belvedere colleges and Superior of St. Francis Xavier's, Upper Gardiner Street, where both he and his brother, Father Tom, spent most of their lives, and where they were stationed at this period. They were both outstanding classical scholars, gifted with prodigious memories, and used to take pleasure in out-quoting one another from the classics, the one eagerly waiting until his brother faltered, when he would triumphantly carry on with the missing line. As a *tour de force*, Father Edward could read down a column of the advertisement page of a newspaper, and then repeat the advertisements in order from memory. The third brother, William, who was then professor of Scripture and Hebrew at Milltown Park, the Jesuit house of theology in Dublin, was an even more universal genius. He was equally at ease in physics, astronomy, mathematics and an amazing range of languages, including Persian and Arabic. He had, at an earlier period, worked at the newly-founded Jesuit college of St. Aloysius in Sydney. Whilst there, he was honoured by being elected President of a Hebrew society in the city, the other members of which were exclusively Jewish, and on one occasion he came to the rescue of a Polynesian native who had got into trouble in the police-court, by acting as his interpreter.

According to Father Cullen, John Sullivan's first leanings were towards the Franciscan Order, no doubt owing to his love of poverty. He frequently visited the Capuchin Friary at Church Street, and formed a close friendship with two of the priests there, Father Peter and Father Fidelis. In fact, Father Angelus, now a member of the Church Street community, recalled how, when a novice at Rochestown, Co. Cork, he heard that Mr. John Sullivan was expected to come to the novitiate. However, the counsels of his Jesuit friends inclined him to join their ranks, and this inclination received further encouragement through his association with two well-known charitable institutions in Dublin.

John Sullivan's sympathy with the poor and afflicted has already been noted. Within a short while from his entrance into the Catholic Church, the young barrister became a constant visitor to the Hospice for the Dying at Harold's Cross, which is under the care of the Irish Sisters of Charity. An old lay-sister, Sister Mary Linus, remembered him as "a lovely young gentleman," and in this case, the phrase was no mere kindly cliché. He had a remarkable gift for putting the patients into good humour, and showed especial sympathy towards the old, bringing them tins of snuff or packages of tea, and reading for them from religious books. In after life, one of John Sullivan's many remarkable traits was a complete disregard for human respect. This is foreshadowed in Sister Linus' recollection of him coming in one day carrying under his arm for some patient a pair of boots, which he had scorned to shroud in the decent secrecy of brown paper. Sister Mary Francesca, now at the Children's Hospital, Cappagh, on the outskirts of Dublin, was then a very young nun teaching in the schools attached to the Hospice. Mr. Sullivan used to visit the schools also, especially the night school. Characteristically, he was most interested in the poorest of the children, and on occasions came to the rescue by bailing them out in court when, in their professional capacity as flower-girls or fish-vendors, they had got into grips with the Law.

In the course of his visits, John Sullivan formed many friendships with the nuns. One of these friends was Sister Mary Joseph Stanislaus O'Brien, who lived on at the Hospice until 1929, dying at the age of ninety. To her he confided that he was thinking of entering the Franciscan Order, but she advised him to choose the Society of Jesus, for which his character and talents seemed more suited. The same advice was given him by Mother Mary John Gaynor, who had been Superioress of the Hospice since its doors were first opened to dying patients in 1879, and who remained in office until her death in 1897, and by Mother Agnes Gertrude

Chamberlain, who succeeded Mother Mary John as Superioress, and was later Mother General of the Congregation.

The other charitable work in which John Sullivan became interested at this time was the Night Refuge conducted by the Sisters of Mercy in Brickfield Lane, to which are attached elementary schools. This interest again led to a lifelong friendship, and would seem to have influenced to some degree his vocation to the Society of Jesus.

The story of his introduction to the good work being carried on in Brickfield Lane is an amusing as well as an edifying one. Some time during the year 1898, the Superioress, Sister Mary Ursula Mooney, happened to be in difficulties over a sum of forty pounds which was due for bread for the Refuge. A Carmelite Father from Clarendon Street, hearing of her embarrassment, remarked that he knew someone who would come to her assistance. A few days later, a slight, handsome young gentleman rang at the door, handed in an envelope containing twenty-five pounds in banknotes, and disappeared without a word. This occurred again, and the Secretary of the Superioress, filled with a holy curiosity as to the identity of the donor, laid an ambush for him. She arranged that, if he came again, the portress was to inveigle him into the hall, and close the door. All went according to plan. The Sister Secretary was then summoned, and Mr. John Sullivan was revealed as the benefactor.

From that on, he frequently visited the convent. The nuns rapidly became aware that this was no ordinary young man about town. His conversation was almost entirely confined to spiritual topics, and he seemed to know the works of St. Teresa and St. John of the Cross by heart. In fact, the good Superioress soon found the spiritual level of his conversation so high that, whenever he called, she used to summon to her aid her secretary—she who had staged the successful ambush—so that their combined efforts might follow creditably the high flights that would be sure to ensue. The Sister Secretary, afterwards Mother Stanislaus Joseph, Superioress of the Mercy convent, Lower Baggot Street, had been reared near the Jesuit novitiate at Tullabeg, and often spoke to Mr. Sullivan about it. He took a special interest in the nuns' school, where there were about 1,500 pupils, mostly children of workmen in Guinness's brewery. There was in the Infant School a little girl named Annie, between three and four years old. Sister Stanislaus Joseph taught her to say "God bless Mr. Sullivan, and make him a holy Jesuit." Whenever he visited the school, this mite used to seize on any book that came handy, run up to him and pretend to read out from its pages this pious and unambiguous wish. He was amused and delighted, and used to say, "Say it again, Annie, say it again." It may be noted that in after years, when Annie came to be married, one of her wedding presents was a statue presented to her by Father John Sullivan, then Rector of Rathfarnham Castle.

On another occasion the good Sister thought things were moving rather slowly, and sent Mr. Sullivan a bogus telegram to Fitzwilliam Place. It ran as follows:

"A block of marble wanted in Tullabeg to be carved into a statue to fill a niche in heaven. Phidias and Praxiteles await reply."

IGNATIUS LOYOLA, S.J.

Phidias and Praxiteles were the Master of Novices and his Socius. John Sullivan replied with another bogus telegram.

"To St. Joseph, c/o Sister Stanislaus Joseph.
Material not up to sample. Phidias and Praxiteles on strike; several chisels broken. General confusion in workshop. Kindly send or call at once for parcel."

IGNATIUS LOYOLA, S.J.

For two more years, the consciousness of his vocation kept growing. It seems evident that at this period his life was given more and more to the things of God, and that it was only a matter of time when he would turn his back on the world altogether. He had at some date after his conversion, visited Carlow in company with Judge William O'Brien who was on circuit. Not long before, in 1893, the Poor Clare Colletines, coming from Manchester, had made in Carlow their first foundation. The nuns were housed, to start with, in a dilapidated house near Graigue Bridge. Judge O'Brien had apparently come to know them, and on this occasion he brought with him Mr. John Sullivan, whom he introduced as being "greatly interested in nuns" Mr. Sullivan spoke very little, but impressed the nuns by the humility of his demeanour.

In July 1900, the Poor Clares moved to their present convent, and John Sullivan, who had apparently become well acquainted with them, came down for the occasion. He served four farewell Masses in the old parish church, creating a flutter of edification even in that recollected atmosphere, and presented a gold ciborium and a *Sacristan's Manual*.

There was a touch of unconscious irony about the

latter gift, for the sacristan of the time was a very vigorous lady, who corrected the eminent lawyer-acolyte for some breach of the rubrics. When remonstrated with by her Superioress, she replied that there was no harm done since "Mr. Sullivan was as humble as a child, and easier to manage than many an altar-boy."

After the Mass, John Sullivan accompanied the Bishop and clergy in the procession to the new convent. Amongst others present that day were Mr. and Mrs. James McCann, whose generosity had provided the nuns with their new habitation. Mr. McCann was the leading stockbroker in Dublin at the time, and played an outstanding part in the development of canal and railway traffic in Ireland. He was a devout and active Catholic, and he and his wife afterwards gave the house and grounds for the first Colettine convent in Dublin, where their only daughter lived for many years as a nun. At the ceremony in Carlow, Mrs. McCann noticed, as she thought, a poor man who had slipped in amongst the crowd. It was John Sullivan. The days of "the best-dressed young man about Dublin" were gone, and the time was fast approaching when Father John Sullivan would have few disputants to the title of the worst-dressed priest in Ireland.

John Sullivan evidently accompanied Judge O'Brien on more than one occasion when on circuit, and the judge took the opportunity to introduce his recently converted young friend to religious communities in the vicinity of the assize towns. The Capuchin Fathers of Kilkenny recalled one such visit to the Friary there, when Mr. Sullivan renewed his acquaintance with his friend, Father Fidelis.

Only a few weeks after the ceremony in Carlow, Miss

Sullivan came in jubilation to the convent at Brickfield Lane to announce the news that John had shaved off his moustache, and was going to the Jesuit novitiate at Tullabeg. He came later himself to say good-bye, and seemed depressed. It was, of course, at nearly forty years of age, and after only four years in the Church, a momentous step. Some time later, his brother, Sir Edward, went down to see him, and found Lord Justice Mathew's late Marshal scuffling the front gravel.

CHAPTER VII

THE NOVICE

THE house in which John Sullivan commenced his novitiate on September 7th, 1900, is officially known as St. Stanislaus's College, Tullamore, but unofficially and far more familiarly it is known as Tullabeg (the small hill or mound), in contradistinction to Tullamore (the large hill or mound), from which it is about seven miles distant. Both names are derived from the low range of *Eskers*, or gravel hills, that runs across Ireland from Dublin almost to Galway. The name Tullabeg is a purely domestic one, and has no roots in antiquity. It is even still unfamiliar to the local inhabitants, who commonly speak of "Rahan College," using the place-name of the adjoining townland, where stand the ruins of the famous abbey. Tullabeg was originally founded as a College for boys in 1818, the second foundation of the restored Society of Jesus in Ireland. It rivalled, or, as was believed by all old Tullabeg men, outshone Clongowes, until the two Colleges were amalgamated, for administrative reasons, in 1886. Like many colleges in Ireland, it consists of a Georgian mansion, to which additions have been made in the course of time. It is surrounded by an estate of moderate size, set in the wild and somewhat lonely scenery that is found bordering on the bog of Allen. Here John Sullivan entered on that daily round of small yet exacting duties that make up the time-table of a Jesuit novice.

It was providential that he should have as his Master of Novices a man of outstanding holiness, the late Father Michael Browne, S.J. From the very start John Sullivan conceived a deep admiration for his Master of Novices, which he preserved all through his life. It was obvious that he modelled himself very considerably, even in his outward demeanour, on Father Browne; he frequently quoted his sayings in retreats and in conversation, and always spoke of him with affection and reverence. This admirable sense of loyalty and devotion to the man who first trained him in the spiritual life will show itself again later in this narrative.

I can recall the first time that I met Father John Sullivan after my own entrance into religion in 1913. I was then a novice at Tullabeg, and he was a priest of some years' standing, making his tertianship (a year of special spiritual training, made by all Jesuit priests after ordination) in the same house. Both novices and tertians made in the autumn what is called the Long Retreat, the Spiritual Exercises of St. Ignatius for thirty days. At the close of this retreat, on the feast of St. Stanislaus, a dinner considerably better than the ordinary was provided, since it was the greatest feast in the noviceship. At that dinner Father John sat on my right, and, as was frequently his wont, ate absolutely nothing except a small portion of a roll, the remainder of which he crumbled all over the table, as if in an attempt to direct attention away from his abstemiousness. It happened that on his other side there was sitting an old Father, whose asceticism was of a milder type than that of Father John. Towards the end of the dinner, this Father, getting rather tired of fruitlessly passing on dish after dish, remarked in a reproachful tone, "You are a regular Father Michael Browne!" I remember well the earnest and embarrassed way in which Father John replied: "I wish I were, I wish I were."

The esteem was mutual. Father Browne valued highly this mature novice who, in spite of his lengthy stay in the world, led the way in observing exactly all the small customs intended to develop self-control and detachment, which must have been more than ordinarily difficult to one who had already developed fixed habits of life. Father Browne spoke after Father Sullivan's death of his extraordinary simplicity and the objection which he had to speaking of himself or of his interesting travels abroad, unless closely questioned. According to Father Browne, his great kindness showed itself also at that early stage. There was one novice who used to suffer from terrible desolations, and the only one who could always console him was Brother John Sullivan.

He made a deep impression on all his fellow-novices. Their testimony to his extraordinary fervour was unanimous. It is customary to put each new novice when he arrives into the care of one who has completed his first year. He is known as the "Angelus," and is supposed to instruct the neophyte in noviceship ways. Father Sullivan's "Angelus" had an easy task. These are his recollections.

"Although I was his 'Angelus,' it was quite evident at the end of a fortnight that he knew far more about the noviceship and infinitely more about religious life than I did. His simplicity and earnestness about every detail were amazing. There was never the least sign of superiority, never the least suggestion that he knew far more than all of us put together. For example, in recreation, one of the most difficult duties of the noviceship, we were always delighted to have him in our company. He would listen with interest to anything we had to say, and if conversation lagged he always came to our assistance with stories of his travels. He knew St. Augustine by the yard, and the Fioretti of St. Francis inside out. I think what interested us most were his experiences as a Protestant. He had many amusing and enlightening stories to tell.

"There was one story on the subject of Hell which seems to me now to be almost too good to be true, though my recollection is that he assured us the incident actually occurred.

"A clergyman was preaching on Hell, and assured his hearers that, though many seemed to doubt of its existence, he had no doubt whatsoever, since he had met people so wicked and base that there was no other place suitable for them. Then in a burst of confidence he added, 'I may as well tell you that I firmly believe an aunt of mine is in Hell.'

"This was too much for one of the congregation, who got up and began to go out.

" 'Look at that man,' exclaimed the clergyman. 'He won't believe my words, but he is heading straight for Hell.'

"The erring sheep was almost at the door, but at this point he turned round.

" 'Have you any message for your aunt, sir?' he inquired politely.[1]

[1] It is unlikely that John Sullivan meant this anecdote to be anything more than a *ben trovato*. As will be seen later, he never had any tendency to ridicule the church to which he had once belonged. Still, it is just conceivable that he had witnessed the incident. Naïveté in the pulpit (which is not confined to the Protestant Church) can at times surpass the efforts of the professional humorist.

"If after some duty or work any of us asked Brother Sullivan how he had got on, he would shake his head and shrug his shoulders and say, 'I made an awful fool of myself, an awful fool of myself.' This phrase became a regular catch-word among us for some time. I remember during one winter the joints of his fingers got very badly cracked and bled profusely. He always refused to put anything on them to cure them. Some novices said he used to rub sand into the cracks to make them worse."

Another of his fellow-novices recalled his ready adoption of the details of noviceship life.

"The chief thing I remember about him was the greedy way in which he wanted to find out all our smallest 'Customs.' To a man of his experience, if he had looked at these with worldly eyes, how trifling and perhaps even silly they might have appeared, but right from the start he seemed to have the appreciation of a John Berchmans for them all. His humility too was remarkable. He would come to us youngsters to send him sweeping the corridor, or whatever else it happened to be, as if he were a young servant newly arrived."

Yet another spoke of his inexhaustible energy, and remarked that his walk, which was very rapid, even along the noviceship corridors, seemed to be an indication of a mental eagerness to advance quickly along the narrowest possible way of the counsels. Some of the more high-spirited of his companions found his conversation rather over-serious, and even depressing. His mind frequently turned towards death, and he had a most vivid sense of the sin and sorrow that abound in the world, but his kindness and sheer good nature endeared him even to those who were slightly overawed by him. He made great efforts to adapt himself to what must have been indeed unfamiliar company for a middle-aged lawyer. At certain times of the day, the novices were obliged to speak Latin, with the purpose of preparing them for philosophical and theological disputations in their later lives. Needless to say, the Latin that was heard was often of a remarkable quality. Brother John Sullivan's Latin alone was strictly Ciceronian, but, in order to encourage his less fluent companions, he frequently interspersed it with deliberate solecisms, "Omne recte" (all right), being a favourite phrase of his.

One of the fellow-novices already quoted added a few characteristic and attractive traits.

"He was a most pleasant companion on walks. His wide experience of life, his cultured mind, knowledge of the classics and of the Lives of the Saints and his constant union with God, all enabled him to be religiously interesting and entertainingly spiritual. He spoke frequently of St. Monica and St. Augustine, to both of whom he had a marked devotion. He had a rather melancholy voice, especially when reading or preaching, and his spirituality was tinged, I think, with a gentle sadness that resulted from his clear realization of the sorrow that the sins of men give to the Sacred Heart of Our Lord. He spoke easily on this subject and on the Passion, which was never far from his thoughts. Occasionally, in those days, he told an amusing story, and, when he did, his face at the climax would light up with an apologetic smile, his eyes would just for a moment glance keenly at you; then his voice would change to a deeper tone, and his hand would be drawn across his eyes as if to obliterate his folly in recounting the story."

It was remarked how completely he had taken on the Catholic mind and ways. The only trace of Protestantism that he retained was that pulpit voice when preaching, which has now become so familiar to Catholics through the medium of the radio, and which is recognized by many of the Protestant clergy themselves as being a not inconsiderable cause of the emptying of churches. Father John never quite shed this tone, but it was redeemed by his utter earnestness.

The life of a novice is essentially uniform, and there is little to chronicle during the two years that Brother John Sullivan spent in Tullabeg. That he practised considerable austerity is certain, for it was known that the novices of that period, with the example of Father Michael Browne before them, required restraint from higher Superiors in that regard. Judging by his after life, it is likely that Brother Sullivan embraced more than the ordinary share of penance. But this, like his prayer, was governed by obedience. Enough, however, has been cited to show that, even in an environment where fervour was almost commonplace, the fervour of John Sullivan's novitiate was above the ordinary.

On September 8th, 1902, he took his first vows in the domestic chapel at Tullabeg. On these occasions every Jesuit scholastic is given a crucifix, known as the vow crucifix, to which is attached a plenary indulgence, granted to any dying person who kisses it and fulfils the usual conditions required. John Sullivan requested that he might be allowed to take as his vow crucifix one which he had brought with him to the novitiate, and which had belonged to his mother. This crucifix, a brass one about nine inches high, he carried with him constantly all through his life. Reference will be made to it frequently later, and he held it in his hands at the moment of his death.

CHAPTER VIII

EARLY YEARS AS A JESUIT

ON the completion of his novitiate, John Sullivan was sent for two years of philosophical studies to St. Mary's Hall, Stonyhurst, the philosophical Seminary for the scholastics of the English Province of the Jesuit Order. The Seminary was situated in the same grounds as and at a short distance from the famous college for boys. These two years, like the three years' theology which followed at Milltown Park, were inevitably somewhat uneventful. The ordinary course of studies essential for the priesthood had to be completed, and the ordinary round of religious duties prescribed for the scholastics of the Society of Jesus had to be followed. Nevertheless, even during these early years, Mr. John Sullivan began to stand out from amongst his fellow-religious as a man of unusual virtue. He rarely, if ever, came into contact with lay people during these years, and our knowledge of him is gleaned almost entirely from the recollections of his fellow-religious. It must not be thought, however, that such testimony is unduly favourable. If no man is a hero to his valet, certainly any man who can win the universal esteem of his brothers in religion must be outstandingly holy. This is no cynical reflection on the spirit of charity existing in Religious Orders, but is simply a recognition of the fact that life in religion is led so much in common that the smallest foibles must rapidly become evident, and virtue must be very genuine and very constant to merit praise or even notice. In accordance with the general principles followed in this Life, the impressions of those who knew John Sullivan at this period will be given to a great extent in their actual words. These were the impressions of Father Patrick Nolan, S.J., who came to Stonyhurst when Mr. John Sullivan had completed the first year of his philosophical course:

"I met Mr. John Sullivan for the first time in September, 1903, at the Seminary, Stonyhurst. I must confess that at my first meeting I was not much impressed, for he was a man who had no showy qualities. He seemed to my unpenetrating mind almost apologetic for his very existence. On and off I met him during the first few months. He was ever the same; diffident, utterly unpretentious, with a regular genius for depreciating himself before others. He spoke openly of his difficulties in his studies, and of the wonderful ability of some of his boyish companions, so much so that we young fellows, thinking too much of ourselves, took him at his own valuation. But I may remark that some who were better able to judge soon detected his fine knowledge of the classics, and observed that, though he was no master of the syllogism, he had a thorough grasp of the Ethics course. Moreover, he seemed to them to be a man of strong purpose, reminding them of St. Ignatius going to school again at Barcelona and Alcala.

"As he did not take part in our games, he was cut off from many of us, but we met him on the 'walk days' and came to know him better, and, before the year was out, he had won a place in all our hearts. He was very fond of long walks, and, on setting out, he let others talk. On the return journey, when bodily fatigue made us silent, he, tireless in mind and body, tried to entertain us, pouring out a wealth of conversation ever fresh, enlivened by a sparkling humour which was all the more entertaining because we had never supposed that he had that gift.

"His unselfishness and thought for others were remarkable. Although forty years of age, he was the first to volunteer for any disagreeable duty, always offering himself as a substitute for the 'fatigues' of the Seminary, such as serving at table. He seemed to live to help others, and when possible did it secretly and unobtrusively. I remember setting out on a cold March day to fish the Hodder. The snow was on the ground and a bitter wind swept down the river. I returned at about five o'clock p.m., weary and wet to the skin, and, on entering my room, found a warm blazing fire to greet me. Others had the same experience, and at length we discovered that the good angel had been Mr. John Sullivan.

"In the Seminary they gave us great liberty, but obedience to the rule was demanded. Mr. John Sullivan was ever faithful, and faithful in a way that did not censure others. When spoken to in English during study-time, he tried to answer by sign, but if forced to speak, it was always in Latin, according to the rule. During my stay in the Seminary I never knew him to transgress that rule or any other. But what most impressed us was his faith and spirit of prayer. He was one of the first to morning prayer and the last to leave the chapel at night visit. At Mass and Holy Communion he was undemonstrative. As far as I can remember, he used the missal at Mass, and no one could notice anything unusual about him. But after receiving Holy Communion he seemed wrapt in prayer. His lips moved, though never a sound came from them to disturb others. One felt that here was a man that lived and walked with God. I spoke to one who had been in the novitiate with him of his wonderful faith, and he told me that Mr. John was a sub-sacristan under him in Tullabeg, and that it was his duty to go to the different chapels in the house to put up the vestments and polish up the chalices and other sacred vessels. One day he went to one of the chapels and found Mr. John on his knees polishing the chalice.

"Mr. John Sullivan was constant in his visits to the Blessed Sacrament during the day. One day I came into the Chapel unobserved, and saw him kneeling in his characteristic attitude, slightly bent both from shoulders and hips, his hands barely resting on the bench, the head on one side, with eyes fixed on the tabernacle and the lips moving. For about ten minutes I kept watching him, for it was a lesson to me. I wondered that any man could have such lively faith, and I recalled what a Dutch scholastic had said some months before, 'Mr. Sullivan actually talks to Jesus in the chapel.'

"On leaving the Seminary in 1904, I went to bid good-bye to the Superior, Father Michael Maher, author of the well-known text-book on Psychology. I thanked him for his kindness to me and told him how much I owed to the English Province. He answered, 'The Seminary owes something to the Irish Province. The Irish Province sent us Mr. Sullivan. To have a man of God living in our midst is a special mark of God's favour to us.'"

The foregoing impressions were confirmed by many others who were at St. Mary's Hall at the time, and further details filled in. There were a number of old Fathers living in the Seminary who through age or infirmity were not easy to manage. Mr. Sullivan was most thoughtful towards them and helped them in many ways. He was the first to greet foreign scholastics when they arrived, and make them at home. In spite of his own difficulty with the philosophy (which was partly due to the difference he found between the classical Latin which he had studied for years and that of the philosophical text-books), he was always ready to help those junior to him when they were preparing for an appearance at a public disputation. In the course of his walks, he came to know many of the Lancashire farmers who lived about the Seminary, and by his sympathy won their affection, thus foreshadowing his later apostolate of the poor and the suffering in his native land.

It was true that, on account of his age and upbringing, he did not fit in completely with the young religious, most of them straight from school, with whom he had to live. Some of them felt that his charity was at times a little overpowering. He was constantly asking others whether he could relieve them of the task of serving at table in the refectory, especially if an unexpected holiday were granted. One of his former companions recalls with a touch of remorse having refused his offers of help rather brusquely, telling him more than once that he was quite capable of doing the work himself. Mr. Sullivan would go away quite unmoved, and on the next occasion be round again to offer his services. Both at that time and in after life he seemed to be absolutely proof against that most virtue-piercing weapon, the snub. His humility was indeed almost startling. It struck some as being somewhat artificial, but the vast majority would say that it seemed artificial only because it was so unusual. One of those who lived with him at Stonyhurst said that he would describe him as having "intellectual humbleness" rather than "intellectual humility," trying by the very awkwardness of the more unusual term to express the positive violence of his virtue.

One small incident of those two years at Stonyhurst is also recorded, as it exemplifies what was perhaps Father John Sullivan's most outstanding virtue, his sympathy for those who were suffering in any way. One of his fellow-philosophers, a fellow-countryman also, was beginning his third and last year of philosophy when Mr. John Sullivan arrived. Possibly as a result of the strain of two years' continual study of an exacting subject, he had allowed himself to get into a groove of depression. The feeling of being a stranger in a strange land had grown upon him, he had given up the usual games and recreations, was losing interest in life, and indulging in a dangerous self-pity. One day Mr. John Sullivan came to him, and suggested to him that he should be his companion for walks, and show him the very beautiful Lancashire fell country which lay all around them. He could not very well refuse such a request, and for some weeks accompanied Mr. Sullivan on his expeditions. At first the walks were somewhat difficult, as he had got out of condition, and found it difficult to keep up with Mr. Sullivan, who was always a splendid walker. However, the latter made the walks most interesting, recounting his many experiences, and giving reminiscences of famous trials at which he had been present, or of which he had heard his father speak. In a short time his companion got back into good condition, and after a few weeks was able for what was considered the champion "hike" of those days, the source of the Hodder.

It was only some years afterwards that it dawned upon him that Mr. Sullivan had got up all this walking purely for his sake, seeing that he had got into an unhealthy groove. When speaking of this experience afterwards, he made the following reflection which was fully borne out by John Sullivan's after life. "The point I would make is this; it appears to me that in whatever surroundings Father Sullivan found himself, he seemed to look round and ask himself, 'Is there anybody here who needs help and whom I can help?' Having found such, he gave himself up to them. To get to know Father Sullivan properly you had to be in some sort of need or distress."

In 1904, at the end of his philosophy in Stonyhurst, John Sullivan went to Milltown Park, Dublin, for his theology. His life there was very much as it had been in Stonyhurst, and there is no outstanding incident to record, nor anything that could throw a fresh light on his character.

He was a sound, but not a remarkable theologian. As might be expected, he was more at home in the problems of canon law and the positive teachings of moral theology than in metaphysical questions. It is a common custom in all seminaries for two students to come together regularly to discuss and go over the matter studied. The Jesuit who "repeated," as it is called, with Father John recalls his thoroughness, and how he would never let his companion pass over any point which seemed vague. The same thoroughness showed itself when they began to practise together the ceremonies of the Mass. Father John allowed his friend to proceed as far as the *Gloria*, and then said bluntly, "You have made about a thousand mistakes. Start again." This downrightness was always a characteristic of his later on in spiritual direction. If consulted about a line of conduct, he never softened down his direction if he saw the penitent wavering, but pointed out that the hardest was usually the best course.

The virtues he had displayed in Stonyhurst shone out just as conspicuously in Milltown. He was never known to deviate in the slightest from any rule. His spare time was spent in prayer, and though not yet a priest, he paid frequent visits to the patients in the Hospice for the Dying and the Royal Hospital for Incurables at Donnybrook. In this latter institution, his favourite patients were those in the men's cancer ward. And, as before, his was the charity that began at home. In those days the young Jesuits who were studying for University degrees lived down in Tullabeg, and used to come up to Dublin for the examinations of the Royal University. One of them recalled how Mr. John Sullivan, though a complete stranger, took charge of them, came to their rooms to see that they had everything they required, and, when they got a wetting coming home from some examination, saw to it that they had a change of clothing.

One amusing as well as edifying characteristic which he had developed at this time was the habit of diverting attention by telling a humorous story whenever anyone began to praise him. The friend who repeated theology with him used to take pleasure in leading on Father John in this way, and got many a good legal yarn out of him. One of these was of a scene he had witnessed when a plaintiff had won a case on some technical point, but had disgraced himself in doing so. The jury gave him damages of a farthing, and the enraged defendant taking a halfpenny out of his pocket, flung it down on the floor of the Court, crying, "Take your character out of that, and give me back the change."

Father Sullivan was ordained by Archbishop Walsh, in the chapel at Milltown Park, on Sunday, July 28th, 1907. The inscription on his ordination card concludes with the words of the cxvth Psalm, "Quid retribuam Domino pro omnibus quae retribuit mihi?" ("What shall I render to the Lord for all the things he hath rendered to me?") It is a stock quotation for such occasions, but few who have used it have repaid more to God for the gift of the priesthood than John Sullivan.

His first Mass was said at the convent of the Irish Sisters of Charity, Mount St. Anne's, Milltown, and his second at the Carmelite monastery, Firhouse, Tallaght. A former fellow-novice accompanied him to Firhouse, and assisted at his Mass. There was benediction afterwards, and Father John had difficulty in putting the Blessed Sacrament into the monstrance, a not infrequent accident with monstrances of peculiar make. There was an awkward delay of about five minutes. When he came into the sacristy after benediction, his friend said encouragingly that he had got on very well. "I made an awful fool of myself," said Father John. It was the old catch-word of the noviceship, and uttered with all the old sincerity.

Immediately after his ordination, Father Sullivan

was appointed to the teaching staff at Clongowes Wood College, where he was to spend most of the rest of his life. He went there that same autumn.

Before he left Milltown Park, an incident occurred which foreshadowed many such in his life. It has been said that he was a constant visitor to the Royal Hospital for Incurables at Donnybrook. One of the female patients there had long been suffering from bad lupus in the head. The disease had begun to affect her mind, and preparations were being made to remove her to a mental home. Father Sullivan came to visit the hospital. It was probably just after his ordination, as it is recalled that he gave many patients his blessing. He was asked to visit the sufferer from lupus, and remained a long time praying over her. The next day her mind was completely restored, and remained so until her death. A witness recalled how this poor patient had, as a result of her mental strain, turned completely against her, though she had done her many services, but after Father Sullivan's visit, their friendship was completely restored.

CHAPTER IX

THE SCHOOLMASTER

WHEN Father Sullivan arrived at Clongowes, the fellow-Jesuit whom he had befriended at Stonyhurst had already been teaching there some years, and one evening just before the start of the term, was invited by Father John to go for a walk. On reaching the entrance gate to the pleasure-ground which adjoins the College, Father John confided to his friend that what he wanted was some hints about the class management of smaller boys. His friend had very definite views on the subject, and proceeded to give them to him. "You must drop from the clouds, be a mystery to them, inspire them with all the fear and awe you can."

As he spoke, Father John's head dropped lower, and the clouds gathered on his brow, so, to soften matters somewhat, his friend added, "At all events I would advise you so to act for the first month." All in vain. Father John answered vehemently, "Surely, that's no way to deal with human souls! Father Michael Browne would never have given us that advice!" His friend then quoted for him a dictum of Father James Daly, the famous Clongowes Prefect of Studies, "Why, if I were to introduce the Pope himself into some of these classes, and he was not stern, there would be pandemonium in no time." But it was all in vain, so the subject of managing boys was dropped. Father John's friend summed up the episode as follows: "That is the last walk, and the last conversation I remember to have had with Father Sullivan. In the light of what I afterwards heard of him, it would appear to me as if his vocation was not to put boys through examinations, but by making a divine and lasting impression on them to help them on towards their entrance examination for the next world."

He was not, indeed, a particularly good teacher. His manner was too humble and self-effacing to ensure good discipline, his speech was somewhat hurried and indistinct, and he suffered from the disability that a scholar is always subject to, of letting his enthusiasm outrun the ability of his class to follow. A subject, for instance, in which he was intensely interested was the discovery of the Muratorian fragment, possibly because he was familiar with the scenes of the learned Muratori's labours. For a while, in fact, he was known as "Muratori" or "Mury," though the name soon died. But the interest of his class in paleography was sadly utilitarian. The Muratorian fragment was a helpful subject to get on to whenever they were not too well prepared to cope with the allotted portion of Livy. Nevertheless, Father Sullivan was most devoted and hard-working, and he had the reputation of being able to pull even the most backward candidate through his matriculation. The boys attributed his success more to his prayers than to his powers as a teacher, perhaps with justice.

He could be severe enough at times with a real idler, but there was never any harshness in his severity. One of his First Arts class of 1908–1909 related how Father John often said to him in the privacy of his room, "I was cross to-day," but added, "He never, however, uttered a really hard word." His most severe reproach was, "You never do a stroke of work," or, for a particularly egregious blunder, "You deserve to be locked up."

He had a great taste for Livy, and often alluded to "Livy's pictured page," a description which was dutifully if somewhat sceptically received by his hearers. The pages really lived for him. A former pupil of his was going to Rome in 1912 to complete his studies for the priesthood, and Father John asked him to sketch Taranto for him so that he might better visualize Livy's narrative of the famous siege.

He was fortunately blessed with a quick sense of humour, which prevented him from taking too seriously the want of response with which his enthusiasm for classical learning occasionally met. On one occasion he gave a dramatic description of the death of Shelley, and wound up with the finding of a volume of Sophocles in the pocket of the drowned poet. One of the class, now a distinguished Dublin surgeon, was heard to growl, "Served him right," alluding, I think, less to Shelley's other shortcomings than to the crowning folly of carrying Greek plays about in his pocket. A quick smile came to Father John's face. On another occasion he had spent a long time dinning into the heads of his class the definition of an oxymoron. The next day he asked the best boy in the class for an example of an oxymoron. There was an unpromising silence and the class began to feel the clouds gathering, but a quick wit from the north of Ireland saved the situation. "A white blackbird, Father," he suggested, and even Father John could not keep serious.

During nearly all his years at Clongowes, Father Sullivan acted as Spiritual Father to the boys. I think that the word veneration is not too strong to use of the sentiments entertained towards him by every generation of Clongownians since 1908. It is, perhaps, the most accurate word, too, for it indicates the natural shortcomings which he had as a boys' man, and over which his holiness triumphed. Veneration does not involve intimacy, rather it excludes it. Father John probably never understood boys perfectly. He took the keenest interest in them, an interest which could only have been prompted by a sincere affection. He was always at their disposal. He corresponded with and helped many of them in after life. Yet, one felt, when hearing him talking about them, that his vision of them, though clear, was from without. He was somewhat severe in his judgment of them, characterizing as "audacious"—a favourite adjective of his—what others would accept as the normal failings of healthy boyhood. But if his judgment sounded at times severe, he was never severe in heart or action. On the contrary, boys flocked to him for consolation in their troubles. His confessional was always crowded, and usually by the least law-abiding citizens of the little world of school.

It was a striking example of the conquering power of true holiness. There is in the hearts of Irish boys a peculiarly responsive chord that throbs in answer to the call of the supernatural, and there was such a call in the very sight of that familiar figure, the head ever bent in prayer as he walked, the worn, emaciated face and hands, the threadbare garments, the low hurried voice that took on a peculiar ring when it spoke of God. Father Sullivan had been only one year in Clongowes when I went there as a boy, and already we took it for granted that he was a saint. It is not surprising to find that at the time of his death one of the boys remarked to a master, "Sir, isn't it a great thing to be able to say that you were taught by a Saint? And the funny thing is that we knew it even when we pulled his leg a bit." And the mother of one of the boys wrote to Father G. R. Roche, S.J., who was Rector at the time:

"Although never having met him, I knew him well through the boys. I think the way they expressed themselves in their weekly letters home plainly tells what they thought of him. 'Father Sullivan (we call him the Saint, Mum) is dying, you will be sorry to hear. By the time this letter arrives, he will probably be in heaven.'

"A strange coincidence—that night, Sunday—and Monday, J (an elder brother who had left school) could not sleep, thinking of Father Sullivan and his devotion to the Sodality; and he told me that he must keep on repeating whatever prayers were usual, seeing all the time Father Sullivan. He was shocked when a friend passed him on a paper yesterday and asked, 'Did you know him?' "

It was on that Sunday night at eleven o'clock, that Father Sullivan died.

That Father Sullivan made a deep and lasting impression on the minds of the boys with whom he had to deal is shown by the following reminiscences, written down after a lapse of nearly thirty years, by two of his former pupils. Their memories are of the years between 1908 and 1912.

Rev. Eric Fair, D.D., professor of education, University College, Galway, wrote as follows:

"I remember hearing, in company with other small boys, in my first year in Clongowes, that Father Sullivan was son of the Lord Chancellor of Ireland. We received the information as a truth which we found it very hard to comprehend. We associated all such high persons as Lord Chancellors—no doubt, unjustly, in many cases—with 'swank.' Now, Father Sullivan was the essence of gentlemanliness. But he was, largely by reason of the same qualities, in his whole bearing, in his gentle courtesy to even the smallest boys, in his simplicity, in his accent, even in his use of the famous word 'audacious,' the very antithesis of 'swank.'

"The first—indeed first and last—quality we got to know in him was his holiness, and a certain attractiveness that went with it. I agree that 'reverence' or 'veneration' is the word, though perhaps just a little bit too cold.

"He taught me pass Latin for a while. He was not a brilliant teacher. Still, he was so in earnest about everything he did that one learned from him. I remember one day feeling very sorry for having vexed him in class, though he showed no more than a kind of gentle surprise and reproach.

"In my later years in Clongowes I was, like many other older boys, often in his room. Looking back, his patience was wonderful. He never seemed to mind when we came or how long we stayed. Even as a boy I certainly found him most interesting when he spoke of his travels and reminiscences. I remember, for instance, his telling how a Protestant minister who had been chaplain to Lord Erne,[1] was first drawn to the Church by the new light in which he saw Irish history when he was commissioned to write the history of the Erne family. He went to Rome, Father Sullivan used to tell,

[1] John Haughton Steele (cf. p. 25).

and there one day entered a church to pray. On rising up he found he had been kneeling on the graves of the O'Neills and O'Donnells, whose sacrifices for the Faith, become known to him through his Erne studies, had first turned his mind towards the Truth.

"In telling us boys of Greece, he spoke little of classical associations, but a great deal of the country folk and of the schismatical monks. He had the greatest quality which makes travel talk good and interesting, charity. He saw the good in everything. He emphasized the kindness of the monks and the old Catholic qualities which had followed them even into the sad schism brought about long ago by their rulers. He dwelt above all on their glorious and loving devotion to Our Blessed Lady, and trusted that one day she would lead them back to the Church. Often in later years, in summers spent in Italian countrysides, Father Sullivan's travel talk used to come back to me.

"He used to speak too of the modern Greek language, perhaps especially to those of us whom he knew to be keen on Irish. I remember him speaking of the different types of Greek, the extraordinary number of newspapers in that country, and one newspaper in particular which was published entirely in verse.

"We boys gradually got to notice too a little of his work in the People's Church—a chance peep at that side of the house would bring it home to us. We were not surprised at the people's veneration for him. It was our own feeling too, then, and is now, combined with the hope and trust that he is praying for each of us."

Captain Sidney B. Minch, of Mageney, Co. Kildare, who was captain of Clongowes in 1911–12, added a few further touches to the portrait of Father Sullivan sketched by Dr. Fair.

"Father John Sullivan will be always vividly in my mind, although memory lets me down rather badly as a rule. Schooldays generally leave outstanding impressions upon us. My two outstanding impressions were, on the one side, the playing-field and its personalities, and on the other, Father John Sullivan. My classroom experiences are mostly remembered, when at all, by his presence there. To me he was different in every way from other masters. In his private room I had many hours with him during my last year. He went to great pains helping me to learn Catiline, which was the Latin text prescribed for the Senior Grade Intermediate examination. The disedifying picture of Roman life seemed hurtful to his delicate and sensitive mind. I noticed very often how, standing, as he always did, he turned this way and that, as if by that means he could avoid the scenes which he was translating. Taking these scenes as his text, he used to denounce and point out the terrible consequences of luxury, avarice, and a misspent life. The many visits which I paid him involved a certain amount of suffering for me. I lost my play-hour, and in winter I knew that I had to face a cold and chilly room. Once I arrived a little before him, and did my best with the fire, which seemed to consist of a little smoke in the centre of a grate half-filled with slack. It was hopeless, and always the same. I found out also how little covering he had on his bed. It was run on the same lines as the grate half-filled with slack.

"I found Father John at his best on walks during that same last year. With his hat crushed any old way under his arm, he started in a half-run, head well forward, praising everything that nature had to show. How he talked! He found out what you were interested in, and then brought God or some saint right into the middle of it so naturally that even our young minds became aware of his constant preoccupation with the things of God. The great scientists, statesmen, and soldiers of those days were well known to him; then, with a jump, he was off to ancient Greece or Rome, the Holy Land, then on to Newman, Sir William Butler, and then to St. Augustine. Every now and again he would slip aside to visit some poor folk living in a humble cottage. We would see him kneeling at the bedside of the invalid. As a matter of fact, he always knelt with us to hear our confessions, also.

"He had a very distinguished face when he really looked at you, but he kept his eyes downwards so much that this seldom appeared. The dried appearance of his cheeks and the semi-parchedness of his lips indicated to us that Father John took very little interest in food or any creature comforts. His hands too were dry, and had a parched feeling.

"He was fascinated by the heroism of great saints, particularly those who had saved themselves from a life of terrible indulgence. How often do I remember him referring to St. Augustine and St. Mary Magdalen. He spoke to me of St. Paul as 'a great fellow, a great fellow.' Father John did admire tremendously the real fighter. He took an interest in the games at Clongowes when he was there, and after an out-match he would sympathize or congratulate as the case might be. His expressions were, 'too bad, too bad, you lost yesterday,' or 'that's great, you won yesterday.' One day he said, 'you win nothing unless you know how to lose.' It was only in after life that the significance of that came home to me.

"I knew him even better when I left Clongowes, during the Great War, and afterwards when I fetched him from Rathfarnham to help my father during his last moments on this earth. I remember him well kneeling at the bedside, his socks, which were badly shrunk, just slightly above his boots—you could actually see his shins. Before he left I realized for the first time how happy an event death could be. In the same old clothes which he always wore, he assisted at my marriage and disappeared immediately it was over.

"When I visited him at Rathfarnham he complained of his appointment as Rector, which he could not account for. I asked him laughingly if he was afraid, and I shall never forget his distant look when he replied: 'When I was told that I was to be Rector I had been for some time meditating on the humility of Our Lord in the stable at Bethlehem, and this doesn't seem to me to fit in properly.'

"As I have said at the outset, his memory is vividly before me. I had a tremendous affection for him, and I know how easy it would be to exaggerate in writing about him, and how much he would hate it. I have, therefore, purposely kept accurately to what I remember of him. There is one thought which to-day I still carry with me and which he alone gave me. It is this. 'You'll never have to fight alone in this world, although we leave Our Divine Saviour to fight alone constantly.'"

The foregoing impressions are those of pupils of Father Sullivan's at almost the beginning of his time in

Clongowes. It is interesting to compare them with those of one who left Clongowes in 1931, only two years before Father Sullivan's death. The lapse of over twenty years had apparently made little difference.

"My friendship with Father Sullivan," wrote Rev. Roland Burke-Savage, S.J., "dates from my first days in the Third Line in September 1926. In the tangled maze of troubled memories of a small new boy's first weeks at school, Father Sullivan stands out as the happiest recollection. From my first few days in the house he began to invite me up to his room from time to time, where he would talk of people we knew, or of books. Strangely enough, despite his most obvious 'differentness,' he always made me feel as if I were talking to an equal with whom I was on the friendliest terms.

"During my five years in Clongowes, I often used to avail myself of the standing invitation to his room. For me the hardest thing in school life was the impossibility of getting away from people for even an hour or so. Classroom, playground, play-room, library, study, refectory, you were always in the middle of a crowd. To me there were only three possible escapes: the chapel, my cubicle in the dormitory at night when the day was over, and Father Sullivan's room. When out of sorts or worried about some little mishap, Father Sullivan's room was the place where I could forget my troubles, not by telling him of them, usually, but by just listening to stories of his travels in Greece, or talking about friends and their doings.

"Why did I like Father Sullivan? Initially I suppose because he seemed to like me. Father Sullivan seemed just interested in you as you were, and not for what you were worth. Besides, he was so extraordinarily kind and understanding that you could not help liking him. The word understanding makes me pause. In what sense was Father Sullivan understanding? I don't think he quite understood the average schoolboy's supreme interest in football; I doubt if he really understood all the difficulties of growing boys; not that he was harsh in his judgments, no, he was kindly and gentle, but gave the impression that grace had made the path of holiness much easier for him than for most. Yet he was very understanding of disappointments, upsets, homesickness, or mere loneliness. These troubles he seemed almost able to sense, and, without any mention on your part of them, he would begin to talk of the Fourth Station or some other scene in the Passion, and, as a result, your own little sorrow would be lost in the larger one. Not that his conversation was normally spiritual in the strict sense; with me, at any rate, I doubt if a quarter of his conversation was strictly on spiritual topics.

"His main topics of conversation were the Latin and Greek classics, and mutual friends of ours. I am a barbarian, and was always told what I was missing; many an evening during after-supper play-hour, I was brought up to his room to hear him read off a translation of Homer, or Aeschylus, or John Chrysostom, and then fondly counselled to take up Greek when I left school. Horace or St. Augustine were his favourite Latin authors, at least the ones he liked to read to you; I often had to listen to my feeble efforts in construing Horace, and then when he thought my patience was coming to an end, he would sit back in the high-backed chair and tell me of Monica and Augustine.

"The only literary, or such-like paper I ever heard from him was a paper on Mahommed, which I persuaded him to read to the Higher Line Missionary Society in 1930–31. I remember the president of the Society asking me to try and get the MS. after the meeting, but when I asked Father Sullivan, he showed me a copy-book covered with hieroglyphics, and said he thought it would be of no use.

"His short talks, given to the whole school, instead of evening rosary from time to time, were very effective. Despite his little mannerisms, the refrains of 'and all that,' and 'out in the world there,' the obvious sincerity, directness, and optimism of his talks impressed me very much at the time. All the talks that I remember could be summed up in the often-quoted passage of Newman, continually repeated by Father Sullivan: 'It is the boast of the Catholic Religion that it has the gift of making the young heart chaste; and why is this, but that it gives us Jesus for our food, and Mary for our nursing Mother?'[1] Love of Christ and of Our Lady seemed to be the topics that came easiest to him, and when during the year he came to talk on the various Jesuit saints, as their feasts came round, he nearly always went off from his hardly-begun narrative to speak of their love for Christ and Our Lady.

"He nearly always had a few words to say before Mass each morning, which gave one the idea that he was perpetually wrapped up in trying to win eternal rest, or grace, or financial help for someone or other. His devotion to the dead, or perhaps better his thoughtfulness, is best illustrated by the fact that, during the

[1] Discourses to Mixed Congregations. Discourse XVIII. "On the Fitness of the Glories of Mary."

two years that I was in the Higher Line Sodality, we never once recited any Office of Our Lady, but always part of the Office for the Dead. This was usually for some old-boy sodalist recently deceased, but if such were lacking, he would tell us to offer the Office for all the Sodality dead, or for the forgotten ones.

"While on the subject of the Sodality, his talks were good, often very striking, but not particularly helpful, nor were they according to any plan. The main impression left on me by them was the enormous amount of suffering people had to put up with. Week after week, we were treated to gruesome descriptions of cancer cases whom he had come across, or for whom his prayers had been sought. He seemed to have the happy knack of always hearing of people who were down on their luck, and seemed always anxious that we should pray for them.

"Personally, I did not go to Confession to him regularly. He had, however, in my time, quite a big following of all types, including not a few of the 'faster element.' This always struck me, as his penances were notoriously stiff. Father Sullivan had a noticeably great devotion to the Stations of the Cross—quite often if one dropped into the Boys' Chapel during recreation one would find him alone in obviously fervent prayer before the Stations. From his giving out the Stations in public during Lent I have an indelible impression of three of the Clongowes Stations, and of the words of the prayers that he used to say at them; these Stations were 'Christ meets His Mother' (to which Father Sullivan was particularly attached), 'Christ is stripped of his garments,' and 'The Crucifixion.' Whenever I make the Stations, and particularly at the three mentioned,

Clongowes and Father Sullivan always come vividly before my mind.

"I never had Father Sullivan as a regular master; on occasion, however, he supplied for someone who was away, or was ill. The most notable fact about him was that whilst he was quite incapable of keeping order, the boys never went their furthest with him, and never seemed to regard him with that contempt they usually had for those who could not control a class.

"While shrewd enough in his knowledge of boys, he either did not see, or did not choose to see the many little deceptions that were played upon him, e.g., if he had set a map to be shown up in class next day, three or four maps, shown up in turn by different boys, seemed to satisfy him, as he never seemed to realize that the same maps were constantly reappearing.

"His idea of the amount of work we should get through was rather alarming to a schoolboy; he would say quite casually, 'take the next hundred pages in Robinson,' which seemed an enormous lesson for First Syntax, a class of boys aged about fifteen.

"His method of dealing with troublesome lads was unusual, and was not always effective. His appeal for order often went this way: 'Keep quiet there, for the love of God keep quiet, there.' His bitterest taunt was: 'You are a disgrace to Clongowes there, ought to be scourged there, ought to be scourged. . . .'

"On one occasion I remember being much struck by a request of his to keep quiet because he had a headache. Coming from one, who, as we boys believed, used to keep stones in his shoes, and never used to dry his hands in winter in order to make them chap, this seemed very human. Thinking over the incident, afterwards, it struck me as requiring a good deal of humility to plead for quiet on such grounds before a crowd of unthinking small boys.

"This story he told me one day with evident glee when visiting my parents' home. A mystery bus tour had come to Clongowes the previous day. Father Sullivan, anxious to help, came on the scene to see if he could entertain some of the visitors. The rest of the story is in roughly his own words: 'I took two old ladies round the New Building. They were real typical Dubliners and appeared to have never been out of the city before. They took in everything and listened to all I had to tell them about the building, chapel, etc. At the end of the expedition one of them opened her purse and produced a half-crown, which she presented me for my trouble. I showed them into the bus, and went off to my room delighted to pick up a half-crown so easily, as it would come in very handy and pay for a number of little things.'

"I remember my mother being immensely taken by this story, and by the great enjoyment which Father Sullivan obviously got from the incident, and from the recounting of it.

"Father Sullivan used often to take Higher Line walks, and as I knew him well, I used often to walk with him. One funny habit of his struck me; normally he used to roll up his hat and stick it under his arm, but whenever he approached a church he used to put on the hat in order to be able to salute the Lord. I remember going up to town in a bus with him, and we had the same procedure all the way.

"What do I owe to Father Sullivan? Much more than I could ever write down. For he was and is for me the embodiment of an ideal of Christ-like kindliness and other-worldliness, the like of which I do not expect to meet again. I still remember vividly the February morning when the Master of Novices began his exhortation to us novices, with a request for prayers for Father Sullivan, who was seriously ill. Two days later news came that he had died the previous night. I had been making a novena for his recovery; I promptly changed it into a novena to beg his intercession for help I needed at the time. Since then I have not ceased to pray to him, and I know that he will continue to be as good a friend to me now as he was to a miserable little Third Liner fourteen years ago."

The long hours which Father Sullivan spent in prayer and his constant visits to the sick and suffering did not prevent him from playing his part fully in the life of the Community. He was always at the disposal of the Prefect of Studies for extra work, and would cheerfully step into a gap and take any class, no mean test of virtue even for one who is not a septuagenarian. On a wet half-holiday, rather than leave the boys on their prefects' hands, he would volunteer to take a couple of classes or half a Line for a walk. It was probably an effort to him to take any interest in games, but he would come and look on for a short time at an important match, then getting an excuse to slip away, and I can remember how one of my own earliest recollections of Father John, in 1908, is of seeing him coming out during the play-hour, tucking up his gown, and bowling at the Third Line cricket nets. His bowling was underarm, and, it must be confessed, not of a very high order.

On Christmas night, when it was customary to call

on each member of the Community to contribute something in the way of a song or recitation, he would always contribute a reading from Aubrey de Vere's memoirs, a tragic murder described in the early pages of the book, which he read with deep feeling. He had a highly developed sense of humour and a fund of witty anecdotes chiefly connected with the Bench and the Bar. A favourite story of his was that of a charming young lady who found herself placed beside a very serious judge at a banquet. She tried to engage him in conversation, but could find no congenial topic. At length she played her trump-card—the great man must be musical, she thought. "Has your Lordship heard Madam Cavallcani sing the 'Voice of the Zephyr'?" "No, thank God!" was the gruff response.

Nor was Father John's humour confined to anecdotes. He could sum up a situation in a shrewd and witty way. On the evening of Union Day (the day when the College entertains Old Boys and parents), a member of the Community who was famous for his conversational gifts remarked to Father John, who was a great friend of his, "I have a pain in my head from all the talking I have had to do to-day." Father John quizzically replied: "And what about the people you were talking to?" But he afterwards feared that he had spoken somewhat uncharitably, and expressed his regret. No-one else regretted the *bon mot*. On another occasion a fellow-Jesuit alluded to a certain lady as Miss So-and-so. Father John, running his hand through his hair and giving his friend one of his half-shy, half-humorous looks, remarked, "Would you call her 'Miss'? She was married three times!" A nun who was a penitent of his, recalled how on one occasion she accused herself in confession of pride. "Ah, well," said Father John drily, "you're in common life there."

It was remarkable that although Father Sullivan was so seriously minded, and although his conversation often ran on not over-cheerful topics such as death-bed scenes and painful illnesses, he always gave the impression of being perfectly cheerful and indeed light-hearted. He had a quaint way of saying, "Cheer up, cheer up, cheer up," and his eyes would light up in a kindly fashion contrasting markedly with his rugged and ascetical face. He did indeed himself give the impression of possessing that happy equanimity which comes from undiluted goodness and indifference to the things of the world.

During his first few years at Clongowes, Father Sullivan used to accompany the Community on their usual holiday in summer. During those periods he was the best of companions and threw himself whole-heartedly into any excursion that was going. One of his fellow-Jesuits, who was then a young scholastic, recalled how Father John, during a holiday in the west, organized an expedition to climb Mweelrea, that fine peak that overlooks Killary Harbour between Galway and Mayo. He took entire charge of the necessary arrangements, and proved himself the most delightful of companions, shortening the ascent of the mountain by telling fascinating anecdotes connected with his Grecian and Macedonian wanderings. The same Jesuit recalled two small incidents of that time which reveal Father John's simplicity and goodness of heart. It was the custom for each member of the community to receive a small sum of money for incidental expenses during the holiday. Father John invariably came to this young scholastic and insisted on giving him half of his own modest store, saying that, being younger, he would have longer trips to make. On a holiday in Donegal this same scholastic mapped out a trip which would include a number of beauty spots which he was longing to see. There was one seemingly insurmountable difficulty. He and his companions would have to get Mass at 2.30 a.m. in order to catch an early ferry across Lough Swilly. With what he now regards as incredible temerity, he put his difficulty to his friend, Father Sullivan, who, though he was not coming himself, cheerfully agreed to rise and say Mass at the required hour, and then helped the party to get ready for the journey.

But even during these holiday times Father Sullivan did not relax in his life of prayer and zeal. One of the college bakers, Thomas Cribbin, accompanied the Community, in 1915, to Annascaul, Co. Kerry, to help with the kitchen arrangements. The kitchen was so small that provision had to be made for washing up in the open air outside the kitchen door. From this spot the baker could see into Father Sullivan's room, the window of which was uncurtained. He used to start work at 4 a.m. in order to have water boiled and dishes washed up from the night before. On only one occasion during the three weeks which the holiday lasted did he see Father Sullivan in bed at that hour, and on that one occasion he was just getting up. Thomas Cribbin used to attend to Father Sullivan's room, and noticed that, although the clothes were thrown back over the end of the bed, the bed itself looked as if it had not been used. During the day, from his vantage point outside the kitchen, he used to see Father Sullivan coming constantly into his room and praying for long periods before a crucifix which he laid on the bed. When out walking in the neighbourhood, Father John was often seen stopping little boys on the roadside and teaching them Catechism.

On other holidays it was a common sight to see him climbing to remote cottages in the hills to visit the sick. At Fintra House, near Killybegs, in Co. Donegal, in 1908, the numbers who came to consult him and get his blessing were so great that he used to interview them in a barn adjoining the house. In 1912 the holiday was spent at Cleggan, near Clifden, in Co. Galway. It was a remote place, and the people in the neighbourhood had leave to come to Mass in the house. Father Sullivan's reputation soon spread, and there was a congregation of fifty or sixty every morning. Yet, apparently, he eventually thought even such apostolic holidays to be too great a concession to human nature, for he gave up going on them after five or six years.

Before passing on to the wider activities of Father Sullivan during his years at Clongowes, it may be recorded briefly that this period was broken for a year, from 1913 to 1914, when he returned to Tullabeg for his tertianship. That was a year which must have been full of inner experiences for him, as it is devoted almost entirely to spiritual exercises, commencing with the Long Retreat of thirty days. But those who lived with Father Sullivan during that year can recall nothing remarkable beyond his constant absorption in the things of God. In view of his age, he was given special latitude in visiting the poor in the neighbourhood, and he devoted a good deal of time to it. But, once again, he did not forget the other and more rare form of charity. Writing of those days in Tullabeg, Father James P. McConnell, S.J., a member of the English province of the Society of Jesus, says:

"Father Sullivan will be remembered by all for his charity, and I can give an instance of this with regard to the care he took of one Tertian, Father Cook (R.I.P.), sweeping his room and doing all sorts of humble duties for him."

Father Cook was in very poor health, and Father Sullivan probably felt special sympathy for him, as he was a convert, and had been a High Church Anglican clergyman.

I was then a novice in the same house. I have elsewhere mentioned one personal recollection, Father John's remark that he wished he were like Father Michael Browne. I may add two others. A section of the Summary of the Constitutions of the Society of Jesus, which is read monthly at table in every house, enjoins that each one should persuade himself "that the meanest things of the house shall be assigned to him for his greater abnegation and spiritual profit." For Father Sullivan, this was no mere pious generalization. Although by many years the oldest amongst the Tertian Fathers, he chose what was by far the worst room in the house for himself, a comfortless recess right under a stairs up and down which heavy-footed young novices constantly passed. Here we used to hear him at all times of the day praying aloud.

The other memory is of August 4th, 1914, a day on which even the remote precincts of Tullabeg hummed with excitement. Father John, who must have finished his tertianship by then, was coming down from Dublin for some purpose—probably to attend to the public church. He walked out from Tullamore, a distance of some seven miles, carrying a shabby portmanteau and wearing his well-known old cape waterproof. Two facts have made me remember all these years his arrival. The first fact was that never before had I seen him carrying any luggage. Normally, he was the embodiment of Juvenal's *vacuus viator*. The second fact was that he was carrying in his hand the stop-press edition of the evening paper, announcing the declaration of war by Austria on Serbia, and that from some remark he let drop, we detected that he had not even opened it.

As has already been mentioned, Father Sullivan's letters were rarely self-revealing. He was, indeed, in this respect, the despair of a biographer. However, a letter may be quoted here which he wrote from the tertianship to a life-long friend, Edward Gerrard, afterwards Captain, Royal Artillery. It gives a few glimpses of Father Sullivan's mind, always interested in scholarship and in the things of God.

St. Stanislaus College,
Tullamore.
St. Stanislaus Day, November 13th, 1913.

My dear Eddie,

We began our long Retreat on October the 12th and emerged to-day. During that time we do not receive or write letters, so I only received yours to-day. I was delighted to hear from you, don't be discouraged about the result of the exam. The reading will have done you a lot of good. I had to teach the Elements of Political Economy for several years at C.W.C. and found it extremely hard.

I have not seen Father Martindale's book[1] though I have

[1] "*Augustine*" *in the History of Religions*, C.T.S.

met him several times. He was one of the most brilliant scholars at Oxford, a convert from Harrow school. Anything relating to St. Augustine has a special interest for me. Some time will you copy out for me the passage describing his reading Virgil. I have no Virgil here, not even our old friend, Book V.

The quotation (The Courtier's, Soldier's, etc.) you mention, is taken, I think, from *Hamlet*; it is part of Ophelia's lament on the intellect of Hamlet whom she supposes to be out of his mind. It is a beautiful passage.

There are twenty-four novices here, extremely fine boys, seven from Clongowes. There is room for more—soldiers are wanting badly to fight Christ's battle which is raging throughout the whole world. It was a sight that stirred all the compassion of His Sacred Heart. "The harvest is great, the labourers few" were His words when He saw the multitude like sheep without shepherds before the ravening wolves. When St. Augustine read the words of St. Paul, "Omnia possum in eo qui me confortat," he called St. Paul a "coelestis miles" and cries out to God, "conforta me ut possim."

Please remember me very warmly to all at home and believe me always,

Yours very affectionately,

JOHN SULLIVAN, S.J.

After the tertianship, Father Sullivan returned immediately to Clongowes, and on February 2nd, 1915, took his last vows in the Society of Jesus at the high altar in the Boys' Chapel.

CHAPTER X

THE FRIEND OF THE AFFLICTED (1)

IF the holiness of Father Sullivan was so apparent to the careless eyes of schoolboys, it was no wonder that it attracted to him countless men and women who were learning the bitter lessons of the larger school of life. It is only possible here to dwell briefly upon the wonderful apostolate that he exercised amongst the sick and suffering in the countryside around Clongowes, and amongst an ever-widening circle of others whom he visited in hospitals and consoled by letter, or who came to him from almost every county in Ireland to ask the intercession of his prayers in their illnesses and misfortunes.

Much of his activity was centred round the public church at Clongowes, commonly known as the People's Church. This church was built in 1819, and served both as a public church and as a chapel for the boys until the erection of the new Boys' Chapel in 1908. It is a building of modest size and of no architectural pretensions, but it has one interesting historical connection. From the time that Daniel O'Connell sent his two sons Maurice and Morgan to Clongowes in 1815, he paid frequent visits to the college, especially in his later years, spending much of his time in prayer in the church seeking strength and consolation in the increasing trials of his strenuous life. Father Joseph

D'Alton, S.J., who was at Clongowes from 1834 to 1836, and was one of the pioneers of the Jesuit mission in Australia, wrote down in 1896 his reminiscences of his schooldays. In them occurs the following passage:

"During the Repeal Agitation, O'Connell spent a week every year at Clongowes. It was the week when the Repeal 'Rent' was collected all over Ireland. . . . O'Connell spent the week in a sort of retreat. He heard the boys' Mass every day. A grand *prie-dieu* was prepared for him outside the sanctuary, and there we saw the great Tribune wrapped in a big frieze coat (it was generally winter) hearing Mass with all the devotion of a novice. It was a very practical lesson to all of us youngsters."

In a letter of O'Connell's to his friend and financial lieutenant, P. V. Fitzpatrick, dated August 8th, 1839, there occurs the following passage:[1]

"My own prospects appear to me to be daily darker and more dark. . . . God help me! What shall I do? I think of giving up my income, save an annuity of a small sum to myself and my two sons, and going, if I am received, to Clongowes, and to spend the rest of my life there. I want a period of retreat to think of nothing but eternity."

Father Sullivan constantly heard confessions in the People's Church[2] and interviewed in the porch those who had come to see him. In later years it was quite a common sight to see several cars waiting outside the door, in which invalids had been brought to get his

[1] *Correspondence of Daniel O'Connell*, edited by W. J. Fitzpatrick, F.S.A. (London: John Murray, 1888.) Vol. II, Chap. 17, p. 195.

[2] His confessional in the People's Church was that on the right-hand or Epistle side, and in the boys' chapel the first on entering on the left-hand or Gospel side.

blessing. One must speak with all the reserve required by the Church of the numerous cures and other favours attributed to his prayers. It is undoubted that extraordinary faith in the power of his intercession was manifested not only amongst the people in the vicinity of Clongowes, but throughout Ireland.

In the following pages accounts will be given of some of the more striking of these alleged cures. At the risk of being tedious, a considerable number have been included, since their mere frequency and their occurrence at all periods of Father Sullivan's life as a priest make them more remarkable. Apart from anything else, they give a vivid picture of Father Sullivan's habitual charity and self-sacrifice. It must be remembered, moreover, that they represent only a fraction of those which have been recorded. It is to be regretted that expert medical evidence was available in only a few cases. At the time when these incidents took place, it did not occur to anyone to obtain such evidence, and when it was sought, most of the doctors concerned were either dead or were unable to recall the cases in detail. However, in practically every instance, either the person concerned has been interviewed or else testimony has been taken from reliable first-hand witnesses. A special note will be found at the end of the chapter, dealing with whatever medical evidence was obtainable.

A few preliminary remarks may be made. Father Sullivan's attitude in dealing with sick or otherwise distressed persons was always one of complete simplicity and humility. He never assumed anything remotely resembling the role of the professional thaumaturgus. He was frequently heard remonstrating with people who came to Clongowes to see him, and asking them why they could not say their prayers as well at home. When he did agree to bless them and pray for their recovery, he would often use a relic or Lourdes water, or ask the sufferers to invoke some saint. He always enjoined prayers and usually some act of mortification. Finally, he was never on any occasion heard to make the slightest reference himself to any of these alleged cures.

Though there is good reason to believe that Father Sullivan was sought after by invalids quite early in his life as a priest, the large majority of the cures recorded occurred from 1920 on. However, in 1911, only four years after his ordination, the following remarkable incident took place.

A boy named Jeremiah Hooks, living in Naas and aged twelve at the time, was attacked by St. Vitus' dance. He was under the doctor's care from November 1910 to April 1911. The disease was so bad that he was unable to use a knife or fork or even drink out of a glass or cup, as everything used to be jerked out of his hand. His father finally brought him to Father Sullivan at Clongowes, who prayed over him and said that he would be all right.

The boy was better after that, but a short time afterwards was frightened by a bull, and the trouble returned. His father brought him back to Father Sullivan, who again prayed over him, blessed him, and assured his father that he would never have the trouble again. When the boy returned home, he sat down to take a meal, and his mother could not restrain her tears when she saw him use a knife and fork without difficulty. From that day on he never had the slightest return of the trouble, grew up strong and healthy and has been working on the railway for many years.

Though it occurred many years later, the history of Mr. Hooks's younger brother may be given here. This boy was delicate from birth and deficient in mind. About 1927, when he was sixteen years of age, he began to get bad tempered and violent. His mother was advised to have him removed to an institution. She determined however, to have recourse to Father Sullivan again. When he saw the boy, he told Mrs. Hooks decidedly that the boy would not be cured. The mother then told Father Sullivan that she asked only one thing of God, that her boy would become quiet, so that she would be able to keep him with her. Father Sullivan approved of this petition and blessed the boy. From that day on, he became perfectly quiet and tractable, and remained so until his death in 1938. A witness who knows the family well confirmed the mother's account, and stated that the change was startling. The boy had previously been positively dangerous, but from the day of his visit to Father Sullivan was always gentle and affectionate.

In April 1918 Mr. W. T. M. Browne, a well-known veterinary surgeon living in Naas, Co. Kildare, was seriously ill with double pneumonia. A very dangerous complication had set in, and a Dublin specialist, who was called in by the local doctor, had tried various remedies to remove the complication without success. He told Mrs. Browne that he had only known one similar case, and that the patient concerned had died.

On hearing this, Mrs. Browne sent her husband's *locum tenens* in a car to fetch Father Sullivan. On his arrival, he went into the sick man's room, requested Mrs. Browne to leave them, knelt down beside the bed and remained for a considerable time. He then left the room, and Mrs. Browne entered. She noticed at once that her husband was much calmer, and in a very short time the dangerous symptom disappeared. Meanwhile, in the confusion, Father Sullivan had slipped away before he could be noticed, and walked back eight miles to Clongowes, though it was raining heavily. Mr. Browne rallied rapidly and made a complete recovery.

Fr. Nicholas J. Tomkin, S.J., who was Rector of Clongowes from 1912 to 1919, recalled two incidents which took place during that period. It is to be regretted that the names of the persons concerned have not been preserved, but it is quite possible that they may still come to light. It must be remembered that it was almost an every-day occurrence to meet persons who had come to Father Sullivan to seek his prayers either for their own cure or for that of some friend or relative, and that at the time it did not occur to anybody to make a record of these events. This is Fr. Tomkin's account of his two experiences:

"One evening, close on ten o'clock in July or August, a glorious summer evening, I was returning from walking with some of the Community through the pleasure-ground, and came out by the little iron gate opening on the walk leading to the castle. I was surprised to see a poor woman with a donkey and cart standing a few yards to the left. No cart ever came that way. I asked the woman what she was doing there and how she had got there. She told me that she had come from Maynooth by Garvey's house, through the fields, and had brought her little daughter with her to be cured by Father Sullivan. This child had never been able to walk since her birth. She said that she had carried her and left her on the steps at the church till Father Sullivan returned from Naas. I asked her in future not to come that way but to come by the ordinary road to the church. Some months after this, I met the woman with the donkey and cart a considerable distance from the College. I asked her how her daughter was. She called to a little girl who ran up to her. 'Father,' said the woman. 'Here is the child that I carried to the church the night you saw me in the College grounds. She is cured. I knew she would be if Father Sullivan blessed her. She is able to walk now like any child.' The child seemed to be about twelve years of age.

"The second incident occurred one morning when I was standing outside the castle hall-door, watching the people leaving the People's Church after Mass. I noticed a man who looked like a prosperous farmer waiting for someone. I asked him whom he wanted and he replied that it was Father Sullivan. I told him that Father Sullivan had just said Mass and had to get his breakfast. We then got into chat, and suddenly he said to me, 'You know, Father, I should be dead now and buried but for Father Sullivan. Last Wednesday two doctors, Dr. O'Connor and another, gave up all hopes of me. I received the last sacraments, and my wife asked me would I not like to see Father Sullivan. I asked her to send for him. When Father Sullivan came to my bed, I told him that all was over, the doctors could do no more. Father Sullivan laughed and rubbed his hands. 'You are not going to die, you will be at Mass next Sunday,' he said. Here Father I am, quite well. You see why I was anxious to see Father Sullivan.' "

During the spring of 1919, a woman living in Co.

Carlow had been suffering considerably for some time from a swelling on her breast. The doctor who attended her strongly advised that an operation would be necessary for the removal of the trouble. Having been a rheumatic for years, her physical strength was greatly reduced, and she dreaded the idea of an operation lest her children, some of whom were young at the time, should be left motherless. Having heard through her son, who was working at Clongowes, of the wonderful sanctity of Father John Sullivan and the many favours and cures attributed to his intercession, she wrote and asked for his prayers. Her son received the letter on Monday morning. On Monday evening he approached Father Sullivan who listened most sympathetically to the whole case. "Tell the good woman not to be discouraged," he said, "I will read an Office for her and offer Mass for her to-morrow morning, and she will be all right in a few days." It was only with great difficulty that Father Sullivan was persuaded to accept a half-crown as stipend for the offering of the Holy Sacrifice; he absolutely refused to take any more, insisting all the time that he would prefer not to take anything, and finally remarking, "Now, are you sure you can spare it?" After celebrating Mass on the following morning, and before he had breakfasted, Father Sullivan was seen by the sick woman's son walking hurriedly towards the house of a poor woman who lived in the locality. There was reason to believe that he had gone to give her the offering he had received for the Mass.

Tuesday and Wednesday passed by. On Thursday morning a letter was received from the patient herself, in which she stated: "When I awoke on yesterday morning (Wednesday) the first thing I did was to put my hand to my breast and see if it was worse (I did not dream that it could be better). To my joy and astonishment I found that the swelling had completely disappeared. I need not tell you how overjoyed I was. I can only offer my heartfelt thanks to God and to Father Sullivan for his prayers and Mass for my restoration to health. See Father Sullivan and tell him everything, and may God bless him eternally."

This woman lived until 1940 and never again felt the slightest trace of the trouble. She was cured, as Father Sullivan had said, "in a few days."

After Father Sullivan's death Mrs. Cruise, of Monkstown, County Dublin, gave the following account of the cure of her mother, Mrs. Williams:

"In 1922 my mother's sight began to fail, and got so bad that she could no longer distinguish faces, or see to read or knit or do needlework, which, as she was an invalid owing to heart trouble, was a very great privation. My sister, Miss Mary Williams, brought her to the oculist, Doctor N. He was away, but his *locum* saw her, and told my sister that my mother had cataract on both eyes and was going completely blind and that nothing could be done. My sister wrote to Father Sullivan, who was Rector of Rathfarnham Castle, asking for prayers. Father Sullivan came out to see my mother at the Salthill Hotel. He prayed over her and touched her eyes with a relic of Mary Aikenhead. My mother's sight improved rapidly, she began to read and sew and no longer complained of not being able to see. I brought her in to Doctor N., who examined her eyes and found no cataract on them. It was eleven years from the day Father Sullivan saw her until she died, March 1933, and she never complained of her eyesight and could see perfectly."

A very similar testimony came from a Dublin Convent:

"Father Sullivan was my Director for eleven years before he died. I should not be able to write now only for him. I had ulcers on my eyes for three years. Some of that time he was Rector at Rathfarnham Castle. He used to come down very often, or as he used to say himself, 'I'll run down next week.' At the end of the three years he said to me one day in an authoritative tone which was very unusual for him, 'How are the eyes?' I replied, 'No better, Father." He said, 'Now you are long enough going to doctors, have no more to do with them, put away all their remedies, and Our Lady will cure you. Make a novena to her, put a cupful of Lourdes water in your eyes, and on her Feast you will be cured.' I asked him then to bless my eyes. He did so, and said Mass for me on the Feast of Our Lady of Lourdes. That was six years ago. I never had an ulcer or inflammation since. Before Father Sullivan spoke thus to me, the doctor had told me that I would get blind. The ulcer was on the sight, the pain was terrible, and I could not read and could scarcely see."

In the early winter of 1923, a young man named Antony Coughlan, living in Sallins, five miles from Clongowes, was dangerously ill with pneumonia and pleurisy. One Saturday night, the doctor attending him told his sister that he would not be alive next day. A friend was sent to Clongowes for Father Sullivan. When he arrived, the sick man was barely conscious, but recalled him coming into the room and hearing his confession. Father Sullivan then left the house but, for some unknown reason, returned almost immediately and went up again to the sick-room. He took out of his breast-pocket a crucifix, gave it to the young man to hold and asked him to repeat some prayer. Mr. Coughlan remembered distinctly that Father Sullivan then put his hand on his shoulder, and said, "You'll be all right." He also promised to ask one of the parochial clergy to come and anoint him. Immediately he had gone, Mr. Coughlan began to feel better, and told his sister and brother, who had been watching up with him constantly, that they could go to bed that night. Shortly afterwards, one of the curates of the parish arrived to anoint him, and he recalled how his feeling of semi-consciousness had disappeared, and he was fully alive to what was going on. Next morning, he told his sister and brother that they could safely leave him and go to Mass, since he felt so much better. He was out of bed within four or five days, and recovered completely.

About two years later, Mr. Coughlan himself summoned Father Sullivan to the bedside of a friend and neighbour of his, John Rourke, who had often stopped up the night with him during his own illness, and who now was dangerously ill, also with pneumonia. This time, no cure was obtained, but Mr. Coughlan's veneration for Father Sullivan was increased in a strange manner. After Father Sullivan had prayed by his friend's bedside, Mr. Coughlan drove him back towards Clongowes. He was very anxious to know what Father Sullivan thought of the sick man's chances of life, but hesitated to ask him, as it was evident that he was wrapped in prayer. At the bridge over the Liffey outside the village of Clane, the car ran out of petrol. Mr. Coughlan got out to pour some petrol into the tank from a can, and Father Sullivan made some trivial remark to him about the quickness with which he carried out this operation. Mr. Coughlan felt emboldened to ask what were his hopes for John Rourke. Father Sullivan replied, "He is not as bad as you were, but he'll do no good." On his return home, Mr. Coughlan mentioned this prophecy to several friends. It was fulfilled within a few days.

In the same year, 1923, occurred the cure of Mrs. Dyer, now resident in Sutton. She was then Miss Nellie Coyne, and was engaged as assistant to Miss Emily Power, who conducted a Catholic Repository in South Richmond Street, Dublin. Mrs. Dyer thus described the incident:

"After an accident I attended the Meath Hospital in regard to a wound in my right hand, caused by a splinter entering between my thumb and forefinger. It was then necessary to have it X-rayed but very little could be found, although the examination covered both hand and arm.

"Actually at this stage only a few very small splinters were extracted, and I was informed that, as far as the hospital could tell, no further splinter could be located, and I was advised merely to keep the wound clean.

"Some months later when I was visiting Miss Power, Father Sullivan called, and on seeing my hand still bandaged, inquired after it. At this time the wound had not healed up and was still very painful. However, it was then that Father Sullivan blessed my hand, and I remember he said he would offer Mass for my cure next morning.

"Two days later, whilst visiting some friends near home, I had occasion to remove the bandage to show them the wound. We were all surprised to see protruding from the wound a large splinter the size of an ordinary match. This was extracted by my mother, who had been sent for, and we then took it along to the Meath for examination.

"The doctors could not understand this, but were quite satisfied that the splinter had traversed my arm from hand to shoulder and back again, and added that if it had not come away I should have lost an arm. You can take it as definite that the entry and exit of the splinter occurred in the same spot in my hand."

Miss Power corroborated this story, and added that she herself saw the splinter the morning after it had come out of the wound "about the size of a flat match, darkish colour and smooth, and the wound it had come from quite healed, no bandage on." She also recalled that when Father Sullivan was told of the cure, he said: "The holy Mass, the holy Mass. *Deo Gratias.*"

Miss Power was well acquainted with Miss Eliza O'Neill, the companion of Lady Sullivan, who has been referred to in earlier chapters. She remembered hearing Miss O'Neill speak of an unusual type of cure attributed to Father Sullivan. It was that of a mentally deficient boy, who had all the outward signs of his infirmity, his hair, in particular, being of a curious streaky quality. When he was about ten years old, his mother brought him to Clongowes to Father Sullivan. A novena was made, and he visited Father Sullivan again on a few occasions. Soon after, he was able to attend school, and at sixteen passed an examination for an important clerical post and made good progress. In appearance he became quite normal, and his sparse hair was replaced by an abundant crop of curls.

Miss Margaret Walshe, of Kilmurray, Enfield, recalled in 1940 the following three favours out of many which she attributed to Father Sullivan's intercession.

"About 1922, I was terribly troubled with neuralgia and a very bad form of headache. I went to Father Sullivan and told him. He said, 'Why should you worry over that? It is but one of the many little ills of life, and should be borne with.' He then gave me his blessing. The pains ceased immediately, and I have never had a return of them since.

"In 1923, my brother was stricken down with a severe attack of sciatica and other internal troubles as well. He was suffering for a long time, and was not getting better. The doctor (the late Dr. John Robinson, M.O., Johnstown) was baffled over his disease. I went to Father Sullivan for consolation. He said, 'Your brother will come all right. It will be slow. Offer up the Rosary every day for his recovery.' It took him six months to recover and he is in perfect health ever since.

"About 1925, my mother had a large lump on her neck. The doctor (Dr. Robinson) said it was a cancerous growth, and was afraid to tamper with it, as it might prove fatal at once. It was dreadfully painful. Again I went to Father Sullivan, who said, 'Your mother will get better. Go home, and with the other members of the family say the *Hail, Holy Queen* and the *Creed* for nine days for that intention.' On the third day of the novena, the lump separated, and before the ninth day, she was completely cured."

The following cure is remarkable for the fact that it was referred to by Father Sullivan himself as a miracle. Needless to say, he took no credit for it, but attributed it to the intercession of St. Anne. The person concerned was a young married woman, Mrs. Brennan, of Dublin, and the story is best given in her own words:

"In September 1925, I happened to be one of the many victims of a fire which happened in Mary Street, Dublin, and in trying to escape, sustained a very bad fracture of the leg below the knee. The fractured portion was held on only by the ligaments. I was removed to Jervis Street Hospital, and after four plaster-casts had failed, no unity having taken place in the broken bones, the surgeon contemplated plating, and, failing that, amputation. At this time I had only heard of Father Sullivan through my mother and sister, who had asked his prayers on my behalf.

"In January 1926, he visited me in hospital, and laid his hand on the place where the fracture was, it being now in the fifth plaster-cast as a last hope. He told me to pray to St. Anne. After his visit, everything pointed to a cure. I felt life beginning to return to the broken half of the leg, and before the surgeon took off the cast I could lift the leg. When the cast was taken off, there was quite a crowd called to see the leg which had at last set after six months.

"I left the hospital in March on two sticks, which broke, one after the other, as if by miracle, there being no apparent reason for them to do so. The surgeon had told me to return to the hospital to have the false tendons broken down that had contracted the knee, but that got all right without treatment, and I was restored the full use of my leg without any defect.

"Whenever I would happen to meet Father Sullivan in after years, he would always ask how the leg was. When I told him that I would never think I had had it broken at all, he would then say, 'A miracle is always perfect.' "

On two different occasions Father Sullivan's prayers were invoked on behalf of a little girl, Kitty Garry, who lived with her parents not far from Clongowes, and each time with happy results. The first occasion was in the spring of 1926. The child was then aged ten, and one day got weak in school. She was examined by her family doctor, who declared that the top of one lung was affected, and his verdict was confirmed by the local tuberculosis officer.

Her parents brought her over to Father Sullivan. He blessed her and, clapping his hands, said, "Don't worry, she'll grow up a great big strong girl." After the lapse of a month she was brought to the doctor, who said that there was a remarkable improvement and that she now seemed quite well. However, he asked that she should be brought to him again in a month's time, when he pronounced her completely cured. She remained in good health until December of that year. She then developed a violent pain in her head and ear. The doctor who had attended her before was summoned. He diagnosed meningitis and gave little hope for her recovery. He attended her for three days and there was no change for the better. On the third day the child's father took a taxi and went to Clongowes for Father Sullivan. When he arrived, the child was lying half-conscious, every now and then lapsing into unconsciousness. On his entering the room, she opened her eyes and recognized him. He spoke to her and said some prayers. Then he asked her mother for a cup of fresh water. Again he prayed, blessed the water, and told her to sit up and take a drink of it. She sat up, took the cup in her hand, and drank some of the water. He then turned to go and the child said good-bye to him. Before leaving, he told the mother to give Kitty a drink of the water whenever she asked for it.

A girl who worked in the same office as Mr. Garry was below in the parlour. She had come, in fact, thinking that the child was going to die. When Father Sullivan had gone, this girl went up to the bedroom, and Kitty immediately put out her hand and said, "I'm well." After that, she frequently asked for a drink, until all the water that Father Sullivan had blessed was drunk.

The next day was Sunday, and the curate called, fully intending to anoint the child. He was astonished at the change in her. The same day the doctor came. He too was astonished at the improvement, and found her temperature much lower. The next morning it was normal. She never looked back and was able to come down from her room on Christmas Day. Though her health in after-life was not over-robust, she never had the slightest return of either of the illnesses from which she was cured on these two occasions.

Early in February 1927, the wife of Mr. Laurence J. Fullam, Assistant County Surveyor, Co. Kildare, was dangerously ill. This is her husband's story.

"My wife was dying of double pneumonia. She had passed through one crisis, and, when the second came, the two doctors who were in attendance told me that very little hope could be entertained for her recovery. She was almost continually unconscious and had been kept alive for two or three days by oxygen. When I heard what the doctors had to say, I suggested getting a specialist from Dublin. On his arrival, the three doctors held a consultation. They then called me into the room and the specialist acted as spokesman. He told me that, though they, as doctors, must keep fighting as long as there was the slightest hope, his own opinion was that it was now only a matter of a few hours.

"Without telling anybody where I was going, I rushed off in my car at full speed to get Father Sullivan. I met him in the College grounds. Without waiting to get hat or coat, although it was winter time, he came with me. Coming along I said to him, 'Father, if ever you worked a miracle, you must work one in this case for the mother of eight small children.' His only answer was to start humming a hymn.[1] When we arrived at the house, he prayed for about half an hour over my wife, who was then completely unconscious. On our way back, he called to Clane Convent to ask the prayers of the nuns, and also made a visit to the Blessed Sacrament in the parish church. Before we parted, he told me to put my trust in God and that my wife would recover. Next morning she was so much improved that I rushed out to send off telegrams to friends and relatives to say that she was out of danger. The improvement continued daily. She was up in about three weeks' time and was able to travel to Dublin on the following St. Patrick's Day."

A very remarkable cure, marked by that peculiar confidence which Father Sullivan sometimes displayed, was that of Mrs. Domigan, of Dunshane, Brannoxtown, Co. Kildare. In 1928, Mrs. Domigan, who was then a very young married woman, got into very bad health.

[1] The explanation of this curious incident may have been that Father Sullivan was confused at the mention of the word 'miracle,' and could think of no other way in which to turn the conversation.

Five doctors had attended her at different times, and all agreed that both her heart and lungs were badly affected. On the advice of the local Medical Officer, it was decided that she should be sent to Peamount Sanatorium. She made arrangements to send her children to a relative in Westmeath. Some two years before, she had visited Father Sullivan and believed that she had been relieved of a minor ailment through his prayers. It now occurred to her to seek his help again. Her removal to Peamount had been fixed for a Thursday, and on the preceding Saturday she drove over to Clongowes. She was so weak that she could not travel alone, and her husband had to accompany her. The proprietor of the car which they hired in Naas required some persuasion before he would take her, as he was afraid that she would die on the way. Father Sullivan interviewed her in the People's Church. He sprinkled her back and chest with holy water and prayed for a long time over her. Then he suddenly said, "The home won't be broken up. You will all be reunited soon again."

On the following Thursday she went to Peamount. On Friday she was examined by three doctors and no trace of tuberculosis could be found. She was kept for three weeks in Peamount and then returned home. Since then she has enjoyed perfect health, has a large family, and has never had any difficulty in attending to her household duties.

In October 1929, an incident occurred which brought out in a striking way the confidence which was felt by those in trouble in the power of Father Sullivan's prayers. A little boy, aged a year and ten months, son of Mrs. Finn, of Naas, was taken ill with appendicitis.

She took him out to see Father Sullivan, who warned her that the child was dangerously ill and advised her to have a second medical opinion. As a result of this consultation, she brought him immediately to Baggot Street Hospital, Dublin, where he was operated on at midnight. His condition was serious, as there was local peritonitis, and he continued to have a very high temperature until the following Wednesday night, the operation having taken place on Monday. On Wednesday night his condition changed for the worse, and his mother became convinced that she must have recourse to Father Sullivan to save her child. She took a taxi from Dublin at 10 p.m. and arrived at Clongowes at about 11 o'clock. The College was almost in darkness, but on her ringing, she was admitted by a priest, who brought Father Sullivan down to her. She told him her story, and he showed great sympathy, gave her a miraculous medal to put on the child, and told her that he would come to Dublin next day to see her little boy. When she got back to the hospital the child was resting quietly, and next morning his temperature was almost normal. Father Sullivan came, as arranged, next day, blessed the little boy, prayed over him, and gave him some Lourdes water to sip. He was very anxious about the child, and had to be let know every day by telephone to the post-office at Clongoweswood how he was doing.

All went well for a week, when the child started vomiting. All efforts to stop the vomiting failed. It continued all night and into the next day. On that day there was Office and Requiem Mass in Gardiner Street Church for Father Peter Finlay, S.J. Mrs. Finn went to the Mass. In the afternoon she visited the hospital again, and was told by the nurse that she had only left that morning when Father Sullivan called and asked to be brought to the little boy. He again blessed him and gave him a little Lourdes water to sip. The vomiting stopped and did not recur.

A cure which had a curious sequel was that of Mrs. Murphy, the postmistress of Ballymore Eustace, Co. Kildare. In February 1929, she was operated on in Dublin for tubercular peritonitis, and after seven or eight weeks in hospital was allowed home after receiving a course of ultra-violet ray treatment. On her arrival home the local doctor again examined her, and found that an abscess was forming where the incision was made during the operation. He allowed it to develop and finally lanced it. All this time she was in very bad health, and the doctor expressed to her husband his concern as to the ultimate outcome of the case. He found that, in spite of all he could do, the abscess refused to heal. During this time he attended Mrs. Murphy twice weekly. She decided to seek the help of Father Sullivan's prayers, and went over to confession to him at Clongowes. He asked her if she believed in Our Lady and in favours granted by her. He then told her to say three Hail Mary's daily in honour of Our Lady of the Immaculate Conception and blessed her, with the request that she would call again on him.

This meeting took place on a Saturday. The doctor's visiting days were Tuesdays and Fridays, and on the following Tuesday, through some misunderstanding, the doctor failed to call in time to meet her. The same unusual accident happened on the Friday. The wound had now not been dressed for over a week, so she called at the doctor's house on Saturday morning. When the dressing was removed, the doctor was astonished to find the abscess completely healed, but he said that it would have to be lanced in about three weeks' time as it could not possibly be healed inside. In point of fact, Mrs. Murphy never had the slightest trouble since. The doctor expressed his astonishment at the cure, especially as the cavity was so deep.

Mrs. Murphy had intended to return to see Father Sullivan as he had requested, but she postponed the visit, and eventually, to her regret, forgot all about it. Some years later she was awakened suddenly during the night with a return of the former violent pain. She was badly frightened and prayed hard for relief. The pain ceased after a few hours, leaving her prostrate. It was not her custom to read the obituary column in the newspaper, but on the following day something prompted her to do so. She was dumbfounded to see the announcement of Father Sullivan's death, which must have taken place either at the very moment that the pain had returned, or shortly afterwards. She immediately made arrangements to visit Clongowes next day, and saw the coffin, but with regret found that she was too late to see once more the face of Father Sullivan, whom she felt to have been responsible for her complete recovery.

It was often Father Sullivan's practice to demand some act of sacrifice on the part of those who were seeking for a cure. Shortly before his death, a maid who was in the employment of a relative of his was suffering from a diseased hand. She was attended to by Dr. C. M. O'Brien, one of the leading skin specialists in Dublin, but without success. The trouble began to appear malignant, and the girl's mistress, with whom she had been for five years, wrote almost in despair to Father Sullivan and asked him to call. He arrived when she was out, but the maid recounted the interview afterwards. Father Sullivan made her kneel down, put on his stole, prayed and made the sign of the Cross over her. He then asked her what she liked best to eat. She confessed to a weakness for the national dish of bacon and cabbage. Father John enjoined on her not to touch it for a month, and then ran out of the house saying, "You'll be all right." Within three weeks the hand was perfectly healed, and the girl's mistress recalls her surprise at seeing her being able to wash up with hot water and soda without the slightest inconvenience.

What appears to have been the most remarkable of all the cures attributed to Father Sullivan's prayers occurred in December 1932, only two months before his death. It is fortunate that in this case it has been possible to get expert medical testimony.

In the last week of November 1932, Mrs. X, a young married woman, prior to the birth of her child, became subject to pernicious vomiting to a peculiarly dangerous degree. She was removed to a Dublin nursing home, and underwent the usual treatment under the care of a well-known gynæcologist. She grew steadily worse, and after about a month the doctor's description of her state was as follows:

"The vomiting was so persistent that she would vomit even drops of water, and then continue dry retching. She became practically a living skeleton, with a dry parchment skin only covering her bones, and did not weigh, I should think, more than about five stone, whereas her normal weight would be about nine stone.

To keep fluids in her system, I had to give her salines and glucose introveinously. Notwithstanding all the recognized treatment, her condition became steadily worse, and I began to think that she was more or less moribund."

About December 17th the patient was anointed. She was in a semi-conscious state at this time, and had a complete disinclination for religious consolations. She had refused to see several priests who were suggested to her, but at last, at the request of her sister, agreed to see Father Sullivan, of whom she had already heard, but whom she did not know.

Father Sullivan came to the nursing home on December 22nd. He was brought to the sick room, which, as was his wont, he sprinkled liberally with holy water from an old lemonade bottle. He then said aloud a number of *Our Fathers* and *Hail Marys*. Mrs. X was so weak that she was incapable of answering, but she recalled distinctly the fervour with which he said the *Our Father*, and how she felt that she had never before fully understood that prayer. Father Sullivan then left the room. Going down the stairs, her sister asked him if the patient would recover. All he replied was, "She is very weak."

The next day, the doctor visited Mrs. X, and found her slightly better. What followed had better be told in his words.

"Although the patient was barely conscious, I told her that I would let her have some dinner on Christmas Day to try and cheer her up, although I had no idea at the time that she would be able to take even a cup of tea. On Christmas Eve, the matron of the home told me that the patient had had toast and tea and did not reject either. On Christmas morning, to my amazement, she had rashers and sausages, and during the day had a full Christmas dinner of turkey, ham, etc., and never vomited anything. I was certainly amazed at the rapid and unexpected recovery, and from that date she continued to put on weight."

This "extraordinary recovery," as the doctor termed it, proved permanent. The child was born on July 25th perfectly normally. He was christened John after Father Sullivan, who, however, never saw him, as he had died in the preceding February.

Even in smaller material difficulties, Father Sullivan's aid was constantly invoked by his friends. One convent in the Midlands recalled a whole series of troubles that vanished when his prayers were sought. A nun was spared a serious operation. Several epidemics had occurred in the boarding-school, but after Father Sullivan blessed the dormitories no serious illness ever recurred. On the farm grave loss was threatened from blackleg among the cattle. Again Father Sullivan's prayers were sought, and the disease disappeared. He was firmly believed to have triumphed even over a refractory range in the kitchen.

It will be recalled how Father Sullivan was originally attracted towards the Franciscans, and at times the accounts given of his simplicity, goodness and evident power with God recapture something of the atmosphere of the *Fioretti*. These are the recollections of a nun who spent her childhood very near Clongowes:

"Father Sullivan directed my home spiritually, and his advice on other points was considered sacred also.

"About the year 1913, when I was eleven years old, I got into a decline as a result of pleurisy, blood-poisoning and other complications. Three doctors gave no hope of recovery. My father asked Father Sullivan to come and cure me. That same day he blessed me, prayed as I have never seen anyone pray, and said, 'You will soon be well again.' He advised a change of air. My removal seemed to be impossible, but when Father Sullivan ordered it, it must be done, no matter what the cost. After about five days away, I returned home for a visit—on my own feet! All agreed that it was a miracle. Father Sullivan, in his saintly way, said to me, 'Thank God continually.'

"At another time something like a plague broke out amongst the cattle on my father's farm. Father Sullivan was summoned, as usual, to the scene. Later he could be seen, in his usual holy attitude, proceeding with my father from field to field, blessing each with water blessed in honour of St. Ignatius, and then burying in each a medal of St. Benedict. Subsequently there was no mortality but greater prosperity than ever.

"His appearance in my home always created an atmosphere of holiness and joy. He always took notice of us small ones, and once asked me to say a favourite prayer of his, 'Soul of Christ, sanctify me!' I was so sorry to have to confess that I could not say it. He saw my great embarrassment and proceeded to teach me. After a few examinations and some help, I proudly said it all alone for him, at which he showed real pleasure.

"At my last confession to him, he gave me a wee engraving of Our Lady with the title 'Ecce ancilla Domini,' and his earnest advice was 'Be humble, child,' which he repeated several times. He also said, 'Just live from day to day. Don't look to to-morrow.'

"Unfortunately, his letters went in the big surrender

before profession. How I regret such destruction. He always wrote briefly, generally described the happy death of someone I knew, and asked for intercession for big sinners.

"He often advised me to imitate St. Brigid, to whom he seemed to have a strong devotion.

"One of my brothers had the honour of taking him on many occasions for a 'joy-ride,' as he called a sick call. Only when his bicycle broke down would he accept of such a luxury, or when my father would take him miles and miles away from Clongowes, often in pouring rain, going to some soul who yearned to see him before starting on the last journey."

Apart from the help he gave by his prayers, Father Sullivan was always extraordinarily kind and thoughtful. He had permission to keep a certain amount of money for alms, and used to run small accounts for tea, sugar and other groceries at one or two of the local shops, distributing dockets for these goods to the very poor. He got many poor children into orphanages or other suitable homes. Almost everywhere he visited some act of kindness was recorded. A particularly touching one occurred on the occasion of his giving a retreat at the Sacred Heart convent, Roscrea. During the retreat, one of the lay-sisters heard of the death of her sister, who was also a Sacred Heart lay-sister, in Mount Anville convent, near Dublin. She asked Father Sullivan for prayers, and he promised that when he was next at Mount Anville he would visit, in her name, the grave of her sister. She was consoled by the assurance of his prayers, but thought that such a busy priest could hardly find time for such a visit. However, some days later, she received a note from him with a little packet of earth. He had not only gone to the grave to pray, but had taken a little of the still loose soil to send to her.

Before closing this chapter, a note may be added on whatever medical testimony was available concerning the foregoing alleged cures at the time of the writing of this Life. Six doctors were called in testimony, of whom four were Catholics and two Protestants, all of whom gave whatever evidence they could with great courtesy and care.

The evidence of the doctor in the case of pernicious vomiting (page 140) has already been cited in full.

The doctor who attended Miss Coyne (page 129) at the Meath hospital had no distinct recollection of the case. He pointed out, however, that fairly rapid travelling of foreign bodies through the human system is common, and that even the fact of the splinter re-issuing through the original wound would not be beyond the domain of natural causes.

In the case of Mrs. Brennan (page 132) the doctor agreed that the fracture was a very difficult one in which to get union, being a comminuted fracture of both bones of the leg, accompanied by shock. He thought, however, that the final union might have been produced naturally, though with difficulty.

In the case of Mrs. Fullam (page 134) the consultant could not recall the details, having been very busy at that period, but the local doctor remembered the consultant looking on the case as a serious one. The consultant pointed out, however, that sudden and dramatic relief is not uncommon in cases of pneumonia.

The only evidence available in Mrs. Domigan's case (page 135) was the record at Peamount Sanatorium confirming her statement that, on admittance, she showed no signs of tuberculosis. But the doctor had died who had made the clinical examination before she was sent to the sanatorium, and his would have been the essential evidence.

The surgeon who operated on Bernard Finn (page 136) had fairly definite recollections of the case. He could not find any definite record in his notes of danger to the child's life, but confirmed the mother's statement that, two days after the operation, the child's condition was quite satisfactory.

It must be acknowledged that the above evidence, with the exception of that given in the first case mentioned, is so slight as to be of little value either positively or negatively. It has been thought well, however, to give it, in order to show that every effort has been made to examine critically the cures attributed so widely to Father Sullivan's prayers.

In conclusion, it may perhaps be useful to note the distinction that may be made between a miracle in the strict sense and what may better be called a favour granted in reply to prayer. A miracle in the strict sense is some unusual effect which can be perceived by the senses, which could not be produced under the given circumstances by natural means, and which can be attributed safely to divine action. It is, however, quite possible that answers may be given by God to fervent prayer under circumstances where the result might have been due to natural causes. Thus a mother prays for her sick child and at the same time secures skilful medical treatment for it. The child recovers. There is nothing unreasonable in thinking that the cure was due wholly or in part to the mother's prayers, yet even if this could be proved (say by a revelation), no miracle would have taken place. Indeed it may safely be said that the Church implies that such favours are frequent. She directs us, even by the official prayers in the Missal, to pray constantly for spiritual and temporal favours. Yet she is far from implying that the answers to such prayers are miracles, since the very definition of a miracle is that it is something unusual.

Hence, when we come across the record of a large number of sudden cures coinciding with the visits and prayers of any holy man, we may lawfully surmise that they are answers to the appeals of one of God's friends without necessarily claiming that they fulfil the strict definition of a miracle. In any case, our surmises will always be made subject to the final decision of the Church.

CHAPTER XI

THE FRIEND OF THE AFFLICTED (II)

MANY cases of spiritual healing were attributed to Father Sullivan. A certain Miss X. had lived for some time in a town in Kildare, and was on friendly terms with the nuns in the convent there. She went to America about 1915. She had evidently known Father Sullivan before her departure, as she used to write to him occasionally to have Masses said. After his death, she wrote to the Reverend Mother of the convent, and enclosed the following statement.

"I had some faith in Rev. John Sullivan's intercession with God, and when I arrived in Y. (a State of America), I learned to my sorrow that my brother and his wife, the mother of a family of six school-age children, were some years absent from the sacraments. Rev. John Sullivan offered Holy Mass at my request in 1915, and on that day, or the next day, they both went to San Francisco all the way up from Y., made their confession, received Holy Communion and remained faithful until their death."

A striking conversion was that of a man who was dying in a town near Clongowes. He had refused to see a priest, though urged to do so by the nurse, and by the doctor who was attending him, the late Dr. Charles O'Connor, of Celbridge, for many years doctor to Clongowes. The latter, who was a great personal friend of Father Sullivan, called over to the College and asked him to go and see the sick man. Father Sullivan was unable to go, but sent word that he would say Mass for him at nine o'clock the following morning. At nine-thirty on that morning, the man of his own accord asked for a priest, and was prepared for death, which took place that day.

Father Sullivan, when faced with the task of bringing a soul back to God, showed all the qualities of the good shepherd, untiring perseverance, complete indifference to rebuffs, and a simplicity and gentleness that disarmed hostility. On one occasion he was the means of bringing peace to an old friend of his who, though he had had an active and honourable career, had grown careless about his religion. An eye-witness recalled Father Sullivan's constant visits to the sick man, his refusal to take any refreshment except a cup of coffee, which he as often left untouched, his recollected attitude as he passed through the house "always praying." Then came the hoped-for day when the invalid made his peace with God. Next day, Father Sullivan said Mass in the house, and it was recalled that his eyes were gleaming with joy afterwards as he said to one of the household, "He's all right now." He was there on his knees by the bedside later when the end came.

In another remarkable case of a death-bed repentance Father Sullivan shared with a fellow-priest the happiness of bringing the wanderer back to the fold. Early in 1926, a man was dying, and had repeatedly refused to receive the sacraments in spite of the zealous efforts of the senior curate of his parish, who was attending him. The sick man was hostile and abusive, and finally the curate decided to enlist the services of Father Sullivan.

He drove to Clongowes and brought Father Sullivan back with him. When Father Sullivan entered the sick-room, he also was greeted with abuse, and told to go. He protested that it was raining heavily at the moment, and asked permission to stay for a short while. The invalid granted this, and Father Sullivan knelt down in a corner of the room and began to pray. But his efforts seemed unsuccessful. He obtained leave to stay in the vicinity for two or three days, and visited the house constantly. Finally, Father John came to the curate with tears in his eyes, and told him that he feared he had utterly failed, the dying man getting even more hostile, and finally threatening to shoot himself if he were not let alone.

Father John returned to Clongowes, but no doubt his prayers continued uninterrupted for the soul in jeopardy. Two days later the curate called again to see the dying man, who, without the slightest difficulty, agreed to make his peace with God.

There were other instances in which Father Sullivan seemed to secure for sick persons the gift of freedom from physical pain or mental suffering, even though a cure did not follow. In 1913 or 1914, Father Sullivan was asked by Mr. Peter Coonan, a near neighbour of Clongowes and well known in Kildare farming and racing circles, to visit his uncle, Thomas Coonan, who was dying of bleeding cancer of the throat at his home, Kilclough, near Straffan. Mr. Peter Coonan drove Father Sullivan over in his gig, and when they got near the house they could hear the sick man moaning and shouting in a most distressing way. Father Sullivan prayed over him for a considerable time. He then rose to go, and said: "Good-bye, Tom, and I promise you one thing, that you won't suffer any more." Thomas Coonan died about a fortnight later, and never once suffered any pain after Father Sullivan's visit. The extraordinary change in his condition was a subject of comment by many neighbours, still living, who visited him.

Another such instance of Father Sullivan's power to console the dying was the case of Sister Crescentienne Debes, a lay-sister of St. Joseph's convent, Mount Sackville, near Dublin, who died in August 1929 as the result of severe burns received from boiling beeswax. After the accident, Sister Crescentienne was removed immediately to a private room in the Meath hospital, in which there was another sister, Sister Mary Joseph, who had undergone a serious operation.

Father Sullivan was already well known at St. Joseph's convent, and had previously consoled the dying hours of another member of the community, Sister Brigid. As was his usual custom, he used to cycle all the way from Clongowes, no matter what the weather, to visit Sister Brigid, and was never known to take any refreshment before facing the return journey. At the time of Sister Crescentienne's accident, he had been visiting Sister Mary Joseph during her illness, which lasted some three months. On August 1st news reached the convent that no hopes for Sister Crescentienne's recovery could be entertained. The Reverend Mother immediately dispatched one of the sisters, Sister Aloysius, to see her. While the sister was on her way to the Meath hospital, she saw Father Sullivan coming out of the University Church, St. Stephen's Green, and walking on before her. She guessed that he was going on his usual errand of mercy to see Sister

Mary Joseph, but he could not have known then of the dangerous state of the other sister. He walked on quickly, and Sister Aloysius had difficulty in keeping close behind him. He reached the hospital several minutes before her. When she got to the steps leading up to the main door, she could hear the screams of Sister Crescentienne, who was quite delirious. She went up to the room and found Father Sullivan on his knees by Sister Crescentienne's bedside, whilst she raved incessantly. He prayed for a long while, then blessed her and went to speak to Sister Mary Joseph. He blessed Sister Crescentienne again before he left. She suddenly became quite calm, and remained so until her death, which took place some twelve hours later. Sister Aloysius was with her to the end, and both she and Sister Mary Joseph, who died not long afterwards, attributed the great change in her state to Father Sullivan's prayers. About an hour after she had become calm, a Holy Ghost Father visited her. She recognized him immediately and was able to speak to him. Sister Aloysius mentioned Father Sullivan's visit to him, and he remarked that he was not surprised that Father Sullivan's prayers had given back her peace of mind to the dying sister.

Father Sullivan's self-sacrifice in these works of mercy was boundless. In 1929, John Nevin, who lived at Betaghstown, near Clongowes, was dying of cancer of the face. The malady dated back for some years and had finally worked terrible ravages, almost entirely destroying one side of the face. The doctor who attended the case recalled it as one of the worst he had known, and found it difficult himself to approach the patient. During the last five weeks of this man's life,

Father Sullivan visited him every day, and during the last fortnight twice a day. He used to kneel by his bed for a considerable time, praying with him and consoling him. The doctor recalled his amazement at seeing Father Sullivan leaning right over the sufferer, with his face almost touching his. A relative added the striking detail that Father Sullivan seemed to have no fear of the cancer, and would put his arms round the poor man in his bed.

Father Sullivan was bound by the closest ties of friendship with the nuns in the Presentation convent at Clane, some two miles from Clongowes, and they have many stories to tell of his kindness towards them and towards the sick and suffering in the country around. He gave four retreats in the convent (including the last he ever gave), acted for many years as extraordinary confessor, and frequently said Mass there on feast-days. In this he was maintaining a long tradition of friendship between the convent and the College of Clongowes. Father Peter Kenney, the first Rector of Clongowes, had given generous help towards the foundation of the convent in 1839, and had presented the altar, carved by the lay-brothers of Clongowes, which did duty in the convent chapel until 1927. Father Sullivan appropriately said the last Mass on that altar and the first Mass, the midnight Mass at Christmas, on the new one.

When coming to hear confessions or say Mass in the convent, Father Sullivan invariably came on foot or on his bicycle, even on the coldest and darkest mornings in winter. One morning in summer he was due to say Mass at 7 a.m. One of the sisters, happening to look out of the window, thought she saw a poor man carrying a tin can approaching the door. When he got near, she could not repress a smile, for she recognized the figure as Father Sullivan. He carefully deposited the can under a chair in the hall and went to say Mass. On being questioned afterwards, he confessed that the can (which he had carried from the College, some two miles away) contained beef-tea for one of the College workmen who was sick. The nuns wanted to insist on having the can delivered for him, but he would not hear of it and brought it to the sick man's house himself.

Father Sullivan's clients were mostly very poor. On one occasion he was summoned to a sick person at Ballymore Eustace, fourteen miles from Clongowes. The family were too poor to provide a car, and apparently Father Sullivan had no bicycle at his disposal. He immediately set out and walked the whole fourteen miles, returning presumably in the same manner.

On another occasion a nun in a Dublin convent had had her arm amputated, and was suffering terrible pain. Father Sullivan was asked by telegram to visit her. In a few hours he appeared on his bicycle (a most dilapidated one), having ridden from Clongowes to the hospital in Dublin, a distance of about twenty miles. He went to the sick room, and remained there for a couple of hours, praying with the suffering invalid. At the end of that time she felt great relief and fell asleep. The nuns then came to offer Father Sullivan some refreshment, but he had slipped away and was off back to Clongowes on his bicycle.

A remarkable feature of Father Sullivan's charity to the sick was its constancy. It is difficult to understand how he managed to get the time for such regular and prolonged attendance, in addition to the fresh visits which he was called on to make daily, often at long distances. A few instances may be given at random. He visited Martin Connolly, formerly head cook in the College kitchen, once a week for about a year, and twice a week when his condition became serious. He visited the former tailor to the College, William Byrne, for three years, during the third year almost every day, and towards the end twice a day. As will be mentioned later, he brought Holy Communion to Mrs. Smyth, wife of the farm steward at Clongowes, every Saturday and feast-day for twelve months.

This apostolate of the poor, the suffering, and the afflicted never flagged during thirty years. Father Sullivan was a great walker, and his figure was a familiar one on the roads around Clongowes or in the Dublin streets during his time as Rector in Rathfarnham, hurrying along with a peculiar half-running gait. But though it may seem a bold statement, it can be said confidently that he was never on any occasion seen going anywhere except to visit some sufferer or to perform some spiritual work. This feature of his life was aptly summed up on the day of his funeral by one of the farm-hands at Clongowes who said, "He seemed to take everyone's sorrow and suffering on himself."

CHAPTER XII

THE ASCETIC

IN 1908, a poor woman was a patient in St Vincent's Hospital, Dublin, suffering from cancer of the face. The physician who was attending her finally pronounced the case to be hopeless. The news was broken to her by Mother Thecla, of the Congregation of the Irish Sisters of Charity, who was afterwards to nurse Father Sullivan in his last illness. Mother Thecla, who was afterwards Superioress, had at that time only just come to the hospital. The woman declared herself quite resigned, but told Mother Thecla that, for the sake of her little children, she was going down to Father Sullivan at Clongowes in the hope of getting cured. It must be noted that he cannot have been much longer than a year ordained at the time. Mother Thecla asked what particular virtue this priest had over others. "He is quite an exception," said the woman earnestly. "He is very hard on himself. You have to be hard on yourself to work miracles. And he does it."

There is no record of the result of this woman's visit to Father Sullivan, but, with the unerring instinct of the poor and unlettered, she had put her finger on the secret of his power of succouring the afflicted.

Any of his religious brothers can bear witness to the fact that he spent every day long periods, often many hours, before the Blessed Sacrament, and that a great part of the night went to prayer also. One night in January of 1925, the college plumber, John Cribbin, was obliged to work late in the boys' chapel repairing the hot pipes. When he entered the chapel at 11 p.m., he found Father Sullivan kneeling on the marble steps before the altar. When he commenced his work, Father Sullivan, so as not to be in the way, retired into a small side chapel. At 2 a.m. the work was finished and the plumber left, but Father Sullivan was still there praying. On another occasion the same witness, accompanied by an assistant, went to repair the railings around the community cemetery. Father Sullivan came to pray there, and began by kneeling at every grave—about twenty in all. He then knelt down on the ground before the large stone crucifix at the end of the cemetery and prayed for about an hour, though an east wind was blowing, so bitter that the two workmen found it hard to endure.

On Holy Thursday of either that same year, 1925, or 1926, Father Sullivan came to one of the scholastics on the teaching staff at Clongowes, and offered to take his hour of adoration before the Altar of Repose. It was the custom that the younger and more vigorous scholastics were asked to remain on adoration during the night. Father Sullivan insisted that this young man must be tired after his term's work, and persuaded him to let him take his place. Next day the scholastic happened to comment to another scholastic on this act of considerateness, and it then came out that Father John had approached all the scholastics with the same offer. As they numbered five or six, he must have spent at least that number of hours in continuous prayer before the Blessed Sacrament during the night.

Many other witnesses could testify to the small amount of sleep which Father Sullivan allowed himself. A servant who looked after his room for about a year noticed that the bed was used only about every second night. Sometimes the bed looked as if Father Sullivan had merely lain down on it without covering himself with the bedclothes. Another servant later wished to satisfy himself as to whether the bed was used or not, and, on at least one occasion, inserted a feather in it, which he found undisturbed in the morning. Two servants who had been delayed by an accident when returning from a football match, had to make their entry after midnight by a window, and found Father Sullivan walking up and down one of the corridors, praying. In the winter of 1918, two other servants, who this time had no legitimate cause for being out late, entered in the small hours of the morning by the only window which they could find open, namely that of the People's Church. As they dropped down on the floor inside, they heard a voice say, "Who's that?" It was Father Sullivan at his prayers. He reproved the servants for their conduct, but, on their promising not to repeat it, told them that he would not report the matter.

In 1916 Father Sullivan gave a retreat to the Sisters of Mercy in Elphin, during which he stopped in the house of the parish priest, the late Canon (afterwards Archdeacon) McDermott. The Canon related to the nuns the following two episodes. Each evening on leaving the convent, Father Sullivan went straight to the parish church and remained kneeling there till the sacristan locked up. He generally came to the presbytery about ten o'clock. One night he did not arrive, and the Canon sent for the sacristan and asked him had he locked the church. On being told that he had, the Canon asked him to open the church again and try whether Father Sullivan was in some corner of it. The sacristan did so, and found Father Sullivan in a corner of the church absorbed in prayer. The Canon's bedroom was on the second floor of the house, and just beside it was a small oratory in which the Blessed Sacrament was reserved for sick calls. Here the Canon used to assemble his household for night prayers. During the course of the retreat he awoke in the middle of the night, and was struck by a doubt as to whether he had replenished the sanctuary lamp. Being a very devout man, he immediately arose and went to the oratory. On opening the door, he stumbled over the form of Father Sullivan, who was kneeling there.

During a retreat in 1919, at the Sacred Heart Convent, Mount Anville, which will be referred to later, the sister in charge of Father Sullivan's room was convinced that he never once slept in his bed during the eight days. When cross-questioned about this, she stated that she found the bed each morning made exactly as she had made it, and that it would have been impossible for anyone else to make it without her noticing the difference. Furthermore, there was no appearance of anyone having lain down upon it. She concluded that Father Sullivan slept either in a chair or on the floor.

Father Sullivan always recited his breviary kneeling in the chapel, often near an open window, apparently oblivious of the cold. When hearing confessions in the People's Church, he was constantly seen to be on his knees, and this was his invariable posture when hearing the confessions of the bedridden. A fellow-Jesuit whom he constantly consulted on cases of conscience, recalls that he always knelt while asking his advice.

Something will be said later of his abstemiousness in food. His room, which he always swept himself, was devoid of comfort. The servants recall the old and broken water-jug which he would not let them replace, until they did so in his absence. In winter he kept a very small fire in his grate—it must be remembered that he had to hear confessions and interview the boys in his room—but the servants described it as an apology for a fire, and used often to slip in and replenish it when he was out. Those in charge of his laundry related that during later years he wore only a thin flannelette shirt. At one time he possessed some under-vests, which had been given him by his brother, Sir William, but when they were worn out, he did not get them replaced. He had no overcoat, only a waterproof, worn and discoloured, and he was never known to use an umbrella or wear gloves. His brother wrote: "On one occasion when I noticed that his hands were all cracked from chilblains, I tried to make him take a pair of gloves, but could not persuade him to do so." One of the workmen at Clongowes recalled seeing him officiating at a funeral with snow falling on his unprotected hands. His boots were old and much patched, and he seems to have managed to do with one pair only. A fellow-Jesuit once accompanied him to a funeral at Glasnevin, and on the way to the cemetery observed that Father John was wearing a pair of old slippers. He thought a word of friendly remonstrance was needed, and Father John, with some embarrassment, explained that his only pair of boots was being repaired. A nun in the Sacred Heart convent, Armagh, recalled having heard that Sir William Sullivan once noticed that Father John's boots were in a bad state and sent him a new pair. Father John wrapped them up in brown paper and went off down to the docks in search of some needy person. (From this detail it is likely that the incident occurred when he was Rector of Rathfarnham Castle.) He soon came across a suitable recipient on whom he bestowed the boots. Some time later he met Sir William, who asked whether the boots fitted. "Perfectly," replied Father John.

During a retreat which he gave to the nuns at Clane, he used to change into slippers when he arrived at the convent, hiding his old boots behind the coal-scuttle in the parlour. The lay-sister who was looking after his meals once happened to examine the boots and found what she described as "a handful of small pebbles" in each of them. That this was a constant practice of his seems to be borne out by the fact that, when he had to go to hospital during his last illness, the nuns and nurses in charge were horrified at the state of his feet, which were much disfigured with corns, and wondered how he could walk at all.

In my day at Clongowes, the boys had a tradition that Father John was still wearing the boots "in which he had climbed the Alps." Apparently, this belief was only slightly inaccurate. Two of the boys, both now members of the Jesuit Order, noticed outside Father John's room his very battered footwear. They held a council of war and decided that it was very stingy on the part of the Jesuits not to give him a new pair. Accordingly, they hid the boots in the boys' boot-press, concluding that now the Order "would have to do something about it." Father John shortly came on the scene, missed his boots and enlisted the aid of the two conspirators in his search for them, adding the disturbing fact that these boots were particularly dear to him, as he had accomplished most of his Balkan tours in them before his entrance into the Society. After a decent interval the boots were found.

What other penances Father Sullivan added to all these acts of self-denial is known only to God and possibly his confessors. All that can be said on this point is that in a box in his room after his death were found two well-worn disciplines and two chains, one large and one small.

Through love of poverty, he wore his clothes until they were patched beyond description, though always scrupulously neat and clean. This poverty of apparel led to several amusing incidents. Once the College tailor, William Byrne, struck and refused to put another patch on Father John's trousers, alleging that the garments were not fit to be seen on a priest of God. "All right," said Father John, "I'll mend them myself," and attempted to take them back. The tailor held on to one leg and Father John on to the other, but finally Father John triumphed and carried off the trousers to be repaired by himself, not—it must be confessed—according to any recognized sartorial canons.

On another occasion Father Sullivan was going to visit a lady who was ill. It was apparently a dark and wet evening. He got a fall when on his way, and the addition of a quantity of mud to the normal dilapidation of his clothes caused him to be taken for a tramp by the invalid's daughter, who opened the door. She was about to turn him away when she caught a glimpse of his collar, and hastily rectified her mistake. An even more embarrassing case of mistaken identity will be recounted later when Father Sullivan's work as a retreat giver is being described.

CHAPTER XIII

THE DIRECTOR (I)

LIKE all his fellow-Jesuits, Father Sullivan devoted much time to the giving of the Spiritual Exercises to Religious Communities. The impression which he made upon those who came in contact with him during these religious exercises was deep and lasting. There is a certain difficulty in expressing how very deep this impression was. In brief, those to whom he ministered testified unanimously to the extraordinary example which he gave of every possible virtue. Now the mere recital of a litany of virtues tends to become monotonous. There is a well-known saying of G. K. Chesterton's that being good is an adventure far more exciting than sailing round the world. The difficulty is that the spiritual odyssey is often less entertaining than the globe-trotter's chronicle. But out of the mass of evidence supplied by those who listened to Father Sullivan's retreats, there emerges the compelling fact that he at all times and in every way practised what he preached. The following typical extracts from letters received after his death could be multiplied indefinitely:

"We had the privilege of having Father Sullivan here (the Sacred Heart Convent, Armagh) several times for retreats. Invariably a post-card would arrive on the day before, stating that he would be with us at such an hour in the evening, that he needed no car to meet him at the station, and would only require a cup of weak tea, having had his dinner before starting. His first question on arriving was, 'Have you any sick in the house?' and once when the answer was, 'Thank God, the infirmaries are empty,' he remonstrated almost indignantly, 'Don't say "thank God,"—the sick are a blessing in the house.' He was indeed devoted to them and during his stay in the convent he visited them every day.

"He gave us the impression of being a very holy man, closely united to God. It was enough to see him come in to give an instruction, his crucifix in his hand, to feel recollected and filled with devotion. During Benediction we noticed that he hardly ever looked fixedly at the blessed Sacrament, but always kept his head bent low in adoration or buried in his hands. While he gave the retreat here we often heard him groan and pray aloud in his room. He must have had the gift of tears, for he gave us a beautiful instruction on Holy Tears and seemed to speak from experience. He several times broke down in the middle of an instruction when speaking of the love of God, the love of Our Lord for sinners. He must have made a promise never to spend a day without speaking about Our Lady, for every day, after the last instruction, he gave us the story of a conversion or of a special favour granted through her intercession. Though his spirituality was very simple, and on great lines, he did not despise little ways and means to help oneself to keep up fervour and to progress in the spiritual life. He engaged each one, for instance, to take up a spiritual hobby that would help her to fix her thoughts and interests in difficult moments, such as studying the mercy of God in the Gospels, praying for the conversion of sinners or the agonizing. I think one of his hobbies must have been praying for the Holy Souls, for several times during the day he was seen going down to the cemetery to pray over the graves, and then making the Stations of the Cross out-of-doors."

From the Ursuline Convent, Waterford, where for many years he was extraordinary confessor, there came the following impressions:

"Father Sullivan's love for the Blessed Sacrament, to which he seemed to be drawn as steel to the magnet, was so great that it was with difficulty he could be induced to leave his thanksgiving after Mass. When the Sister, after some delay, went to call him to his breakfast, he was usually found making the Way of the Cross. Then when she thought he was following her to the parlour for breakfast, he would be seen hastening to visit a Calvary which stands in the grounds.

"He usually heard Confessions in the sacristy, and could be seen through the aperture in the screen clasping his crucifix in his hands as he listened to those who trusted to him for guidance. It was with a certain sense of awe that, as frequently happened, the penitent realized that he, too, was on his knees while he heard her confession, for this seemed to have been a special practice of his.

"He never spared himself when there was question of helping a soul, and would hardly take a short interval for a walk during his stay at the Convent.

"An unwonted atmosphere of prayer, calm and recollection seemed to pervade the house during Father Sullivan's visit as extraordinary confessor. It was the unconscious reflex of his own deep, simple spirituality, for he was ever an adept at self-effacement. He seemed to seek contempt as he knelt in prayer on the lowest step of the Sanctuary. Utterly lost to all but God, he embodied in visible form the prayer of the Publican. Despite the rugged asceticism of his appearance, there was a singular attraction in his simple genial manner in the parlour. He was delighted to tell you of the Fathers who were well known at the Convent. He was generous and lavish of his praise of his fellow-Jesuits, and indeed of anyone whom he believed to merit commendation.

"His direction was simple, strong and impersonal. He did not give his own opinion. It was usually thus he gave advice: 'Now, St. Teresa advises this',—'St. Ignatius urges that'—and he even quoted the advice of the Fathers of the Society who were well known to the community. 'Father N. recommended this practice in a certain difficulty; it proved most efficacious.' Once a sister asked him what she could say to a sister who was suffering acute pain in her last illness. He replied: 'Father N. answered a similar question thus: "Tell the sufferer that when he gets to heaven he will be sorry he had not greater pain to endure."' "

It will be recalled how, shortly after his conversion, and whilst he was still in the world, he had visited the Convent of the Poor Clares, at Ballyjamesduff. In 1920 he returned to give the annual retreat and also gave the Christmas triduum in 1921. A member of the community gave the following impressions:

"His lectures were long—he never spared himself—but most interesting, and above all, full of the love of God. He loved to talk of the mercy of God, and seemed to have great veneration for the holy women in the Gospel. He often emphasized the fact that they never left Our Lord, but were faithful to the end. But his spirit of prayer and mortification preached even more eloquently than his words. He prayed all the time. After the last lecture, he remained on praying until the convent door was closed at 8 p.m. He went straight to the town church, and remained there for a long time in prayer. He always walked backwards down the avenue so that he might face the Blessed Sacrament. His spirit of mortification was wonderful. He ate very little, no meat, a little rice pudding without eggs for dinner. How he lived was a mystery. The sister who looked after his simple wants always found him absorbed in prayer when she entered the parlour. He never used the arm-chair, but always knelt upright on the floor.

"At Christmas, 1921, the weather was very severe. Snow fell continually during the days of the triduum, Father Sullivan's boots were broken, and when Mother Abbess tried to get him another pair, or at least to have the old ones repaired, he would not hear of it. At the same time he gave her to understand that the broken boots were his own choice, and that he could have had others if he wished. The sister who looked after the parlour often saw his wet socks drying before the fire. He evidently had but one pair and when they were wet he just did without any. At the close of the retreat, Mother Abbess wanted to know the hour he would require a car to get to the station. He told her he would walk to the station, a distance of five miles, in the rain! Needless to say, he did not gain his point for once.

"He was kindness itself to everyone. Twice at least when some of our sisters were in hospital, he put himself to great inconvenience to visit them. This inconvenience we heard of from another, but for himself he was very punctual, and once when he could not come at the appointed hour he wrote an apology. As soon as it was known that he was in the hospital everyone, nuns, patients and nurses came to get his blessing. He once remarked when talking of operations, that sanctity was the most painful of operations. Once when he was visiting one of our sisters in hospital, she went to the parlour to see him, and found him wrapped in prayer, quite unconscious of anyone present."

Another convent where Father Sullivan was well known was the Carmelite Monastery, Firhouse, Co. Dublin, where his second Mass had been celebrated. One of the sisters of that community thus recalled her impressions:

"Father Sullivan, S.J., was a very dear friend of our community. We first made his acquaintance in July 1922, when he gave us our annual retreat, and from that on he paid us frequent visits. He was kindness itself to the sick, and would think nothing of riding up all the way from Clongowes on a bicycle if any sister needed his help and advice. He came to see us for the last time less than two months before his holy death. His retreats were always prayerful, but he excelled in the confessional. I cannot say how much good he did my soul. He was a man of prayer, a real saint, but then so natural and approachable. His great remedy for all ills was the ejaculation, 'Sacred Heart of Jesus, I place all my trust in Thee.' A visit from Father Sullivan was always as good as a whole retreat."

Yet another convent where Father Sullivan made a deep impression was the Presentation Convent, Castleisland, Co. Kerry.

"Father John Sullivan conducted our eight-day retreat here in 1925. There was nothing particularly striking about it, as a retreat. His delivery was poor, and rather indistinct, so that it was a strain to catch what he said. He emphasized devotion to the Holy Ghost, called attention to the riches and beauty of the prayers of the missal and urged the use of them at Mass and in time of prayer.

"It was the character and demeanour of the man that impressed us all. One could not come into contact with him and fail to realize that he was truly a man closely united to God. In his manner of acting and speaking he seemed to belong to another world. If humility is a test of sanctity then Father Sullivan was a saint. He seemed to consider himself at everybody's service, and would actually run if anybody expressed a wish to see him or get him to do anything. He spent much of his time at prayer, generally kneeling erect on the step of the altar. One evening a sister had pity on him kneeling on the cold hard marble, and she placed a little prie-dieu cushion beside him. But Father John almost immediately stood up and went off, and a few minutes later another sister who was doing some work in the parish church saw him come in and continue his prayers. He liked visiting the parish church, for he said that he loved to see so many come in to pay a visit to the Blessed Sacrament. He was charmed to see young children come in and kiss the feet of a large crucifix, one holding up the other so that they might reach it. Some months later, a boy from the town, home on holidays from Clongowes, called to see the sister who had attended to Father John and told her that he wished to be remembered to her. She could not think whom the boy meant, and asked, 'Is he a holy man?' 'Oh, yes,' replied the boy, 'he is a class of a saint.' "

It was remarkable that Father Sullivan's holiness made an equal appeal to contemplatives and to those who were engaged in the active life. These were the impressions of the Reverend Mother at the Convent of Mercy, Swinford, where he gave the retreat in 1926.

"I had the privilege of following Father Sullivan's retreat in the summer of 1926. Personally, I am convinced of his great sanctity and it is a pleasing task to supply all the details at our disposal.

"Evidence of Father Sullivan's great holiness was given by his spirit of extreme abstinence. Contrary to his express wish—or rather, owing to some misunderstanding of his wishes—the usual dishes were served him at dinner. One day I surprised the venerable Father engaged over a small dish of rice. This he ate out of the dish, evidently reluctant to cause trouble to the sister by using a plate in the ordinary way. The other dishes served were untouched.

"On another occasion I went to his sitting-room to beg of him to speak just a little louder, as there was quite a big number of sisters following the retreat lectures. He expressed his gratitude for the reminder with all the genuine humility of a saint, and begged me to remind him in case of a similar failure.

"The sister who attended Father Sullivan during his stay here assures me that his spirit of prayer was extraordinary. She found him frequently on his knees absorbed in prayer.

"Father Sullivan's presence in the community created an atmosphere of sanctity, much more efficacious, we agree, than mere eloquence could ever effect."

His spirit of prayer made a deep impression at the Convent of Mercy, Rathangan, in 1929:

"I thought his attitude during the whole time of the retreat was very saintly. I must say in all truth that the very tone in which he recited the prayers after Holy Mass moved me to contrition. His reverence in presence of the Most Holy Sacrament was profound and striking, and his modesty at all times edifying. He seemed to have a special devotion to the sacred Passion, as he kept the crucifix clasped in his hands whilst giving the lectures, and he looked as if he were drawing the beautiful thoughts to which he gave expression from the book of books, the crucifix."

At yet another Mercy Convent, that in Athy, in 1931, his humility was the virtue which made the deepest impression.

"Father Sullivan was himself, in person and conduct, a constant exhortation to higher things. His practice of holy poverty was evident at first sight, and his humble demeanour marked him out at once as a truly mortified man. One felt instinctively that here was a true religious who had long ago made the complete holocaust of self. Closer contact deepened this impression, as was shown by the declaration of the sacristan after the retreat. She gave it as her opinion that Father Sullivan was the most humble man she had ever had to deal with. He was so ready to put himself at her service that she had to be on her guard not to make a request at an unseasonable moment."

Half the work of a successful retreat is done in the confessional, and enough has been said already to show that Father Sullivan never spared himself in that regard. A retreat given by him in 1919 at the Sacred Heart Convent, Mount Anville, near Dublin, stands out in the memories of those who made it for the impression he left as a confessor. One of the exercitants wrote thus:

"Beyond the fact that he ended many sentences with what came to be accepted as a formula, 'and all that', (for instance, 'there was Peter there, and the nets there, and all that'), I am ashamed to say that I do not remember one single word he said. But *what he was* struck me, and the impression has never been effaced; a man of real sanctity, deep humility, intense love of our suffering Lord, a priest full of charity and the desire to help souls, especially in the confessional.

"He held his crucifix, rather a large one, in his two hands, tightly clasped, right through every instruction, and he constantly cast what I might call furtive glances at it. There was nothing dramatic or studied in this action; it was just the outcome of intense love. Beyond these glances at his crucifix he never raised his eyes, never looked at his audience. He gave the impression of being thoroughly ashamed of his existence.

"Confessions during this retreat have remained legendary. Father Sullivan's kindness and devotedness and charity were inexhaustible. He spent every moment between the instructions in the confessional. One soul, young and inexperienced, and at that time in a certain state of interior distress, went to him six times, and even after the sixth effort was invited with extreme kindness and sympathy to come back again. However, she left the holy man this time, filled with peace and consolation."

Another added, "It was like a mission. Everyone went to confession three or four times."

A third said: "Father Sullivan was also most helpful in confession, not soft, but kind, encouraging, uplifting.

Austere to himself, he was most compassionate to others. I well remember the rush up to confession, as many stayed for a long time with him and waiting became a tedious affair. All kinds of dodges were tried to get up quickly after the instructions. Some started almost before the last word had been said, others slipped out by a side door, others even hurried up the sacristy stairs to reach the chapel quicker."

Some years later, one of the sisters, not then at Mount Anville, but who had made this retreat, became very ill and suffered much. She made a novena to Father Sullivan, and, having obtained a relic, wore it with much faith and prayed earnestly for her cure. One night, towards the end of the novena, she dreamed that she was walking along one of the convent corridors, when she saw in the dream Father Sullivan coming quickly towards her, his head slightly bent, his hands joined on the big crucifix. As he came close to her he stopped, did not speak, but taking the crucifix, put it in her hands. At that moment she awoke, and realized that suffering was God's Will for her, and that she would not be cured."

A few more impressions may be added of this retreat, which made a lively impression on all who heard it.

"J'ai suivi la retraite donnée par le Rév. Père Sullivan, S.J., en 1919, et je puis dire que son extérieur recueilli et perdu en Dieu, était prenant. Il ne cherchait point du tout à être éloquent mais persuasif. Tout en suivant étroitement les exercices de St. Ignace, il nous donna un exposé complet d'une vie chrétienne et religieuse. Je crois qu'il voulait surtout augmenter notre confiance en Dieu, et des sentiments d'une contrition aussi parfaite que possible, nous excitant à apprécier le *don des larmes* et nous exhortant à implorer cette grâce par l'intercession de Sainte Monique."

"Speaking of the Examen, he said it did not mean going so many times round the same place, or scraping and rooting in our souls. We should take just a small look at our faults, and spend most of the time thanking God.

"I and Sister X. made our vows at the end of the retreat, and Father Sullivan preached the sermon at the ceremony. He took for his subject the two Irish Princesses whom St. Patrick baptized, and who went straight to heaven!

" 'Father Sullivan is a saint,' was the general sentiment in this house after that retreat. His almost palpable union with God could not but impress all those who came in contact with him. His humility was startling. It was not that he had a lowly opinion of himself, he had no opinion at all of himself. And his kindness was something very special. He seemed never to weary in his efforts to help individual souls. He spoke hesitatingly, fluency in words seemed not to be his. This raised some questions in the minds of those who knew of his early life. There had been days when he was an able and eloquent speaker. But he had apparently now deliberately put all that behind him, and he seemed to have made his own the manner and way of speech of a man who is unsure of himself, who does not count for much, if for anything. But his words remained and bore fruit, and by their fruits did we know them."

Some of the above impressions were confirmed and a few fresh details added in the recollections of a member of the community of the Sacred Heart Convent, Lower Leeson Street, Dublin.

"The impressions made on me by Father Sullivan

are indelible, and what struck me most was his utter unworldliness, together with his humility and extreme mortification. His clothes, though neat, were of the poorest. I have seen him travel a long train journey on a most bitter winter's day with no protection against the cold, not even a pair of gloves. Half frozen at the end of his journey, he made nothing of it. I suppose it was the price he offered for the souls he came to preach to.

"Though so hard on himself, he was wonderfully kind to others. I had the great grace of making two of my annual retreats under his guidance, and though there was nothing beyond the ordinary in the lectures, yet there was a hidden power at the back of every word that went straight to the heart and made one wish to give Our Lord of one's very best. That was the impression of each one of the retreatants, without an exception. But it was in the confessional that he excelled. Time or trouble were nothing to him, if only he could bring souls to love and serve Our Lord more intensely. His penitents came away filled with fresh courage and confidence. The power that Father Sullivan exercised over souls was bought by his prayers and extremely severe macerations, prayer and penances that could be heard at a great distance from the room he occupied.

"Father Sullivan had a wonderful devotion to the Sacred Passion of Our Lord and tried hard to instil the same into the hearts of others. He and his crucifix were never separated. It was on his table during his lectures, at his meals, in his hands during his walks, in fact, everywhere. He had a very marked devotion to the dead. He visited the cemetery every day, and oftener when he could."

CHAPTER XIV

THE DIRECTOR (II)

A RETREAT which Father Sullivan gave at the Presentation Convent, Mitchelstown, Co. Cork, in August 1925, was marked by a series of edifying incidents, some of which were not without a touch of humour.

The priest who was originally to give this retreat was called away to his mother's death-bed, and Father Sullivan had to step into the breach at short notice. His letter to the Reverend Mother was, as usual, not easy to read, only two words, "car" and "luggage," and the hour of the train being decipherable. The Reverend Mother accordingly sent a note saying that a car would meet him at the railway station. To this a speedy reply was received announcing, "no car" and "no luggage." This missive gave rise to lively conjectures during the nuns' recreation hour regarding the unknown director.

It had been arranged that Father Sullivan should stop at the house of the parish priest, the late Archdeacon Rice, himself a most saintly man. Father Sullivan presented himself at the presbytery door apparently without any luggage. It was his custom when travelling to carry his scanty toilet articles in one pocket and his breviary in the other. His much-worn waterproof, green with age, and his equally venerable hat created grave misgivings in the mind of the housekeeper who opened the door, and she came to the conclusion that this was some irregular cleric in difficulties. She tried to get rid of him, and finally left him standing on the doorstep while she went up to tell the pastor of his suspicious-looking visitor. The good Archdeacon, full of compassion, hurried down and said to Father Sullivan: "What can I do for you, my poor man?" in a tone which was meant to imply that it was never too late for the erring sheep to return to the fold. Father John was obliged to reveal himself, and it is hard to say whether he was more confused than his kindly host, who lavished every mark of reverence on him for the remainder of his stay.

The Archdeacon told the nuns that when Father Sullivan introduced himself to him he immediately felt that he was "in presence of superior sanctity." One incident during the week must have helped to confirm this impression. The Archdeacon was a very early riser, and one morning he noticed the door of the guest's room open at an hour considerably before that of the convent Mass. Wondering where Father Sullivan had gone, he entered, and found his guest asleep on the floor, with the bed untouched.

The unequal competition in virtue which took place during the course of the retreat between the Archdeacon and Father John was humorously commented on by one of the curates, who, echoing his pastor's words, said that "the Archdeacon was fading away in the presence of superior sanctity."

The expectations which the nuns had formed as to their director were not disappointed during the retreat. He seemed to them, as one of them put it, "to breathe sanctity." They noticed that he kept before him at all times, whether reading, writing or eating, the large crucifix already mentioned as having belonged to his mother. Once when the sister who attended him delivered a message, he presented the crucifix for her to kiss, telling her that he was very fond of it. This sister's constant fear was that he would starve as, except for his meagre breakfast, the only food which he ate during the eight days was a tablespoonful of rice and half a cup of tea each day. On some days he took less rice and no tea.

It seemed to the nuns that he positively lived in the chapel while they were elsewhere. One of them accidentally saw him at prayer, and still recalls the sense of awe and reverence which the sight inspired. During dinner, she left the refectory to secure a door that was banging, and, entering the organ gallery of the chapel, she heard a noise and saw Father Sullivan enter. He prostrated inside the door, remaining in this attitude on the tiled floor for several minutes. Then, apparently with a great effort, he dragged himself to a kneeling position. His absorbed expression and his attitude, as of one completely lost in God, will always be among this nun's most precious and inspiring memories.

Father John's typical dry humour appeared in the manner in which he used to announce before every lecture of this retreat that some other community, contemplatives generally, were praying for the conversion of the good Sisters of Mitchelstown. "They are praying for us in the convent of Perpetual Adoration at X.," he would announce. "So I think we'll pull through."

The impression made by Father Sullivan during that week in Mitchelstown was not confined to the convent. One morning a maid, sent to cut vegetables in the garden, returned excitedly to the kitchen, exclaiming, "The holy Father is prostrate on the ground, his arms stretched out, saying his prayers." From maid to man, from kitchen to garden, and thence to friends in the town the talk spread about "the *real* holy Father," as one maid described him. As a result the convent chapel was filled with townspeople during evening Benediction. A gentleman who met Father Sullivan on his way to post some letters questioned the Reverend Mother afterwards about him.

"I was very much struck by his appearance," he said. "He must be a very remarkable man."

"What did you consider remarkable about him?" asked the Reverend Mother.

"I cannot say," he replied, "but there seemed to be an air of greatness about him. I stood to look at him and thought to myself that he must be a great saint."

One morning a sister, whose cell was situated over the parlour, overheard voices conversing in loud tones. Father John had seen a poor beggarman returning from the kitchen hall, and addressed him through the window:

"Well, my poor man, have you had breakfast? Is it long since you got a chance to make your confession? Kneel down there and I'll hear you."

And there and then, through the parlour window, Father John dispensed the riches of God's mercy, and sent the poor man on his way at peace with his Maker.

The memory of this retreat is still strong in the convent, and the sisters continually invoke the aid of

Father Sullivan. One nun was a martyr to nerve trouble. She had suffered intense agony for over three years, and at times seemed to lose all power of movement. One day she suddenly thought that she would ask Father Sullivan to cure her. She began to keep on her person a picture of him with a small relic of his clothing attached. From that day on, whenever she found this nervous trouble coming on, she had only to touch the relic and all inconvenience ceased.

About two years after Father Sullivan's death, the Sister who had witnessed his intense prayer in the convent chapel had been suffering for over three months from a discharging knee, which resisted all efforts of the doctor to cure it. One Saturday she told the doctor that she had now entrusted herself to Father Sullivan, and that the knee would be healed when he saw it next.

"While I respect your faith and confidence in prayer," said the doctor, "I fear your hope of the trouble healing will be disappointed."

"My novena will end on Tuesday," replied the sister, "and Father John will obtain my request."

The wound required dressing several times a day, and each time the sister placed between the bandages a tiny fragment of cloth taken from the Jesuit gown worn by Father John, which she had secured during the retreat.

On Tuesday, the knee was perfectly healed and normal without the least sign of any kind. The doctor was astonished and said, "You must certainly have prayed well. I did not expect it to heal."

The hospitality of convents is proverbial, and Father Sullivan's abstemiousness, though highly edifying, must often have been a source of heart-burnings to the generous sisters who were put in charge of him. We find repeatedly in letters the same admiration for his austerity, mingled, one would gather, with a slight tinge of disappointment at the failure of the highest culinary efforts to conquer his virtue. In the summer of 1921, he was at the Convent of Mercy, Skibbereen, Co. Cork, and all during the retreat took only two meals each day, a very moderate breakfast and rice and milk for dinner. The following year there was very much the same story at the Carmel of the Nativity, Tranquilla, Rathmines. "His diet was a little boiled rice with a little milk and dry bread for dinner, and in the evening dry bread and tea. Once the sister baked the rice, so he only took one spoonful. He would not touch anything else that was on the table, his serviette was just the same at the end of the retreat as when he first got it."

The dish of rice for dinner figures again and again in accounts of his retreats. Once at the Mercy convent, Baggot Street, the sister in charge of his meals remonstrated: "But, Father, you'll never be able to keep yourself up on that." "That's just it," replied Father John. "I want to keep myself down."

Between 1921 and 1929 he gave at the Carmelite monastery, Hampton, Drumcondra, two eight-day retreats and three triduums. During all these exercises, the rice-pudding was again in evidence. Sometimes he did not trouble to go to the parlour, but ate his meal in a small room off the sacristy. The sister in charge used to send in the pudding on the usual "turn" which is used in contemplative convents. On one occasion she heard the bell ring and sent in the pudding. She heard a surprised voice saying, with obvious amusement, "Is this for me?" It was the late Canon Pettit, a well-known and beloved figure in the archdiocese of Dublin, who had come to the sacristy on business. On hearing that this was the Director's entire dinner, the Canon smilingly remarked, "Oh, that would never do me," and with characteristic good-humour carried the pudding to the parlour and handed it over to its proper owner.

During these retreats Father Sullivan's other meals consisted merely of a cup of tea and some bread, and received scant attention. One morning, when at Hampton, he did not come to his breakfast, and the sister in charge went back to the chapel where, through the grille, she saw him still praying before the altar. Another sister entered the choir at that moment and both nuns were awestruck by his appearance, as he looked up at the tabernacle, his face radiant with a heavenly smile and his hands uplifted after the manner of the priest at the canon of the Mass.

But it would be superfluous to multiply testimonies as to Father Sullivan's indifference to food. His religious brothers were witnesses of it daily for many years. Only twice during his life in religion was he known to take meat, once about 1911 when giving a retreat in the convent at Clane, at a time when he was very exhausted, and again in the Infirmary at Clongowes during his last illness. When he was Rector at Rathfarnham his daily fare was noted by the young students under his care as being abstemious in the extreme. His breakfast consisted of a large plate of porridge with milk and some dry bread, his dinner of potatoes and dry bread, and he seems to have taken no other meal.

After his return to Clongowes in 1924, he mitigated

this severity. He had begun to suffer a great deal from stomach trouble, which prevented him from sleeping. He was ordered by his superiors to consult the college doctor, who told him he must eat more or he would die. He accordingly began to take boiled eggs and bread and butter at breakfast as well as porridge, and added a small dish of rice to the potatoes and bread at dinner. On greater feast-days he fared very badly, partly because he did not ask for the rice which formed a large part of his diet, and partly, I believe, in order to practise more austerity on those days. Several witnesses recalled him to have dined on dry bread alone on such occasions. He used to say that before he entered religion, he had been advised by a Harley Street doctor to adopt a meatless régime. It is quite possible that there was something in this, especially in view of the anxiety about his health which had troubled him as a young man. But one could not help feeling that his interpretation of the specialist's advice had made a virtue of necessity, and with a vengeance.

The only retreat which Father Sullivan ever gave to priests was given in 1925 at the Cistercian Abbey, Roscrea. It is not surprising that Father Sullivan's austere life and austere type of retreat-giving made a strong appeal to men following a life so essentially austere. The following impressions were given by Father Columban, the present Sub-Prior:

"Fifteen years ago was my first retreat as a Cistercian novice, and I looked forward to it for an odd reason. I had made many retreats under the Fathers of the Society of Jesus, and may I be pardoned for saying that I was just then a little tired of the Ignatian exercises. As the time of the retreat drew near this desire for something new expressed itself. 'Thank God,' I said to the Novice Master, ''Tisn't a Jesuit we will have, anyway!' 'Who told you it wasn't?' he replied. I confess I was appalled and could only face the retreat with dispositions far from ideal.

"Then Father Sullivan came. I can see him still, seated in the Abbot's throne, a six-inch brass crucifix grasped in his two hands. He seemed to just meditate aloud, speaking to his crucifix, rather than to address his listeners. Frequently he made a funny gesture with his left hand, running his fingers through locks of hair that did not exist. But one at once got the impression that here was an unusually holy man speaking, and that other little matters did not count. He followed the order of the Exercises closely, as I can still see from rather skimpy notes taken at the time. He spoke in simple short sentences with a directness that reached both mind and heart. Father Sullivan seemed wholly absorbed in God and yet I found him very affable when I approached him for confession and spiritual advice, and have ever since remembered his parting words, 'Brother, you have a wonderful vocation. Always serve the Lord in great joy.' I don't know how that simple sentence has remained for fifteen years in a bad memory, but I think it will be there for ever."

Another of the monks, Father Oliver, added the following recollections:

"I can honestly say that the aggregate impression of the retreat given by Father Sullivan, S.J., in 1925, was just this, that one felt virtue going out from the Father Director, although every possible natural reason therefor was utterly and palpably lacking. Father Sullivan's appearance was abject. His shrunken figure, his tense and rugged features, his time-worn and time-coloured garments, which fitted his person much as do those of a scarecrow, breathed forth an unction which was in inverse ratio to those naturally unattractive features. To this day his voice still echoes in my ears. It was raucous and absolutely devoid of intonation, but his very words come back to me precisely because they were so unadorned, so poor in phrase. If all members of the Society of Jesus must become adept at painting 'compositions of place' then Father Sullivan must have been the solitary exception. The gospel lines are themselves fragmentary. The tremendous call of fishermen by the Incarnate God is so wonderful that human word-weaving would be an insult. The Holy Spirit dictated no such fine phrasing, and Father Sullivan certainly emphasized the Divine element by increasing the human weakness. The text is unadorned. He made it uncouth. 'There was Peter there'—such were his reiterated parable-pictures.

"And yet while Directors have come since who brought to God's word every human elegance and grace, it is not to their discredit, but a testimony of fact, that of nearly all, I, at any rate, have forgotten both features and phrases.

"It is my conviction that only the most intense union with God, the almost complete absorption of the human and natural element could account for Father Sullivan's power. It would strike one as approaching blasphemy even to permit one thought critical of just those natural defects which I have mentioned. Never yet have I seen exemplified so completely in a creature those strange boasts of St. Paul that human wisdom is folly before God, that the divine truth is not a matter of persuasive words, that the Cross, the standard of Christ, is the only motive-power in the world of grace. Father Sullivan spoke as one who knew he was commissioned from on High, who knew that the truth would gain nothing from merely natural embellishments. One of the brethren—the late Brother Malachy—died during the retreat. For many this event would have afforded legitimate matter for a magnificent sermon on the Last Things. I can remember Father Sullivan's simple but repeated phrase: 'What does that Brother think of it all now?' And when poor Father Sullivan had put the question, the Holy Spirit answered it. Let that be the final eulogy on that humanly needy instrument which was Father Sullivan, that quite obviously God spoke with him, finished his broken utterances in His full divine way, echoed his uncouth and jerky sentences, and it is that echo of God which is the surest sign of the interior preacher."

To these testimonies of the Cistercian monks there may be added appropriately the impressions of Father Charles O'Sullivan, parish priest of Adrigole, Co. Cork, who met Father Sullivan when he was giving a retreat to the Presentation nuns at Castleisland, in 1925, Father O'Sullivan being then a curate in that town.

"At each day's close, when his work was done, his gentle knock at my door was a signal for a most welcome conference of no usual character. From the outset he struck me as a man of extraordinary interior perfection. I found myself explaining him as being one of those favourites of the Master, because of some physical suffering endured with a saintly resignation and rewarded by an unusual insight into the secrets of the Higher Life.

"Like most men of his kind, he was more of a keen listener than a talker, and all his interests were in the Kingdom of Our Lord. I thought that I would engage him on the Holy Land which I had had the privilege of visiting in 1924. One evening, as I remember well, he listened with rapt attention to my account of a memorable day on the Sea of Galilee. I told him of my reactions to that privileged visit, and its crowning on my return next morning to say Mass on that spot which appears to me to be the most authentically hallowed by the footsteps of Our Lord. The climax was reached; I saw the tears welling in the eager, sunken eyes and a light rejuvenating the haggard face, and I heard my poor saint reciting as a hymn the sixth chapter of St. John's Gospel. At the Words of Promise, his voice, his manner, his whole attitude appeared to me to be the confession of his own ardent faith, and of his readiness to go to prison and death as complete as that of Simon Peter himself.

"He then stood up, and, overcome by emotion, embraced me and left the room in silence. That was the last I saw or heard of Father John. But the impression that he left with me of being a man of most saintly character and of most lofty perfection survives the years."

CHAPTER XV

INNER VISION

FATHER SULLIVAN had at all times a great gift of calming and consoling those who were suffering mental or physical pain. At times his power seemed to go further. He seemed to be able to see into the minds of those who consulted him, and he spoke of future events with an abrupt and almost disconcerting confidence, which was all the more remarkable in view of his great humility and his normal reluctance to obtrude his own views.

This gift manifested itself at all periods of his life. It will already have been remarked in his dealings with sick persons who sought his prayers. A few further instances may be added.

About 1912, a Jesuit novice was troubled by some spiritual difficulty which he found hard to express to his master of novices. In a casual conversation with Father Sullivan, the latter, without any prompting, brought up this very difficulty, and so spoke of it as to give courage to the young man to go and have his doubts solved.

Another novice, a nun, was greatly worried about a violent pain which she used to get in her side. She said nothing about it, fearing that she might be sent away from the convent. In the end, she told her mother, who wrote to Father Sullivan and asked him to say Mass for her daughter. Father Sullivan called at the convent, asked to see the novice, and said to her in a most abrupt way, "You won't be sent away." The pain never recurred, and, though not over strong, she has always been fully able for the duties of religious life.

An almost startling allusion to the future was made by him at the opening of the retreat, already mentioned, which he gave at the Sacred Heart Convent, Mount Anville, in 1919. After a few moments' silence he looked up and gazed round the room—the only occasion, it was noted, during the whole retreat on which he raised his eyes. Then he said very quietly, "Of those who are listening to me now, and who are about to make this retreat, one, at least, will be dead before the next community retreat." His prophecy proved quite correct. One of his listeners, then apparently in quite average health, was buried on August 4th following, very shortly before the opening of the community retreat of 1920.

When Father Sullivan was Rector of Rathfarnham Castle, a well-known social worker in Dublin brought out a number of poor neglected boys to make a retreat. This gentleman was a great admirer of Father Sullivan's and used to allude to him as "Saint Sullivan." The thought had been in his mind for some time that he was getting too old for this sort of work, and he secretly made up his mind that this would be the last batch of boys he would organize for a retreat. During the retreat he went himself to Father Sullivan for confession. As usual, Father Sullivan was clasping his crucifix in his emaciated hands. His penitent said nothing of his intention, but Father Sullivan, after having given him absolution, pointed to the crucifix and said, "You are doing the very work *He* would do if He were in your place. Persevere. You are a Redemptorist in the truest sense of the word." The words deeply impressed his hearer and he resolved on the spot to persevere in his good work, a resolution which he carried out until his death.

Sister Mary Joseph, one of the Irish Sisters of Charity at Donnybrook, was a witness of two of Father Sullivan's predictions. In May 1922, her sister, who had been a Sister of Charity for twenty-seven years, was dying of a painful disease in the Hospice for the Dying. Father Sullivan visited her frequently, and after hearing her confession at his last visit, he went over to a small altar, and prayed earnestly, and loud enough for her to hear the words, "Dear Lord, in Thy pity, take this child." When Sister Mary Joseph next went to see her, she said, "I have not long to live now, for I know that Father Sullivan is a saint." In fact she only lived for two days more.

Four years later, a brother of Sister Mary Joseph was seriously ill and had been anointed. Father Sullivan was called to see him and remained a considerable time praying beside him. On leaving, he told the sick man's daughter not to fret, as he would not die during that illness, and next day he called to see Sister Mary Joseph and told her the same thing. Actually the patient recovered and lived for another two years, though he was eighty-four years old.

In 1923 a postulant entered the convent of Poor Clare Colettines at Simmonscourt Road, Ballsbridge. Her health, although she had a slight cough, gave no serious cause for anxiety. She derived great help from Father Sullivan's direction, and, before making her temporary profession, remarked to him how much she felt that she was only going to bind herself for three years. "Who has told you you are going to live three years?" he said. "Make your vows now as if they were for life." She did so interiorly. A few months later she developed rapid consumption, and died in January 1923, just a year and a half after her conversation with Father Sullivan. A few days before her death she recounted these facts to her Mistress of Novices.

About 1919, a lady living in Dublin went to visit Father Sullivan at Rathfarnham Castle, and told him that she was worried about her son, who was not settling down to any career. Father Sullivan expressed interest in the boy, but no opportunity occurred to bring them together.

In 1923, the boy, then aged twenty-one, fell dangerously ill and, on his removal to hospital, was found to be suffering from peritonitis. Quite spontaneously he asked his mother if it were not true that Father Sullivan worked cures, and demanded that he should be sent for. Father Sullivan arrived at 7 a.m. When he entered the room, the young man said, "Father, won't you cure me?" Father Sullivan replied, "No, X, it is better to go to heaven."

The young man showed no dissatisfaction, and died a holy death after ten days of suffering.

His father felt his loss keenly, and in his presence, the mother asked Father Sullivan why God had permitted such a thing. Father Sullivan replied, "This boy would have had to bear a cross he would not have been able for."

The mother used frequently to ask Father Sullivan to say Mass for the repose of the soul of her son, but after a couple of years he refused to do so any more.

Father Sullivan's sympathies were wide, and though spiritual needs claimed his first attentions, he could interest himself in a very human way in the material difficulties of those who sought his aid. A nun in a convent near Clongowes had failed three times in the special qualifying examination in Irish for primary teachers. In 1930 she was making her last attempt, as she would be over the required age for qualification in the following year. She was very despondent, as she had got lower marks at her last attempt than at the previous one. Someone recommended her to write to Father Sullivan and ask him to say Mass for her. Father Sullivan wrote back, "I said Mass for you this morning. Do not fear. You will get on well at the examination this year." His assurance proved true.

Father Sullivan always preserved a deep interest in the boys whom he had known at Clongowes, and it was when they were sick or otherwise afflicted that he was most assiduous in looking them up. One of these Samaritan visits was the occasion of another of those confident predictions which were always in such marked contrast to his ordinary diffidence. In June 1932, an old Clongowes boy met with a serious accident, and had to have his leg amputated at the hip. After the operation it was clear that he had only a slender chance of life. His brother wrote to Clongowes for prayers, and the Rector asked Father Sullivan to call to the hospital. On his arrival, there was a group of friends and relatives present, but he had nothing to say to them, asking only the one question, "Where is he?" He went straight to the injured young man's bedside, blessed him, held his hand and said a few prayers. Then he turned away, said abruptly to the patient's brother, "He will be well," and walked out. The young man made a complete recovery.

The following experience of a nun in a contemplative Order is best told in her own words.

"As far as I can remember, this incident took place in November or December 1929. It was not during the retreat given us by Father Sullivan that summer, but some months later, when some of the sisters had asked to see him. When I heard he had come to the convent for confessions, I decided that, if I got the opportunity, I would speak to him about a matter which I knew he would understand, and about which he would be able to tell me what I might safely believe.

"Later, I was told that he had to leave at 6 p.m., and when my turn came, it was ten minutes or so to that hour. I gave up the idea of consulting him, as the question would have taken some time even to ask.

"However, I went to confession, and, on going into the confessional, said that I was sorry he had to hurry away, as I would have liked to consult him about something, but that I would wait for some other time. Father Sullivan said nothing, but when I had made my confession, he answered, almost abruptly, but completely and fully, the question I had wished to ask him. While he was speaking, I did not say a word, as it seemed that he knew exactly what was in my mind, and in those few minutes he satisfied me completely. Then the Angelus rang. He said it, and rose at once to go, saying, 'I must go now, but I think that's all now.'

"This incident made a deep and lasting impression on me, and confirmed my belief in Father Sullivan's nearness to God."

A very similar experience was related by another nun in a contemplative Order.

"Father Sullivan's very presence and words used to bring something like the peace and joy of Heaven to my soul, and I always thought that he was gifted, somewhat like what I had read of the saintly Curé d'Ars, in being able to read souls. At one time in particular, I think it was about three months before his death, I was very worried and in doubt over something , so much so that it seemed to crush my very soul. I had said nothing to anyone when, to my great surprise and joy, who ran in but Father Sullivan. He said to the portress that he wanted to see me, and then ran round to the sacristy. I went to him at once, and when I knelt down, he gave me a big blessing, saying, 'Now, my poor child, my poor child, fear nothing! That trouble or worry you have is direct from the devil. Your soul is very dear and pleasing to God.' Needless to say how grateful I was, but he wouldn't hear of thanks for anything, always saying, 'It's nothing at all, I wish I could do more.'

"His next visit was his last, and he seemed to know that it would be his last. He stayed longer than usual speaking to me, and then said, 'Listen to me now, listen to me now. Fear nothing, I tell you, now, you are very dear to Our Lord. Keep very close to His Heart.' As I was going away, he called me back to say good-bye. Three times he did the same, and asked for prayers for someone dear to him, so that I really thought he knew it would be his last visit."

An even clearer presentiment of his death seems to have been manifested by Father Sullivan in an interview recalled by a nun in Gallen Priory, Ferbane.

"Father Sullivan gave us a retreat here in 1925, and since then I often went to confession to him as Extraordinary Confessor. His kindness and patience as confessor were admirable. The fervour and determination of his voice when giving absolution always touched me and made me feel the presence of God. When saying good-bye he always added, 'Please God, I will see you soon again.' But at my last interview, in July 1932, he omitted this phrase, and said, 'good-bye' about four times, which was most unusual for him. Also that day, in the course of a conversation on a conscience matter, he suddenly said, 'Fix up this matter now, as it may be the last chance.' I took this to mean then that God might withdraw His grace, but when I heard of Father Sullivan's death, I came to the conclusion that he had a presentiment that it was near at hand."

It will have been noted that in many cases when appealed to by sick persons Father Sullivan urged them confidently to seek a cure through prayer. On the other hand, he sometimes, with equal confidence, recommended natural means, or, less frequently, urged the sufferer not to hope for a cure.

In 1932 Sister Delphine de St. Paul, one of the Community of Little Sisters of the Poor, at St. Patrick's House, Kilmainham, became blind as the result of cataract. Having heard of Father Sullivan's reputation, she conceived a strong desire to see him. The Reverend Mother Provincial wrote to him asking that she might bring Sister Delphine to Clongowes. Father Sullivan replied that, as the weather was very cold, he would come and see the sister, asking her in the meanwhile to say certain prayers and practise certain mortifications.

There was at the time in St. Patrick's an old woman from near Clongowes named Bridget Keena, whom Father Sullivan used to visit. When he next arrived to see Bridget, he asked for Sister Delphine. She told him that there was question of an operation and that she dreaded going to hospital. She begged him to ask Our Lady to cure her. Father John replied with decision that he could not cure her, and that an operation was necessary, but he promised she would be cured. At this the good sister began to weep, but Father John sprinkled some Lourdes water on her eyes, blessed her, and again repeated that she would recover her sight and use it for the glory of God. The operation was performed very shortly afterwards in the Royal Victoria Eye and Ear Hospital and proved completely successful, although the sister was then seventy-four years of age, and the cataract was of long standing. Her sight has been perfect ever since.

At the time of this visit of Father Sullivan to Kilmainham, there was in the convent a young and promising sister, who was confined to bed with a mysterious malady which the doctors could not diagnose. The Reverend Mother asked Father Sullivan to see and console her. After some conversation, he said to her, "My dear child, have patience. You will never recover your health here, but in Paris you will be cured." Shortly afterwards the sister was transferred to Paris, and almost immediately on her arrival she was pronounced completely cured.

On the other hand, there was at the lodge of the convent, acting as portress when she was able, an American sister, Sister Euphrosiné du Sacré Coeur, who had been for years suffering with tubercular disease in her arm, hand and foot. She was quite helpless at times, but always cheerful and generous. She called Father Sullivan aside and asked him if he could do anything for her. The sisters recall exactly his answer.

"My dear sister," he said. "I can do nothing for you. It is the Holy Will of God that you should suffer. I pity you. Your sufferings will be long and painful. Have patience and courage, for a beautiful crown awaits you. I will bless you and pray for you."

This was in May 1932, and the sister continued to suffer until her death in March 1934.

Once he seemed to be completely wrong in a prediction, but even in that case, there seems to have been an inner truth in his words. A nun in a convent near Dublin was stricken with total blindness. She had been all her life a friend of Father Sullivan, her family having been intimate with his. On hearing the news of her affliction, he came up from Clongowes to see her. She was in bed at the time and, approaching her bedside, he said, "You're not going to be blind," and sprinkled her eyes with holy water. He then spoke to her of the loveliness of doing God's will, and she was so filled with enthusiasm that she lost all her desire to be cured. She always remained convinced that his promise of a cure would have been fulfilled had she not had the grace to ask for the greater gift of renunciation. On the day of his death she had an almost irresistible inclination to go into the hospital and get his hands laid on her eyes, confident that she would receive her sight. But she succeeded in keeping the resolution she had made years before of not asking to be relieved of her cross.

CHAPTER XVI

TEACHINGS (1)

THIS account of the life of Father John Sullivan would be incomplete without some record of his spiritual teachings. But to compile such a record was a difficult task, and has been accomplished only imperfectly. It has been said already that Father Sullivan did nothing in his lifetime to facilitate a possible future biographer. With regard to his spiritual teachings, it may be said that he put every obstacle in the way. One might well compare him to the commander of a retreating army who, on his way, blows up every bridge and blocks every road that his pursuers may use.

Father Sullivan's death was unexpected, and he had no time to destroy any of his papers if he had so wished. No record whatsoever of his own spiritual life was found amongst them, and it may be taken that the only diary he kept was written in his heart. He left behind him some one hundred and fifty note-books, but these contain nothing personal whatsoever, only useful extracts from well-known spiritual books, and notes taken of retreats by other Jesuits which he had attended. Even the note-books which he kept when a novice are marked by that characteristic of complete objectivity.

It may be remarked, in passing, that even if these note-books had contained illuminating matter, it would have been the work of years to extricate it. Father John was, in his later years, one of the worst penmen that ever existed. Many of his sermon notes are in such a hand, and full of such abbreviations that at first sight it is not apparent that they are written in English. In many convents there were nuns who specialized in deciphering his handwriting, and who were called in to help to make out even the hour at which his train would arrive. This illegibility was a late development in his life. The handwriting of his novitiate notes is almost copper-plate. Those who knew his character well will agree that it is not far-fetched to see in this curious characteristic another outward manifestation of his habitual self-depreciation. His thoughts seemed to him to be so poor that they deserved nothing more than to be hastily scribbled.

The only writings of his that ever appeared in print were the preface to *The Dilemma of John Haughton Steele*, already alluded to, and the preface to *The Life and Work of Mary Aikenhead*, by a member of the Congregation of Irish Sisters of Charity, published in 1926. When a philosopher at Stonyhurst, he wrote a study of Crashaw's poems for the *Blandyke Papers*, a domestic periodical. These fragments show that he could write excellent, plain, nervous English, but, unfortunately, he never saw fit to unwrap that talent from its napkin.

His numerous sermons and exhortations were never committed to paper. One Jesuit recalls being present at a sermon preached by Father Sullivan on the occasion of a profession at the convent of Poor Clare Colettines, Simmonscourt, Dublin. It struck him as the most beautiful piece of oratory that he had ever heard. On the way back to Rathfarnham Castle he asked Father Sullivan if he could have the manuscript. Father Sullivan produced an old envelope with a few almost illegible notes scrawled on the back of it. This seems to have been his customary mode of preparation. He must have had a very extensive correspondence with friends, penitents and invalids who invoked his prayers, and yet he was in no sense a letter-writer. I have been privileged to read about a hundred of his letters, but again they contain the minimum of self-revelation. They are very short, usually promising prayers or a visit, or sending some consoling message, but though they invariably contain some spiritual thoughts, these are of the simplest.

In order, therefore, to get some idea of the spirituality which he preached, we are obliged to fall back on notes taken of the retreats which he gave. Even these are scattered and incomplete. All agree that his retreat lectures, as a rule, lacked form, and that it was difficult to retain any complete memory of them. Their efficacy lay in the peculiar power Father Sullivan possessed of giving a new meaning to old truths, and of inspiring his hearers with the desire of putting those truths into practice. It will have been noticed in other parts of this book that many of those who knew him could remember his words *verbatim* over long periods of time. Yet what they remembered was often some spiritual truism. It was the utter sincerity with which it was said or the effect it had on the hearer's life that made its memory so permanent.

I can recall two instances of this myself. In 1913, when a novice at Tullabeg, I recollect speaking to him about the difficulty of making an hour's meditation. He said, "Keep on. Use bits of the Our Father or the

Hail Mary. Say anything. But keep on." I remember being profoundly disappointed at this apparently kindergarten solution of the difficulties of prayer. But in after life I realized that, at any rate, as applied to the ways of ordinary prayer, Father John's advice, by its very jejuneness, was sound. On another occasion I told him that I was feeling depressed. He replied, "A great cure for depression, there, is to make the Stations of the Cross. When you have finished the Stations, you will find all the depression gone." The only remarkable thing about this remedy for depression is that I have never known it to fail.

A nun in the Dominican convent, Wicklow, writing in 1940, recalled how in 1919 Father Sullivan recommended to her the following aspirations:

"Sacred Heart of Jesus, I place all my trust in Thee."

"Sacred Heart of Jesus, I believe in your love for me."

"Sacred Heart of Jesus, I believe you love me *now*. (Useful when God sends crosses.)"

"I believe in God. I hope in God. I love God. I am sorry for having offended God."

Father Sullivan added, "Say these frequently and you'll become very holy."

Although the aspirations suggested were nearly all well-known ones, the nun was so struck by Father Sullivan's tone in recommending them that she never forgot his words, and never allowed a day to pass since without saying them.

I have been able to get notes of only one complete meditation taken from a retreat given in 1926. This will be followed by stray extracts from other notes, arranged roughly, for greater convenience, under the headings of various virtues. It is quite likely that many of the thoughts are not original. No apology is required for this. It was Father Sullivan's own way to rely largely on the teachings of saints and other spiritual writers.

The Gospel Gem

(*Lecture given in a Retreat*, 1926)

Commentators on the Scriptures sometimes call the first chapter of St. Luke the Gospel gem, around which all the other gospels revolve as its setting. It is, as it were, a pearl of great price, a treasure hidden in a field. It is the Marian gospel. St. Luke must have heard all the things related therein from Mary's own lips. The best proof that it is Mary's own gospel is the fact that no one was present at the Annunciation but Mary and the Angel Gabriel. Zachary and Elizabeth must have been dead when St. Luke wrote it, twenty-four years after Our Lord's ascension. The Gospel says that "They both were well advanced in years" when these things came to pass. The sound of a mother's voice is in the telling. How the disciples must have gathered round her, eagerly listening to every word as she related it. Let us sit among them during this lecture. We cannot get better company. We can never hear enough about it. The more we seek the more we shall find in it. The greatest act of all time is recorded there.

(Read verses 1–25.)

Mary was the first eye-witness and minister of the Word. This is a great thought for God's priests. They, too, have care of Him in the Blessed Sacrament and take Mary's place when they put Him on the corporal, the swaddling bands of His sacramental life. When making anything for His use on the altar, make it in the company of Mary as she makes the little garments prepared for His coming.

What kind of people were Zachary and Elizabeth? "They were both just before God, walking in all the commandments and justifications of the Lord without blame." (Verse 6.) There is no small praise in that one verse which indicates the fidelity of a lifetime.

Notice the time at which the angel appeared to Zachary. "In the order of his course before God." (Verse 8.)

It was in the time of ordinary prayer. There are great graces going at the appointed time for prayer. You do not know what depends on fidelity to it. In it you get light to see the difficulties of the day and you get the strength to overcome them. How do you know but that God has some special message for you as He had for Zachary?

"And Zachary seeing him, was troubled; and fear fell upon him." (Verse 12.) All God's saints feel fear and mistrust when any unusual message is sent to them.

The angel comforted him, "Fear not, Zachary, for thy prayer is heard." (Verse 13.) When Our Lord spoke to St. Teresa, she was troubled, until He consoled her with the words: "It is I." Look at the way in which Zachary was punished for one small doubt: "And behold thou shall be dumb . . . because thou hast not believed My words which shall be fulfilled in their time." (Verse 20.) How many times have we sinned more grievously than Zachary by our doubt? How great is the mercy of God to us, one absolution washing out all stain.

"And after those days Elizabeth his wife conceived

and hid herself five months, saying: Thus hath the Lord dealt with me in the days wherein He hath had regard to take away my reproach among men." (Verses 24–25.)

How did she know the things that were to come to pass? Zachary was dumb, and so could not relate them. She was a house of prayer. She was filled with the Holy Ghost. In silence she heard His small voice speaking in her heart. Is this house a house of prayer? Is my own soul a house of prayer? Or is it filled with the buyers and sellers of worldly trifles? How can I hear the Holy Ghost if there is not silence there?

(Read verses 26–38.)

It is the same messenger who comes to Mary, Gabriel the angel of the Incarnation. Mary, too, was at prayer when God's messenger came, and she too was "troubled at his saying." (Verse 29.) In her humility she lived like all the Jewish maidens. Nothing external marked her out from her companions or showed her to be "full of grace." The angel comforted her, too, "Fear not, Mary, for thou hast found grace with God." (Verse 30.) Mary is still troubled, for she had made a vow of virginity in her lowliness, thinking herself unworthy to be the mother of the Messiah, an honour to which all the Jewish maidens at the time aspired.

The angel gives her a sign to reassure her: "And behold thy cousin Elizabeth, she also hath conceived a son in her old age, and this is the sixth month with her that is called barren. Because no word shall be impossible with God." (Verses 36–7.) Mary was not punished like Zachary when she asked for a sign. Why? Her cousin answers the question: "Blessed art thou that hast believed. . . ." (Verse 45.)

What answer will Mary make to the angel? Listen: "Behold the handmaid of the Lord: be it done to me according to thy word." (Verse 38.) How great is the humility of the Mother of God. She was the one person who filled the greatest position in all time. The handmaid! She must indeed have been full of grace, not to have any feelings of pride when she was told so suddenly that she was to fill such a high destiny. Occasion proves the man.

If we receive special graces in prayer, do we act and think like Mary? Or do we go around relating, with vain self-complacency any supposed grace we have received, which is a gift from God without any merit on our part. We are sinners by creation.

When the humble maiden had said her *fiat*, the Word was made Flesh and dwelt amongst us. If Mary had not co-operated with grace, the hand of God would have been detained. If we do not co-operate with grace as Mary did, we shall have to give a strict account of it before God.

This Word of God is life. There were once two Protestant children, a boy and a girl, who were told to read the Bible. They happened on this chapter. When they came to the apparition of the angel to Mary they were so delighted that they joined the words of the angel and the words of Elizabeth together, learned them off by heart, and ran in glee to tell their mother of the prayer they had made. Consternation followed. They were forbidden to read that part of the Bible again, but the words are life, the seed was sown by the power of the Word of God, the Gospel. The Word was made Flesh mystically in the heart of a little child. The seed grew and produced flowers and fruit in due season.

The girl entered the Catholic Church and became the Foundress of a religious Order.[1]

What effect has His coming on Mary? Did she sit idle, contemplating the great things done in her? The Gospel tells us: "And Mary rising up in those days went into the hill country with haste. . . ." (Verse 39.) Charity knows no delay. "Into the hill country." She faces the fatigue and weariness of a long journey to render service to her cousin in her needs. Do I rise up in haste when charity or obedience calls me to go into the hill country of trials and difficulties? The great pity is that Mary's salutation to Elizabeth is lost for ever. We can imagine what it was like from its effect. "And it came to pass that when Elizabeth heard the salutation of Mary, the infant leaped in her womb. And Elizabeth was filled with the Holy Ghost. And she cried out in a loud voice and said: Blessed art thou amongst women, and blessed is the fruit of thy womb." (Verses 41–2.)

How does she know the greatness of her visitor? Again she is filled with the Holy Ghost. "And whence is this to me that the Mother of my Lord should come to me? For behold as soon as the voice of thy salutation sounded in my ears, the infant in my womb leaped for joy." (Verses 43–4.) What kind of a salutation indeed,

[1] This incident is related, though not in such detail, in the *Life of Mary Aikenhead,* to which, as has already been mentioned, Father Sullivan contributed the Preface. The children referred to were Letitia Bradshaw and her brother, whose parents owned considerable property in Co. Tipperary. Father Sullivan is incorrect in one point. Letitia Bradshaw did not found a Religious Order, but she was one of the early companions of Mother Aikenhead, entering the Irish Sisters of Charity in 1833. In religion she was known as Sister M. Emilian. (*The Life and Work of Mary Aikenhead, Foundress of the Congregation of Irish Sisters of Charity*, by a Member of the Congregation, p. 227.)

when the infant in his narrow prison was sanctified by Mary's Son through Mary's word.

Mary brought Jesus into the house of Elizabeth, the greater to the lesser, Jesus to John, Mary to Elizabeth. Do I bring Jesus to those whom I visit? Is this retreat a visitation?

Mary breaks out into a glorious song of praise. The highest prayer is praise.

(Here read verses 46–55.)

Since that day her prayer rings down the ages in holy Church at Vespers, will continue until the end of time, and will fill heaven with harmony for all eternity.

It is difficult to leave the company of the two cousins so full of joy. Has my intercourse with my friends any of the qualities of this heavenly scene? Is it a joy to meet me? Has my word the power to move my hearers to break out in prayer? If not, learn the lesson from Mary and Elizabeth.

(Here read verses 56–64.)

An act of obedience loosed Zachary's tongue. Do we hear from him any complaints about his infirmity? His first words are: "Blessed be the Lord God of Israel." (Verse 68.) This is how God's friends act in time of trial. Compare Zachary with Job: "The Lord gave, and the Lord hath taken away. As it hath pleased the Lord so it is done. Blest be the name of the Lord." (Job. i. 21.)

This first chapter is the gospel of prayer.

1. Zachary was at prayer when God's angel came.
2. The people "understood that he had seen a vision in the Temple," (verse 22) because they were at prayer.
3. Elizabeth's was a house of prayer.

4. Mary was at prayer when the angel appeared to her.
5. The exchange of greetings between the two cousins was prayer.
6. Mary's hymn of thanksgiving was a prayer.
7. Zachary's prophecy was a prayer.
8. John the Baptist was a child of prayer. "Thy prayer is heard." (Verse 13.)

Do you want to know how to pray? Listen to the salutation of an angel, the response of God's own mother, or the greetings of Elizabeth. You say that you cannot make a meditation. How could Mary tell St. Luke the great things he related? Because she "kept all these words, pondering them in her heart." (ii. 19.) Ponder all these words in your own heart with her. You too will learn how to meditate.

Do you want to know how to make your thanksgiving after Holy Communion? Kneel at Mary's feet whilst she sings her thanksgiving after the first Holy Communion.

Lest we forget the brilliancy of this gem, our true Mother the Church recalls it for us morning, noon and evening in the Angelus, in the Magnificat at Vespers, and in the countless Aves of her rosary. She could find no better hymn to finish her official prayer of praise, the Divine Office, than the "Blessed be the Lord God of Israel" of Zachary. Isn't it grand, all the prayer that is in it?

Who is the teacher of prayer? God the Holy Ghost. It was because Zachary and Elizabeth were filled with the Holy Ghost that they were just before God. Then we have the promise of the angel concerning the child.

"And he shall be filled with the Holy Ghost, even from his mother's womb." (Verse 15.) And the angel's words to Mary: "The Holy Ghost shall come upon Thee and the power of the Most High shall overshadow Thee. And therefore also the Holy One which shall be born of Thee shall be called the Son of God." (Verse 35.) When Elizabeth heard the salutation of Mary she too "was filled with the Holy Ghost." (Verse 41.) Zachary "was filled with the Holy Ghost. And he prophesied, saying: Blest be the Lord God of Israel." (Verses 67–8.)

If you want to know how to pray, cultivate devotion to God the Holy Ghost.

The highest virtues are practised in these scenes. Zachary and Elizabeth were both "walking in all the commandments and justifications of the Lord." (Verse 6.)

We see exemplified in this chapter:

Fidelity to duty.

Persevering prayer, "and they were both well advanced in years." (Verse 7.)

Resignation and patience.

Silence and retirement. "Elizabeth . . . hid herself five months." (Verse 24.)

Faith. "And blessed art thou that hast believed." (Verse 45.)

Conformity to God's will. "Be it done to me according to Thy word." (Verse 38.)

Humility. "Behold the handmaid." (Verse 38.)

Charity. "And Mary rising up in those days, went into the hill country with haste. . . ." (Verse 39.)

Forgetfulness of self.

Zeal. St. John was sanctified at her salutation.

Generosity. She shared her joy with others.

Simplicity. She appeared outwardly like those around her.

With all these virtues, no wonder it was that the angel hailed her "full of grace."

Apart from this first chapter, St. Luke's whole gospel may be called the gospel of prayer. In other chapters we find the beginning of the *Gloria in excelsis* (ii. 14), Mary's example of meditation, "Mary kept all these words, pondering them in her heart" (ii. 19), the *Nunc Dimittis* of Compline spoken by Simeon (ii. 29–32), the *Domine non sum dignus* of the Mass spoken by the Centurion (viii. 6), the Lord's Prayer, and the parables teaching perseverance in prayer (xi), the parable of the master and his servant, warning us to watch and pray (xii), the parable of the unjust judge, teaching us that we "ought always to pray and not to faint," and the prayer of the publican, "O God be merciful to me a sinner" (xviii), Our Lord's Prayer in the Garden (xxii), the Forty Days' Prayer of Our Lord in the desert, the whole night spent in prayer, etc., etc.

CHAPTER XVII

TEACHINGS (II)

Blessed Sacrament

When an unexpected humiliation come to me, I should go to Our Lord in the Tabernacle and tell Him all about it, and all will be right. I should take all my troubles to the Tabernacle. Nothing is too big for Our Lord and nothing is too small.

Charity

The Angel Gabriel said to the Blessed Virgin who was sinless, "Hail, full of grace!" (Luke i. 28), and to Mary Magdalen Our Lord said, "Many sins are forgiven her, because she hath loved much." (Luke vii. 47.) We should never criticize sinners. Our Lord rebuked those who did so.

"Little children . . . love one another." (John xiii. 33–4.) "By this shall all men know that you are My disciples, that you have love one for another." (Ibid., 35.) Should I not take these words to heart as a precious legacy and put them into daily practice. It was His charity that urged Him to leave heaven and become man for my sake. It was His charity that urged Him to suffer and die to save me. It was His charity that urged Him to institute the Blessed Eucharist which is, of all the proofs of His love for me, the greatest. Because a higher and better gift Jesus Christ could not give me than His own Flesh and Blood. Through the whole gospel we have proof of the power of His love. Love, and love alone, was the secret of the saints. Charity is the lily, all other virtues are but common flowers. Charity is the purest virtue of all. It was the favourite virtue of Our Divine Lord. Even when Magdalen fell at His feet weeping and anointing them, He said to Simon, "Many sins are forgiven her, because she hath *loved* much." (Luke vii. 47.)

Want of kindness is a great fault in religion. We meet with many heroic acts of kindness on the part of people in the world, even amongst those who are not Catholics, and especially amongst the poor. It would be a shame if religious were less kind than those in the world, and if their fellow-religious received more kindness before they entered religion than after they have entered.

"Little children . . . A new commandment I give unto you: That you love one another as I have loved you. . . ." (John xiii. 33–4.) Consider your own faults and you will not have the courage to launch out against others. One cannot be religious, a good Catholic or even a Christian if uncharitable. Charity is greater in God's sight than poverty, chastity, or even martyrdom. The world gets a shock at want of charity in a religious.

CHILDREN, TRAINING OF

Teach the children to cling to the Heart of Christ, to cling to the Cross of Christ, to cling to the Mother of Christ.

Prayer and work are necessary in order to lead a sinless life. Impress this on the children, give them Mary for their imitation. Make them marvels of prayer, and not marvels of learning. Give them true and solid devotion, love of the Blessed Sacrament, devotion to the Holy Ghost, to Our Lady and St. Joseph.

The shepherds were watching their flocks when they received the heavenly message on the birth of Our Lord. We have to watch over the children, and if we do that faithfully we shall undoubtedly receive lights from the Holy Ghost.

The scene of Our Lord with the little children is the sweetest in the whole gospel story. (Matt. xix. 13–15; Mark x. 13; Luke xviii. 15–17.) The soul of a child is a most perfect image of God. God wills that no child be lost, not even one. There is nothing grander on God's earth than teaching children Christian doctrine.

Teach them piety. Impress on them that God is their Father. Tell them about His love for each one of them.

Teach them humility. Tell them they can do nothing without God's help.

Teach them self-restraint. How they must overcome their passions.

Teach them fear of hell. What happens to them if they commit sin. It is very necessary to impress them with a fear of hell. They should be taught that God is in earnest about mortal sin. If they often think of hell, they will never go there.

Consecrate children to the Most Sacred Heart of Jesus. Train and teach them on the lines of the Sacred Heart. Take them to the Sacred Heart and teach them there His gentleness, His love. But before this is done, we must ourselves be full of the spirit of that Divine Heart.

One good girl can change a parish. We do not want crowds.

If we fail in our work for children, so did Jesus fail in

the eyes of the world. His pupils did not always turn out well—Judas—the disciples who went away.

The Church

Apart from religion, at all times Jesus Christ was the greatest man who ever lived. The very date we write proves it. All things date before Christ or after Christ. This fact alone should set non-Catholics thinking. If we were sincere, the natural conclusion would be that He was no ordinary man. That leads to the institution He founded, the Church. It is unlike all other earthly institutions, world-wide, irrespective of peoples and nations, in all nations alike. It stands the test of time and is unchanging. There must be something more than human in it. All things human change. The greatest personalities are forgotten in a short time. That fact alone should lead men to the truth, but "with desolation is all the land made desolate, because there is none that considereth in the heart." (Jer. xii. 11.)

The Cross

(*Lent*)

"I send you two little books. Possibly you have them already. The larger one is by Father Michael Browne, S.J., and I am almost certain that the smaller one is by him too. The Stations of the Cross in the larger book are very beautiful. The smaller one will teach you to love your crucifix and to make it your favourite book. It is the only book that we can read at the hour of death."

(*From a letter.*)

Forgiveness of Enemies

On Calvary Our Lord said, "Father forgive them, for they know not what they do." (Luke xxiii. 34).

One would think that there could be no excuse for the wickedness of the Jews, but Our Lord found one.

Prayers for our enemies are the most powerful of all prayers, and will bring untold blessings on those who utter them.

God

Introduction to a Retreat

God and I—my soul and its Maker. God alone—to sanctify my soul, to bless my work, and to possess me for eternity. God and my soul together now—". . . I will lead her into the wilderness; and I will speak to her heart." (Osee. ii. 16.) Yes, Jesus has led me into the wilderness now, i.e., silence of retreat, *there* to speak to my soul. Listen! Can I hear Him?—No! He does not speak in a very loud voice. It is in the silence of retreat He will speak to me—I must wait and pray. Humility will be the fruit of this meditation. What is that? It is the knowledge of what *I* am and what God is—God and my soul—Who art Thou O Lord and what am I? You are my Creator; You brought me out of nothing and gave me the precious soul, which I am to save for Your greater glory and honour. You are Lord of *all*. You make out of nothing, and *I*——? Who am I? A worm of the earth that can do no good of myself. Without the aid of the Holy Spirit I cannot say, "Jesus." The Holy Spirit is the Spirit of Jesus. Seeing the guilt of my past life, with my deep ingratitude to my Creator for all His wondrous favours to me, I should shrink with horror at the sight of myself as I am really before the Omnipotent; but God's mercy intervenes, and I am spared and given this opportunity of removing the obstacles that draw me from my God. If I only look at *any moment* of my life I must admit, "the Mercy of God is with me." I must pray the Mercy of God to show me myself as I am, not often, but continually. If often, knowledge of self comes too; but if continually, I shall grow in knowledge and contempt of my wretched self, and attain intimacy with Jesus, which should be my only aim.

GOVERNMENT. ADVICE TO A SUPERIOR

1. Be always accessible. Leave Christ in order to find Him in your subjects.

2. Always trust those in your care. It is better to err on the side of too much trust.

3. Always be kind.

4. Give praise sometimes. In some convents the faults are always come down on, but there is never a word of praise.

5. Say a prayer to the Holy Ghost every day to ask a right understanding in all things.

GRACE

The Holy Ghost will write in invisible ink on our hearts. If we are only faithful to His inspirations we shall do great things. It is on account of our unfaithfulness to His inspirations that we remain so imperfect.

HEAVEN

We should be homesick for heaven, since it is our home.

The Hidden Life

Consider the influence this life has had upon the world. All the strength of manhood, all the beauty of the homes of Europe were but images of the home at Nazareth. The true Christian mother is but an image of Mary. Since Mary left the faith of England so did the love of Jesus, for He cannot be where Mary has not got a home.

It was here in Nazareth that Jesus got His parables, the leaven in the bread, the good shepherd, the sparrows, the eagles.

Here we see the perfect model of home-life. If the home is holy and pure, the nation will be likewise. How great a work is then to be done in Ireland to preserve the home and thus the nation.

The Holy Ghost

If nuns spoke more to the Holy Spirit of their anxieties and their aims in their instructions, there would be fewer falls amongst the girlhood that goes through their hands.

The Holy Ghost is dwelling within us, and this thought of the presence of God within us was the greatest help to the saints in acquiring sanctity. Have recourse to the Holy Spirit in all trials, and teach devotion to Him. Never undertake any work without asking in prayer for His light.

Try to realize the indwelling of the Holy Ghost in our souls. Live by Him. Pray by Him. Turn to Him in all difficulties. Think well over the prayers to the Holy Ghost. "Come" means for us "Come closer." We already have Him, but want Him more.

Humility

Try to imitate Jesus. Meekness is all-powerful, few can withstand it. A religious made his meditation for a year on the words, "Learn of Me, because I am meek and humble of heart." (Matt. xi. 29.)

Do not speak outside confession of your interior life. The devil does much harm that way.

Introduction to a Retreat

On the front page of the Life of St. Teresa, translated from the French by Lady Lovat, there is a picture of the saint seated at a table, with an open book before her. If one puts a magnifying glass on the words written there, one will find them to be: "Unless the soil is cultivated, it will bring forth nothing but thorns and briars." That great saint loved to compare the soul to a garden in which the bridegroom loved to take his delight. That is the work of this retreat. We must cultivate the soil of our souls, pluck up the thorns and briars of passions and vice from the *roots*, and plant flowers of virtue in their place.

Love of Our Lord

Jesus in my soul to sanctify it, in my heart to possess it, and in my work to bless it.

Jesus loves to get outward marks of attention when they are accompanied by inward love.

The great antidote for sin is personal love of Christ.

Mercy of God

(*From a meditation on the Prodigal Son*)

God always leaves the door unlatched.

OBEDIENCE

We should totally abstain from criticizing Superiors. They have light and grace from God, which the subject may not have. It is obedience God wants, not our work. A murmur was never heard in the holy house of Nazareth. All was submission to God's Will. The angels hovered over the head of St. Joseph as he performed each lowly act in the humble workshop.

"And he went down with them and came to Nazareth and was subject to them." (Luke ii. 51.) Jesus Christ, the eternal Lord of all things, went down to Nazareth and was subject to his own creatures. Mary and Joseph were both very holy and dear to God, yet they were only creatures, the work of God's hands. The little Jesus went to learn the trade of Joseph. He is told by Joseph to make a chair; surely He Who made Joseph and Mary knew how to make a chair in the best possible way. Still He made it in no way but that which He was taught by Joseph. Here again is our model of obedience and humility. He, the great God of heaven before Whom the angels veil their faces, was obedient to His own creatures both in execution, in will and in judgment.

Is my obedience like His? Why not? What are the obstacles that make it not so? How can they be removed? I am only a creature of the slime of the earth. When that immortal soul leaves the human frame, very soon those around the corpse will realize that it is only dust, for the smell of the clay will shortly return.

It is of no consequence to me who commands. All things here are passing, and, when the hour of death comes, it will not matter to me if I have done the will of Him Whom I came into religion to serve. On the contrary, obedience relieves me of much responsibility. Once I do what I am told, my part is done. If asked why I did so, "I was told" is the only answer that removes all responsibility from me.

The cause of most sins is that men forget that they are creatures. If a Superior tells me to do something I do not like, I should at once blindly respond to the command, taking it as if Jesus Himself told me to do it. There is no need to question or examine the value of obedience. In it the only sacrifice man has to give is given to his Maker. Our Lord has said, "He that heareth you heareth me." (Luke x. 16.)

The devil said to Eve, "Why hath God commanded you, that you should not eat of every tree of paradise?" (Gen. iii. 1.)

When we question God's commands, "Why so-and-so?" we may be sure that the devil is always knocking around.

Superiors stand on a height and see fifty reasons to our three or four. The Holy Ghost is *bound* to help *them* with special light, as it is not our business. *They* will be responsible for the work or apparent failure, not we. God does not command success, only goodwill.

Keep the rule, and the rule will keep you.

Perfection

Take life in instalments, this one day now. At least let this be a good day. Be always beginning. "Now have I begun." (Ps. lxxvi. 11.) Let the past go. Now let me do whatever I have power to do. The saints were always beginning. That is how they became saints.

Poverty

On Christmas night the heavens were opened to the poor shepherds, and a beautiful angel sent to convey to them the glad tidings, but the rich Magi had only a single star to guide them. Caesar Augustus had couriers on all the roads that night to bring him tidings from all parts of the world, but not one messenger to bring him news from heaven.

Prayer

Perseverance in prayer is necessary if we want our petitions answered. We begin a novena with great fervour on the first day. Do we continue with the same fervour for nine days? Not at all, we want miracles, if you please, from God Almighty. We will not do the little required of us.

In a letter received from a poor woman in great trouble she says: "Please pray for me and put your whole heart into it." There is a great lesson from that poor woman. Put your whole heart into it. Now, when you pray, think of her, and put your whole heart into it.

Even people of the world acknowledge the power of prayer. Lord Russell of Killowen objected strongly to his daughter becoming a nun. On his deathbed he wrote to her saying, "I know now what it is to have a brave young heart praying for me."

If we only turn towards the tabernacle, God is pleased. He does not need words. Just as an earthly father is satisfied with seeing his child, so is God with us.

We may never be called upon to do anything more heroic than make our morning meditation well.

In prayer, if your thoughts rest on a single word,

stay there as long as you can get anything out of it. Imitate a dog with a bone. If you study the dog, you will see that he goes back and back again, gnawing on something that seems to you to be a dry useless bone. You wonder what he can get out of it. He has the secret.

Prayer is the greatest power on earth. What a void there would be in the Church to-day without the prayer of St. Paul for the Church, the prayers of saints like St. Ignatius, St. Francis and St. Clare, for the members of their orders. St. Patrick's prayer converted the Irish nation. St. Teresa kept the reformation out of Spain by her union with God in prayer. St. Francis Xavier owed his vocation as apostle of the Indies to the prayer of his sister, a Poor Clare Abbess. We have in our hands a great power. See that we make good use of it.

We find one of Our Lord's days in St. Luke (vi. 12–19). After Our Lord's prayer, people with all manner of diseases came to Him, and He healed all. After our prayer, we assist at Mass. There Our Lord comes down on the altar, and we can present to Him the whole world with its wounds of sin; our own country with its festering wounds, and our own souls.

In temptation, turn your back on it, and throw yourself into prayer.

Get the *Magnificat* into your life. Live it, and always be praising and blessing God.

In prayer, don't mind the scaffolding. Get at God.

THE DISCIPLES AT EMMAUS

(*Conclusion of a lecture given in a retreat,* 1915.)

The whole story of the disciples' deeds and words may be regarded as the various parts of a meditation.

Our Lord in this case sets the points Himself, and develops them too. No wonder the disciples afterwards said, "Was not our heart burning within us, whilst He spoke in the way?" (Luke xxiv. 32.) And we—what about our meditation? Well, our hearts will burn, too, if we, patiently, persistently, keep turning to the Holy Spirit for help.

Having reached Emmaus, Jesus "made as though he would go farther. But they constrained Him, saying: Stay with us, because it is towards evening and the day is now far spent." (Ibid., verse 29.) And Jesus stayed. This petition, "Stay with us," is like the colloquy of the meditation. Had the disciples not made that request Our Lord would have gone, and then what favours they would have missed! So, it may be that if we omit the colloquy in the progress, or, at least, at the conclusion of our meditation, we shall miss great favours. "Our hearts may have burned within us" during the meditation, but we shall miss knowing that we had Jesus with us, we shall not know Him "in the breaking of bread."

The disciples returned to Jerusalem, to the Upper Chamber and told all that had happened. With what joy and enthusiasm they related it all—and they would not have known that Jesus had been their fellow-pilgrim only for that petition, "Stay with us!" What a lesson for us as to our method of action at the close of our morning meditation! If we ask Our Lord to "Stay with us" throughout the day—specifying the times or duties of special difficulty we foresee—He undoubtedly will. Thus we shall be borne through our difficulties when we are on the point of failing, as were the disciples at Emmaus.

One thing more we must note in connection with the above: these disciples, like all Jews, must have read the prophecies concerning the Saviour, the Messiah. But their own reading did not convince them—another proof of the necessity of grace for the understanding of Divine truths, and hence of the necessity for invoking the Holy Spirit before, and often during meditation.

The Presence of God

God is everywhere, but He does not dwell everywhere, only in faithful souls.

Purity

In the Presentation of Mary we see a picture of recollection and peace. Beside her grows a spotless lily, the image of her purity. In this picture we see, first, the results of intimate union with God, and, second, the result of constant prayer and diligent work. It reminds us that the lily, if uncared for, will fade and die. Tepidity and sloth are the enemies of purity.

The Religious Life

When Mary went to visit, where did she bring her Divine Child? She brought Him to a home away in the hills of Judea, away from notoriety and worldliness, to silence and prayer, a figure of a convent.

Resignation

To say *Deo Gratias* to all things is to be a saint.

Rosary

Have great devotion to the Rosary, and teach it to the children. It is the greatest prayer, as it contains the three greatest prayers of the Church. It works miracles. It goes straight up to God's throne in heaven.

St. Mary Magdalen

Some Lives of saints repel us, but the lives of the saints written by the Holy Ghost attract us, as for example, that of Mary Magdalen. She anointed Our Lord's feet with a most precious ointment and broke the vase. The ointment was a holocaust of herself, soul and body, no reserve. After she had washed Our Lord's feet with her tears, she made her first vows. The anointing was her final profession. The vase was the world, empty and hollow, and she had broken with it. Our Lord commended her act as she came to His feet. Cling to Our Lord's feet by prayer. No matter how dry, keep on the prayers. Aim at personal holiness, it will do more for souls than talents and great gifts.

How did Mary know that tears had power over the Sacred Heart? Perhaps she had witnessed the raising of the widow's son, and had seen the tenderness of Christ. She saw the poor mother leading the funeral of her only son, saw the two crowds meet, saw Christ the Author of life—and death. Christ said: "Weep not. . . . Young man, I say to thee, arise." (Luke vii. 13–14)—and the boy was once more in his mother's arms.

St. John, in writing his gospel years afterwards, recalls that when Mary Magdalen poured the ointment on the feet of Our Saviour, the house was filled with the odour of the ointment. So her virtues have filled heaven and earth with their perfume, which has remained for so many centuries. We should strive to imitate her and to diffuse the odour of sanctity about us.

Our Divine Lord always defended the penitent Magdalen. For example, He defended her when Simon wondered how He suffered such a sinner to touch Him, and also when Martha complained that she had been left alone to serve. Again he defended her when Judas pretended to be scandalized at her extravagance, and He chided the apostles for not crediting her evidence after His resurrection.

Our Divine Master has not changed. He is still the Friend of all penitents. What He has forgiven He has forgiven; and those who are ever, as it were, throwing the penitent's sin into his or her face, are offering a grievous insult to God Himself and may expect His wrath to come upon them. This is not acting in a Christ-like manner. No! Let us *forgive* and *forget*. It is said that next to the Mother of God, no creature ever loved Him as did Mary Magdalen. Her love exceeded that of the Seraphim.

St. Mary Magdalen is said to have done penance for thirty years in a grotto high in the mountains to the south of France, and to have been buried there. The Dominicans now have charge of this shrine. When the Papal seat was at Avignon, in one century no fewer than seven Popes came to venerate the holy relics. St. Louis of France himself came to seek her aid in the Great Crusade to recapture the tomb, as it was she who arrived first at the tomb on that first Easter morning. St. Bernard made her patroness of the Crusade.

Scruples

When God forgives me my sins, He buries them beneath a large stone. It is desecration to root them up again.

People forget that "I believe in the forgiveness of sins" is an article of faith.

Anything that causes uneasiness is from the devil.

Self-Denial

Try to lead a comfortless life. Every victory over self is a victory for God.

Self-Love

We shall acquire personal love of Our Lord by going against our own self-love, rooting it out of our hearts. The two cannot exist together. God is jealous of our love. Anything that denies self is an act of love.

Sin

The devotees of the world range themselves around Eve, but we stand with Mary at the foot of the Cross, where her Divine Son makes reparation for Eve's sin.

Union with Our Lord

The short road to perfection is to keep in close touch with Jesus. ". . . virtue went out from Him, and healed all." (Luke vi. 19.) This happens each morning at Mass. The sick and blind had Him only for a while, whereas we have Him always.

Worldliness

Worldliness brings a blight on a community and dries up union with God, the fairest flower of religious life.

Zeal

As artists carve the statues of great men, so should religious try to carve the image of Christ in the souls of children committed to their care.

This chapter on the teachings of Father Sullivan may

be closed fittingly by some impressions of a retreat which he gave to the Jesuit novices at Tullabeg in 1930.

"This is not a detailed account of Father Sullivan's retreat, but rather an impression. Father Sullivan, emaciated and ascetical, began all his lectures with the prayer, 'Come, Holy Ghost, replenish the hearts of Thy faithful, etc.' Then, reaching into the breast-pocket of his gown, he took out his crucifix, which he held in his hand during the greater part of the lecture. He seldom shifted his gaze from it except to give an occasional quick glance at his listeners. He was very fluent, but often interrupted what he had to say with the words, 'And all that, and all that,' meanwhile running his fingers through his hair.

"The opening lecture took for composition of place the scene which took place after Our Lord's ascension into heaven, when the two angels accosted the apostles and disciples saying, 'Ye men of Galilee, why stand you looking up to heaven?' (Acts i. 11), and telling them, 'Stay you in the city till you be endued with power from on high.' (Luke xxiv. 49.) These words he took for his text, and, enlarging on them, exhorted his listeners to go into this retreat as the apostles went with Our Lady into the Supper-room, to bar all the doors and windows of their senses, shutting out all distractions, and as the apostles did, to pray that the Holy Ghost might come down to give them light and succour during the retreat. This was more or less the refrain of the whole meditation.

"The retreat which followed was exceedingly interesting, full of devotional ideas, scholarly, with a wonderful choice of quotations from Greek, Latin and English literature. Most of these quotations he had by heart, so that at times we had to marvel at the memory that could so easily retain these long and beautiful passages. His knowledge of Scripture and the Fathers, especially St. Augustine, was, as one would expect, even greater. With all this ammunition to help him and his own undoubted sanctity, the retreat was easily one of the best his hearers ever heard in the Society.

"When speaking of the mercy of God, he used an unusual and striking illustration. He recalled the tragic story of 'Little Em'ly' in *David Copperfield*, picturing with feeling David's friendship for the humble fisherfolk living in the old wreck on the beach at Yarmouth, and the agony of mind of the big, kind-hearted fisherman when he found his little niece betrayed and stolen from him. Father Sullivan described Dan Peggotty's heart-broken search and his injunction to his sister that the little door of their humble house was always to be left on the latch, so that if the child, in her misery, should return, she should at once find admittance. Then at last came the happy day when uncle and niece were reunited. 'If such could be the love and forgiveness of an earthly relative,' said Father Sullivan, 'what must be the love and mercy of God for the poor sinner who goes astray and for whom He laid down His life.' When telling this story of Little Em'ly and her uncle, Father Sullivan quoted long passages of Dickens' narrative.

"Then came the story of the conversion of St. Augustine, and the terrible struggle which took place before that great soul was won for God and the Church. How St. Monica prayed and wept bitterly that Augustine might be won for God, how when all seemed in vain, the person whom she consulted told her to weep no more, because God could never refuse to hear the prayers of a mother that with her tears were offered up for her son. Very often during the retreat Father Sullivan spoke about St. Monica and the power of a mother's prayers to move the tender Heart of Our Divine Lord.

"He reminded us how different the mercy of God is from the cruelty of the world that is ever ready to point the finger of scorn at the weakness of sinners. To exemplify this he told the story of a down-and-out who once came to him in Clongowes. As a boy, this man had been well educated and sent to a good college, but had fallen into bad ways. He was either turned out of his home or else he ran away on some mad exploit which left him stranded, starving and ragged. This poor prodigal, thinking of his home where his father, a rich man, ruled with a rod of iron, made his way home, only to be sent from the door by his father himself. He managed to send a message to his mother, a poor kindly creature who was heartbroken about him. She tried to give him something at the back door, but the father again sent him off, shutting the door in his face. The boy in his despair and rage broke every window in the house, cursed the father that had given him life, and then left to be a tramp upon the road, because of the folly of his youth. What a contrast the father's action was to the mercy of God.

"Father Sullivan warned us that it was not only people of the world that were unkind. At times, whether unwittingly or otherwise, religious could be very cruel. Religious houses where charity had grown cold were, he said, hells upon earth, where cruelty existed of a refined nature that the world did not dream of. Then followed a particularly feeling exhortation to be charitable. If we were not charitable in thought, word, and deed, then woe to the religious life, woe to the safety of our own souls, for when we prayed, 'Forgive us our trespasses,' we brought on ourselves our own condemnation.

"The cross which he lovingly held in his hand was, he said, something for which we should have a personal love. It signifies so much that we ought always to cherish it and love it with a strong personal love. Our crucifix should always be near us, ever ready to teach us the lesson that Christ meant it to teach, namely, that if He suffered so much, we should gladly suffer the little things that afflict us in life. Then, too, it is the badge of our salvation, because by the cross we are saved. He told one story about the power of the crucifix in bringing home to man the love of God. An actress in Paris one night, after leaving the stage and going to her dressing-room, did not reappear until the next morning, although many people tried to gain admittance. When her attendants knocked at the door they were told to go away. In the morning, she left the theatre never to return again. She told her confessor that on that night something disturbed her, and, thinking of the crucifix, she began to realize how much God loved her. Then for the first time in her life she realized what a happy thing it was to love God. She who had loved the world so much and in sinful ways now saw that the happiness which it gave was mere vanity. The thought of the love of God so preoccupied her that she knelt all night in prayer, never noticing the time pass.[1]

[1] This passage suggests an allusion to the conversion of Eve Lavallière, which created a sensation in the theatrical world in 1917. The precise incident described, however, does not appear in the published accounts of her life.

"In his meditation on the beautiful and homely scene where Mary Magdalen anointed Our Lord's feet, he commented on the fact that St. John, after so many years, should have remembered all the little details of the scene, and how the odour of the spikenard filled the little house. He told the novices that they too should try to remember all the small details of the scenes in the Gospel, and live them over and over again in their meditations. He made very real for us the places in which Our Lord had lived. Listening to him, one could see for oneself the lakeside of Galilee, and the little country villages round Nazareth, all of which had been made holy by the prayers which Christ had prayed there, while all nature looked on in reverence. When Christ climbed the hillside to pray at evening, the birds hushed their evensong, the very trees and grasses, swaying in the gentle breeze, seemed to bow in humble adoration. The foxes peeped silently from their holes, and the wild beasts in their lairs must have been all struck with reverence while He Who made them, and made to shine the stars that already were beginning to twinkle in the sky, and the sun that was sinking behind the hill, knelt down to pray to His eternal Father. Who could forget the beauty of such scenes or the wonders of the God-Man as told by Father Sullivan? They were the outpourings of a heart that was truly dead to the world, the thoughts of one who lived only for Christ."

CHAPTER XVIII

THE SUPERIOR

ON July 27th, 1919, Father Sullivan was appointed Rector of the Juniorate and Retreat House at Rathfarnham Castle on the outskirts of Dublin. This office he held until May 20th, 1924. The news of his appointment undoubtedly came as a great shock to him, and the burden was rendered peculiarly heavy by his habitual diffidence. On the day of his appointment, he paid a visit to his friends in the convent at Clane, and seemed to be quite overwhelmed by the sense of his own unfitness for the task which had been entrusted to him.

His primary duty as Rector of Rathfarnham was the care of about twenty young religious, fresh from the novitiate, who were engaged in their University studies. It must be admitted that in the carrying out of this duty he showed certain marked shortcomings. He never quite seemed to understand the difficulties of these young men, or the somewhat complicated situations in which they found themselves at times, owing to the necessity they were under of taking part in University life whilst trying at the same time to observe the reasonable restraints of religious discipline. He had not sufficient trust in himself to make promptly decisions which were immediately required. Owing to his great spirit of recollection and his personal austerity, he often did not advert to deficiencies in matters concerning the material welfare of the young scholastics.

But in spite of these shortcomings, the impression left on the minds of those who were in his charge during those five years was a very inspiring one. He had in a high degree many of the most important virtues required by a Superior. He was always most accessible, ready to listen to reasonable argument, and ready to be convinced. When troubles arose, he was very calm and, being almost completely free from personal feeling in such matters, was able to take a very objective view of the failings of any of his young subjects. His diffidence has been alluded to, but when he once did make a decision he could be firm in keeping to it. His kindness was literally boundless, and he was a model to the young men under his charge of every possible religious virtue.

The intense life of prayer which he had lived in Clongowes continued unabated in Rathfarnham. If any of the Juniors, as they are called, wished to find the Rector, they always went first to the chapel and almost invariably found him there. The recollections of one of them may be quoted.

"Father Sullivan rose at the same hour as we did, 5.30 a.m., took a shower and was in the chapel before most of us. He used to say Mass with great devotion and always seemed quite absorbed in it. As far as I can recollect, he nearly always said the Mass of the Sacred Heart on days when votive Masses were permitted, at any rate he used to say it very often. Devotion to the Sacred Heart seemed to be one of his great devotions. Whenever Juniors were serving Masses later than the hour of the Community Mass, Father John was sure to relieve one or other of them. During the day he constantly made visits to the Blessed Sacrament, running into the chapel for a moment and kneeling on the step of the altar. I remember that he used to say almost the whole of the Office in the chapel, kneeling near a window and not resting his arms on the bench."

Another of these young men, whose room was immediately under the Rector's, constantly heard him praying aloud at all hours of the night. When travelling in a tram, he would take off his hat and tell his beads into it with a complete lack of human respect which was rather embarrassing to the less heroic young religious who happened to be travelling with him. It was, in fact, quite obvious that he was always praying when going anywhere.

It has already been mentioned that Father Sullivan's mortification in the matter of food was at its height during his time as Rector of Rathfarnham. During all that five years he refused to have a fire in his room, although he never appeared to be wearing enough clothes, and looked intensely cold during the winter. There was near his room a hot press containing a boiler for drying clothes, and he would occasionally relax so far as to step into this press and say his Office there for a short time until he had warmed himself up somewhat. The poverty of his room and of his dress gave a striking example of detachment to the young men who were commencing a life professedly governed by a vow of poverty. One of them recalled that he never saw his superior carry a bag when going away to give a retreat. Whatever scanty luggage he brought was packed away in the pockets of his old-fashioned cape waterproof.

Apart from his example, the Juniors at Rathfarnham

derived great help from the spiritual exhortations which he gave once or twice a month. One of them thus described his talks:

"These exhortations often took the place of points for meditation, e.g., on the eve of the feast of a saint of the Society, and Father John would hold up for our imitation some particular virtue of the saint. The impression I always got from him was that he seemed to see no reason why each of us could not rival the saint in the practice of that virtue. He never used notes at these exhortations, though he often quoted from memory long passages in Latin from the writings of the Fathers of the Church to illustrate a point. At other times he spoke about a rule or some point of observance which he wanted to bring to the notice of the Juniors. I remember once that, when discussing the matter of rising with the bell, he said that the sound of the bell in the morning delivered the same command to us as the words of Our Lord, 'Zachaeus, come down.' He then added a characteristic remark of his own. 'Great graces going in the morning, there.' When speaking about diligence in work, I remember that he said that silence should be as strictly observed in the study hall as in the chapel. He often exhorted us to hard work, but when one had occasion to go to his room he nearly always said, 'Not working too hard, there?' when the business which was the object of the visit was finished. At the beginning of the exhortations he used to take his crucifix from his pocket, and keep it in his hand till he had finished. He usually kept his eyes closed while speaking, and when he opened them it was to look at the crucifix or to give a glance heavenwards."

The deep spirituality of their Rector was rendered

all the more attractive to the young students at Rathfarnham by his unfailing kindness. One of them recalled a very painful illness, when his tonsils were so swollen that to swallow even the smallest particle of food was agony. Father Sullivan literally made himself the servant of the sufferer. At 4.30 or 5 each morning he would slip into his room in his socks, bringing him a cup of tea. Later he would come with breakfast. Then he would order the young man out of bed and make him sit at the fire rolled up in blankets. He would proceed to make the bed, taking off his gown, pulling sheets and blankets off the bed, and turning the mattress. He was in and out all day, and each night gave the patient his blessing and, as was his wont, a generous sprinkling with holy water.

Another recalled with a certain amount of humorous compunction that whenever he wished to obtain some little favour, such as leave to visit his family, he used always to try to get the Rector to postpone his decision until the morning. At night the tone of Father John's remarks would be somewhat as follows: "I think not, what? Think better not, there. Keep to monastery, there. People would be disedified, there, what? Come back in the morning there." In the morning there would be quite a different story. "Certainly, there. Must be very anxious to see you, there. Long time since you saw them and all that. Go out there and see them, there." Then there would be a touch of Father John's inimitable quaint humour. "Need some money, there? Here's a half-crown, there. Spend lavishly—and bring me back the change, there!"

The Father who recalled this youthful finesse of his towards his saintly Superior was convinced that it was

Father Sullivan's severity towards himself during the night that begot his almost reckless kindness in the morning hours.

Almost everyone of those who were under his care during those five years could recall some striking act of kindness. One of them, whose sister was a Sister of Charity working in the Children's Hospital at Temple Street, used occasionally to ask Father Sullivan for flowers from the garden for the hospital. He was always told to take the very best. Another had a brother who had been very badly injured in the European War of 1914–18, and who was confined to his bed for some eleven years. It is quite understandable that these young men, just beginning their religious lives, were only permitted to visit their relatives at comparatively rare intervals. Yet in this case Father Sullivan gave leave to the young Jesuit to drop in and pay a short visit to his invalid brother any day on his way home from the University if he liked. He himself often called in to see the invalid, and was his most anxiously expected visitor.

It has been remarked that Father John's holiness was made attractive to his young subjects by his kindness. It may be added that it was made further attractive by another very precious virtue, though one of a lower order, namely his sense of humour. The Junior whose invalid brother he befriended was in charge of the seismological station at Rathfarnham. It was the custom that each young man was obliged during the year to preach a sermon on some appointed subject in the refectory during dinner. For most this was a considerable ordeal. The young seismologist was dreading the approach of his turn to preach, and went to Father John to try to get off. He gave a number of excuses which he could not help feeling were rather insufficient. But Father John, seeing his real distress, helped him out most unexpectedly. "In God's Holy Name, how could you preach, there? Haven't you charge of the seismograph? It would be a terrible thing, there, if there was an earthquake during dinner. If you were preaching, you would not be able to do anything to stop the earthquake!"

This same young man one day went into the Rector's room, and saw to his astonishment on the bed a bottle of whisky and a bottle of wine. "It's all right," said Father John. "I'm not going on the booze. Those are for a poor old woman. They do more to keep her heart up than I can."

Dubliners take an amused pride in the product of Guinness's famous brewery, and have invented scores of good stories to extol its potency. Father John related one such story to the young men in Rathfarnham, which I have never heard elsewhere.

In a certain travelling circus there were three performing elephants. One night the weather was bitterly cold, and the three elephants were so numbed that the ringmaster was afraid they would be unable to perform. He got the brilliant idea of ordering a bucket of Guinness for each elephant. The results were marvellous. The elephants performed as never before, and could hardly be got out of the ring. The next night was oppressively hot. The men were working in their shirt-sleeves, the animals overcome by heat, ladies in the audience fanning themselves. But in a corner stood the three elephants—shivering with the cold.

Those who knew Father Sullivan will be all the more

amused by the two preceding anecdotes since his views on the subject of drink were very strong—almost extreme. Yet there was no trace of the kill-joy in his make-up. Any over-severity which he may have betrayed in this regard may be attributed confidently to that extraordinarily vivid sense which he always possessed of the evil of sin.

Father Sullivan did not take any very active part in the direction of the studies of the young men at Rathfarnham. This was certainly not due to lack of interest, nor to lack of ability. His distinguished University career was well known to everybody. It was more probably due to that extraordinarily poor opinion which he held of his own talents. Yet, on occasions, he could give useful help, and he actually did do a good deal of coaching for the weaker students. It was, moreover, clear to all that he was deeply interested in scholarship, and he would give at times unexpected signs of that interest, such as handing on the modern Greek "Messenger of the Sacred Heart," which he read regularly, to those students who were studying ancient Greek.

There is a rule of the Jesuit Order by which, where circumstances permit, every newly-appointed Superior must teach Christian doctrine to children or unlettered persons for forty days. Father John, needless to say, interpreted this rule in its strictest sense. On Sunday mornings it was customary for the young scholastics to go in turn to the parish church at Rathfarnham to help in the catechizing of the children of the parish. Somewhat to the discomfort of the young catechists, they were joined by their Rector, who himself taught the catechism, instructed the children, stayed to listen to the Juniors' talks and often thanked them for them and begged to have his own instructions criticized.

In addition to the Juniorate, there is at Rathfarnham Castle the well-known house of retreats for working-men. In 1921–22 this project was in its initial stages, and Father Sullivan took the deepest interest in it. Father R. S. Devane, S.J., who was giving the retreats at the time, recalls that Father Sullivan's attitude was always one of encouragement. "You're doing splendidly," was his constant phrase. Though such a strict observer of poverty in all that concerned himself, he would spare no expense where the work of retreats was concerned, often pressing Father Devane to accept sums of money for his expenses, alleging that they could not be better spent. With his usual humility, he refrained from offering advice about the retreats, but would frequently beg the favour of being allowed to serve the retreatants at table. Father Devane objected that it might embarrass the men to have the Rector serving them. "I'd be very grateful if you would let me do it," Father John persisted. "I so like doing anything for these poor fellows." He often gained his point, and, donning an apron, acted as server. He was not an adept, and his efforts hardly helped from the practical point of view, but his charity and humility made up for his want of skill.

In connection with the retreats for working-men and for poor boys, Father Sullivan came into touch with Mr. Frank Duff, the well-known Dublin social worker and founder of the Legion of Mary. Mr. Duff gave this impression of Father Sullivan at that period.

"Father Sullivan was always very kind to me personally. He invariably stopped in the street whenever he saw me, in order to exchange a few words, to assure me of his deep interest in the things which I had in hand and to promise his prayers for them. The chief notes which struck me in Father Sullivan were his extreme prayerfulness, his gentleness and his humility. Moreover, he gave the impression of being a very mortified man. My chief picture of him is in his miserable, threadbare garments on a wintry day. I got the impression that he had nothing on underneath. As he walked along (or sometimes ran), he always seemed to be lost in thought, or I suppose it would be more accurate to say, in prayer. I found him an utterly lovable person. The first time I ever saw him in my life was on his knees in the domestic chapel in Rathfarnham Castle. That was typical, for I was assured that such was the way in which he spent much of his time. I also heard from different quarters that he had the reputation of healing, but I never had any direct knowledge of this."

During his five years at Rathfarnham Castle, Father Sullivan kept up his former apostolate of the poor and suffering, as far as his duties as Rector permitted. He also did much spiritual work for other religious communities, some of which has been mentioned elsewhere. He gave regular instructions for several years to the novices of Loreto Abbey, Rathfarnham, where his humility and unadorned eloquence made a deep impression. He took a great interest in St. Mary's open-air hospital for children at Cappagh, near Dublin, which was then in its very early stages. It was an enterprise about the success of which many doubted, as it was feared that the Irish climate was unsuited to open-air treatment. Father John was one of those who were confident that it would succeed, and he was invited by the Sisters of Charity in charge to bless the foundation-stone of the first large extension which was begun about the spring of 1923. He did this task in his usual thorough way, climbing down into the cavity where the builders were working, placing some religious medals under the stone, and drenching it with holy water. He was a familiar figure at the hospital, hurrying up the avenue, giving the children a blessing as he passed, inquiring about the progress of the work, and invariably departing without accepting the slightest refreshment.

One strange occurrence during this period is worthy of record. A certain Father was transferred to Rathfarnham Castle, and, on his arrival, found that he had been assigned a room underneath the Rector's, which was situated in a wing somewhat isolated from the rest of the house. He found himself kept awake every night by Father Sullivan's prayers, which were audible in the room above until a late hour. This was not all. Frequently he heard sounds as if Father Sullivan were struggling on the floor and being dragged about the room, whilst he groaned and cried, "Oh, oh, oh!" as if in terrible fear. The sounds were most awe-inspiring, and after a while the Father could stand it no longer and went to take counsel with the Spiritual Father. The latter volunteered to tell Father Sullivan that his prayers were disturbing the rest of the other Father. From that day on, the sounds ceased entirely. The Father who related this experience was strongly inclined to think that Father John was wrestling with some diabolical power. Another explanation may have been that in the dead of night his meditations became so vivid as to cause these groans and struggles. But whether he had to pray to be delivered from some preternatural attack, or whether he voluntarily abandoned his nocturnal prayer, it is remarkable to note that he was willing to abandon the mystical combat the moment the convenience of another was in question.

CHAPTER XIX

THE END

ON his return to Clongowes in 1924, Father Sullivan continued for another nine years his apostolate in the countryside around, many incidents of which have already been set down. In spite of the severity of his life, he always enjoyed robust health, but some time about 1929, when talking to a doctor, a friend of his, he mentioned that a certain priest of his acquaintance had had an internal hæmorrhage that morning, and asked if that would indicate some growth. The doctor put a few questions about the case, and from the readiness of Father Sullivan's answers, began to suspect that the priest in question was himself. In view of the nature of his final illness, the suspicion was probably correct.

A more definite sign of failing showed itself about two years before his death. For over twelve months he had been in the habit of bringing Holy Communion every Saturday and on feast-days, even on the coldest and darkest winter mornings, to Mrs. Smyth, wife of the Clongowes farm-steward, who was an invalid. This involved a walk of some five minutes through the pleasure-ground to the adjoining farm. On one occasion he did not arrive at the accustomed time, and was found wandering around the pleasure-ground suffering, apparently, from a sudden loss of memory. He recovered rapidly, but this trouble recurred again on a couple of occasions, once forcing him to abandon his Mass just before the Gospel.

Some time early in the new year of 1933, he was talking to one of the nuns in the convent at Clane, and the conversation turned on the number of people who came to see him. "They have me killed," he said. The words were half-jocose, but they may have been prompted by a sense that his strength was being undermined. Nevertheless, he was working as usual up to within a fortnight before his death. On Saturday, February 4th, he asked to see the doctor about a swelling in the elbow. This proved to be due to bursitis, which necessitated having the arm lanced on the following Thursday. After this he had to remain in the infirmary for about a fortnight.[1] During that time he showed the greatest patience and cheerfulness. He never spoke much, except to make inquiries about other patients, or to thank the Matron for all that was being done for him. Two small but significant facts stood out in her mind in recalling those days, the first that she never recalled going into his room but he was meditating on his crucifix, the second that he never rang the bell for attention except on the last morning, when, as it proved afterwards, he was in danger of death.

At some time during this last illness, a particularly touching pilgrimage was made to Clongowes by a young girl accompanied by her father. She had been a nurse in England, and had had a mental breakdown. While she was receiving treatment in a home, her parents had written to Father Sullivan for prayers. The girl had recovered completely, and was now on her way home with her father. They broke their journey at

[1] The room he occupied was No. 3.

Sallins to call and thank Father Sullivan, but he was too ill to see them.

On the morning of Friday, February 17th, he was suddenly attacked by a violent internal pain. The doctor was summoned, and saw that it was a case for a surgeon. It was thought dangerous to give the patient any injection and so he suffered intense pain. Yet he remained perfectly calm, and to distract his attention from the pain, began to read his breviary. Father Kenny, the Father Minister of the college, who was with him constantly all this time, tried to dissuade him from this, but he persisted. He then said to Father Kenny, "You had better anoint me, I may die at any moment." He received Extreme Unction, and made arrangements for the saying of Masses which he had undertaken. When the surgeon arrived, he diagnosed a dangerous obstruction, and ordered the patient to be removed at once to hospital.[1] Two injections were given, but the pain was so great that this had no effect, and Father Sullivan suffered severely whilst travelling in the ambulance to Dublin.

He was operated on that afternoon at about five o'clock, and it was at once clear that his condition was desperate. During the remaining two days of his life, he continued to display the same extraordinary courage, selflessness and humility that had always characterized him. The surgeon who operated was a former pupil of his at Clongowes. "I am left," he wrote afterwards, "with a very vivid memory of his supreme courage and fortitude when suffering the shocking pain which he must have had in his last illness. The cause of his death

[1] He was brought to the private nursing home of St. Vincent's Hospital, No. 96 Lower Leeson Street, and occupied room No. 2.

was mesenteric thrombosis, causing gangrene of an extensive length of his small intestine. I think it would be very hard for those who have not had a similar type of experience to imagine the appalling intensity of the pain that he had to endure. After his operation he was cheerfulness itself. He was extraordinarily grateful for what poor service I had been able to give him, and was humorous and confident. His morale was so good that I cheated myself, hoping against hope that he would survive."

The next morning he was quite conscious. His brother, Sir William Sullivan, had arrived from England by the mail-boat. The nun in charge went into Father Sullivan's room at about six o'clock to see whether he would be able to interview Sir William. Finding him conscious, she was going out to summon his brother, but before she could leave the room the Angelus rang in some neighbouring church. Father Sullivan heard the bell and said, "The Angelus," as if calling her back. They recited the prayer together. At about ten o'clock that morning she suggested that he might receive Viaticum. He answered, "Yes, Yes," and received Viaticum without difficulty. He spent almost the whole of that Saturday, and of the following Sunday, the last two days of his life, in continual prayer. Frequently one or other of the nuns in charge would say, "Don't mind praying any more," fearing that he would wear out the little strength left to him. His invariable reply was, "But you pray."

One of the nuns thus recalled these two days. "I think that what most struck me and those who were privileged to nurse Father John Sullivan during his last illness was his perfect conformity to God's will and his marvellous patience. Because of the latter, it was impossible to know what was the extent of his suffering. He placed himself in the hands of others with an entire abnegation of self, receiving everything with gratitude and asking for nothing. His obedience was faultless, and he never showed by the least sign that he was not ready to comply with every injunction of doctors and attendants. The latter realized that every instruction to the patient had to be well weighed before utterance, so complete was his compliance with every wish. His recollection and spirit of prayer were very striking, so that on entering his room one felt that he dwelt always in the conscious presence of God."

On Sunday morning he was able to receive Viaticum again with ease, and continued praying in quite a strong voice almost continuously up to about midday. On either this or the preceding morning, after he had received Holy Communion, he was lying quite still in bed and one of the Sisters of Charity was kneeling by his side reading the thanksgiving prayers, he apparently taking no notice. When she said the *Anima Christi*, he lay, still unheeding, until she came to the words, "That with Thy saints I may praise Thee." Then a light shone in his eyes and a new happiness filled his face. She thought that this was perhaps just imagination, so she went through the same prayer a second time with the exact same result.

About midday, Mother Thecla, the nun in charge, again wished to conserve the little strength left to him, and it also occurred to her that Sir William Sullivan, who had been present all this time, would think that this continuous prayer was excessive, in view of the very weak state of the patient. Accordingly, she said to Father John, "I think you have done enough praying, and you have offered up your sufferings to God, and should now rest." He agreed, but immediately added, "But you go on." The nuns themselves were almost wearied by these continual prayers, but could not refuse his request, and continued with the Litany of the Holy Name, the *Anima Christi* and other usual prayers.

Some time during the afternoon Father Roche, his Rector, who had been with him constantly during the two days, asked him to give him a message to the boys in Clongowes. He whispered, "God bless and protect them."

At about three o'clock he became half-unconscious. Two of the priests of the Clongowes Community who had come up to see him arrived at that moment, and one of them gave him the last Absolution. Meanwhile the whole countryside round Clongowes was praying and awaiting each fresh bulletin. The post-mistress at the College gate was kept constantly occupied answering the anxious queries of those whom Father Sullivan had helped and befriended. At six o'clock he was quite unconscious. Father Roche, Sir William Sullivan, Mother Thecla and a nurse remained on with him until the end. As the night drew on, Sir William began to look utterly worn out. Mother Thecla suggested that he had now done all that was possible, and should go down to his club for the night. He agreed that he would wait until 11 p.m., and if there were no change then that he would go. It would almost seem that, at the last moment, God gave to Father Sullivan one more opportunity of exercising that selflessness that had always characterized him, and of sparing his brother any further burden of weariness. At about five minutes to eleven there were signs of a change. Father Roche gave him a final Absolution, and he was dead at eleven o'clock, passing away most peacefully.

The next day there was a continual stream of clergy and laity touching the body with rosaries and other pious objects. The nuns of a Carmelite Convent rang up and asked for a bit of bandage stained with blood from the operation. Some of the hospital students were found cutting off pieces of his hair. He was buried in Clongowes on the following Wednesday. At 9 a.m. Mass was celebrated by Father Rector in the People's Church. After Mass the entire congregation quite spontaneously filed up to the coffin, and all, many kneeling, kissed it repeatedly, placing on it rosaries, crucifixes and prayer-books. At 11 a.m. there was Office and Requiem Mass in the Boys' Chapel. His Lordship Dr. Cullen, Bishop of Kildare and Leighlin, presided, and afterwards said the prayers at the grave. When the grave was filled in, and Bishop, priests and boys had gone, many of the people came to carry to their homes some of the earth that covered the mortal remains of him who had been such a true friend.

CHAPTER XX

RETROSPECT

IN this concluding chapter, an attempt will be made to add a few details to the portrait of Father Sullivan that stands out from his life, and to emphasize one or two of its more remarkable features. Character study is a task which must be approached with diffidence. The material is elusive, and there is the danger of falling into either of two extremes. One may over-refine, over-analyse, over-qualify, over-explain, in the effort to present exactly the many facets of the subject of study. On the other hand, in the endeavour to keep to broad and clear outlines, one may easily disfigure and misrepresent.

The task is especially difficult when dealing with such a character as that of John Sullivan. For it was definitely an unusual character, yet it was anything but strange. And between the unusual and the strange, the line of demarcation is hard to determine.

Even those who had the greatest reverence and affection for him discerned in him a certain quality that can best be described by coining a word "apartness." One certainly could not call him aloof, and he was the very opposite of self-centred. He was intensely sympathetic towards others and interested in their spiritual and temporal welfare; he was reasonably well informed about matters of the day, and followed them intelligently, especially where the Church was concerned. Still, one could not help getting the impression that he was living himself on a separate plane, and that there was a constant element of effort in his interest in the things and persons of this world.

It may, indeed, be asked whether even the greatest saints, granted the defects of fallen nature, were able to combine with keen supernatural vision a perfectly easy, natural and at all times unrestrained approach to the things of this world. Hagiographers often vindicate this gift for their heroes or heroines with a facile phrase or two, yet it would seem to postulate an extraordinary combination of gifts of grace and gifts of nature, which would not be at all necessary for the attaining of heroic sanctity. That God gave this remarkable blend of the natural and the supernatural to some of the greatest saints, so that their sanctity might be peculiarly attractive, we may well grant. But it is no grudging belittlement of sanctity to think that many of them betrayed at times traces of the struggle that human nature must go through in trying to satisfy at the same time the claims of God and the claims of the world in which He has put us.

It must further be recalled that John Sullivan did not become a Catholic until he was thirty-five. There are converts who, whether as a result of great graces, or because they are helped by their natural mental make-up, take on Catholicism without an effort. They grasp each feature of it, from the sublimest theological truth down to the homeliest devotional practice, with eager and accurate appreciation and make it their own. They rapidly out-distance their friends who have been Catholics from their childhood in both the understanding and the practical exercise of their Faith. Others there are who make the fundamental change completely and generously, but who have, perhaps all their lives, to struggle with little clingings to old ways of thinking and old practices of devotion, and who suffer constantly from small jars and shocks and discomforts, as they slowly settle down into their places in the Church.

Father Sullivan belonged decidedly to the first class, yet there was in his spirituality just a shade of that quality of effort that makes the second type of convert. There were some, it cannot be said many, who found it difficult to penetrate his reserve, and who thought his self-control somewhat unnatural. Yet even these had no doubt about his sanctity. Thus, one of his fellow-Jesuits who lived in the same community with him on three occasions between 1908 and 1932 wrote:

"My impressions are peculiar. The first time I looked on him as being 'half a Protestant,' the second as 'rather artificial and forced in his spirituality,' the third as 'a Saint—one who had come in for his full heritage.' "

But the vast majority of those who knew him, though recognizing that the *agere contra* played a large part in his spiritual make-up, did not find it repellent or oppressive, because it was found in company with such very lovable qualities, boundless kindness, transparent sincerity and complete forgetfulness of self. All through this Life, Father Sullivan has appeared as the friend of the poor, the suffering, and the afflicted. It is evident that to them, at any rate, his heart was open enough. I have a vivid recollection of the first anniversary of his death when his brother, Sir William, came down to visit his grave. Afterwards I said a few conventional words to him about how we missed Father John. The tears flowed unrestrainedly down his cheeks as he said, "He was the best brother a man could have had." Father John's love of God had evidently done nothing all those years to lessen the ties of human affection.

Father Sullivan had certain outward peculiarities which caused innocent amusement to his friends. He had a number of little clichés in speech, all quite his own. His habit of saying "Cheer up, cheer up, cheer up" has been mentioned already. He would often resort to it under circumstances that were anything but cheerful—thus on a holiday which had been a disastrous fiasco—and by a curious mental process, the fact that it was so incongruous on these occasions helped it to produce its desired effect. He had another most amusing habit of exclaiming "Nonsense!" when told some most obvious piece of news, such as that the Pope had said Mass in St. Peter's on Easter Sunday. It was only his equivalent for the almost equally senseless "Is that so?" but it could be at times somewhat disconcerting. One of his favourite descriptions of a person whom he wished to praise was that he was "a lovely character." This became a regular catchword amongst his friends, especially as his charity often led him to apply the description to persons whose qualifications or it were decidedly low. His habit of interjecting "there" or "and all that" between phrases has been noticed earlier, and the strange thing is that though it was so remarkable, it did not interrupt the flow of his words, and indeed gave a curious and not unpleasing cadence to his sentences. Allusion has also been made to his use of the word "audacious" when condemning youthful shortcomings. He always gave to it the peculiar pronunciation "owdacious," which was possibly a survival of an older usage.

He had a very characteristic walk, hurrying along almost at a run, and occasionally giving a sort of limp as he increased his pace. He was a truly amazing walker, going everywhere on foot when he did not use the bicycle, and covering the ground usually at what appeared to be about five miles an hour. I remember a friend telling me how Father Sullivan came to see him at Ballsbridge, and left him at about a quarter past five, saying that he must be back for dinner at 6 p.m. at Rathfarnham Castle, a distance of about four miles. "I did not believe he could do it," he concluded, "until I saw him going down the road."

A very characteristic habit of his was that of running his hand through his hair, or rather appearing to brush his hair at the side with the tips of the fingers of his right hand. This was such a familiar gesture with him that when his friends were repeating one of his good stories or quaint sayings, they would instinctively dramatize the anecdote by imitating it.

Those who knew Father Sullivan will not think it trivial to record these characteristic mannerisms. They were so much part of himself that to omit them would leave his portrait incomplete. Yet it must not be thought for a moment that there was the slightest trace of the eccentric in him. His spirituality was essentially sound, based on the teachings of theologians, the writings of the Fathers and Holy Scripture. His views on general topics were not original, and tended to be somewhat conservative. He would have been the first to laugh at the idea of himself as a great thinker, and to acknowledge that he sometimes made mistakes. But he was always worth listening to and never superficial. It may, however, be granted freely that, as a director and adviser, he shone out not by the brilliance of his thought, but by the power he possessed of making ordinary ideas extraordinarily operative.

There were those who, during his lifetime, thought his poverty in dress eccentric, but I fancy that, looking back, they now remember that there is a thing called the folly of the Cross. Certainly when one holds in one's hands the much-patched coat which is preserved at Clongowes, all furrowed with Father John's deplorable needlework, one does not now think of smiling.

There was just one characteristic of Father Sullivan which was somewhat difficult to understand, and that was his unusual devotion to holy water. The sick who came to him and the sick whom he visited came in for the most large-handed aspersions, and when he had to bless pious objects, they were drenched liberally. This practice was not due to mere absent-minded awkwardness, but was an evidence of his own devotion. It was remarked during his last illness that he asked for holy water again and again.

Possibly one might discern here a trace of the exuberance of the convert who has all his life been deprived of such natural and legitimate, though minor helps to devotion and the acquiring of grace, and who is inclined to revel in his newly-acquired heritage after a manner somewhat incomprehensible to the born Catholic. Yet perhaps the lavishness of Father Sullivan's aspersions was simply due to a peculiarly keen realization of the power of a sacramental, hallowed by its association with most of the greatest functions of the Church and the administration of several of the sacraments, as also by the constant practice of the saints in their combats with the powers of darkness. It is interesting to note that, in the retreat which he gave to the Jesuit novices in Tullabeg in 1930, of which some impressions have been recorded earlier, he devoted one of the "considerations" to "the power of pious objects and practices against the onslaughts of Satan." And in one of his note-books there is an extract from the Life of some saint (the name is—characteristically—undecipherable) who at the hour of death often used holy water. The extract concludes: "It relieves body and soul," and Father Sullivan had underlined these words.

It is regrettable that so little, almost nothing, indeed, can be recorded of Father Sullivan's views concerning the faith in which he was reared, or the intellectual path he trod on his way towards the Catholic Church. All that can be recollected is that, whilst seeing in the clearest light the defects of Protestantism, he always spoke kindly and with understanding of those to whom the great gift of the Faith had not been given. "There is light outside the Catholic Church," he once said in a retreat to nuns. And never for a moment did one detect in him any tendency to ridicule or belittle the sincere service of God of those outside the Church, imitating in this his Divine Master, to whom those who were not of His fold were yet "other sheep."

Several of the appreciations of Father Sullivan already recorded were given by non-Catholics. Two more may fittingly be added here, of especial interest because of the contrasted ages of those from whom they come.

John Garvey, D.L., of Vevay House, Bray, who was

a lifelong friend of the Sullivan family, wrote in 1939 (he died in the following year):

"I had left Trinity before Father John entered, but I met him later on many occasions, through my friendship with his brother, Sir William. It was difficult to show him any hospitality, as he scarcely ever partook of the comforts of life. He never touched meat and usually took nothing except a slice of bread and butter. I never knew a man who practised such self-denial. He really was one of the greatest saints we ever knew, and we often observed his great friendship and affection for his brother William."

The other impression came from his grand-nephew, Desmond Lloyd, who at the time of Father Sullivan's death was a boy of sixteen.

"Although I never saw Father John at all often or for any length of time, I think I can say that he was one of the most charming men that I have ever met. He was always so saintly, and withal intensely human and kind. I often think of him as the nearest approach to a living Christ on earth. Like Our Lord, his life's ambition seemed to be to help his fellow-men and serve his God truly."

A last word may be added to emphasize what, in the opinion of many who knew him, was Father Sullivan's greatest virtue, his humility. His outward manner, as will have appeared from many of the testimonies cited, expressed complete contempt of self, and this was a faithful reflection of his inner convictions. It has been noted that his conferences and sermons were, in their composition (though not in their delivery) markedly impersonal. That this was due to a sincere belief that the thoughts of others were better than his own is borne out by his constant attendance at sermons, and the eager way in which he listened to them. He was frequently seen kneeling at the altar-rails in the People's Church during the ordinary Sunday sermons. He once helped for a few weeks on the staff of Gardiner Street, and it was noted there also that he heard all the sermons possible. The priests of the Jesuit Order are free, after their tertianship, to make either a private or a public retreat annually. Father Sullivan usually, if not always, made one of the public retreats given in the Jesuit houses, and was seen daily in the chapel after the conferences, re-reading the notes he had made and obviously making them the background of his prayer. A Jesuit Father recalled his astonishment when, as a young scholastic, he was approached by Father Sullivan, who asked if he had any notes on the subject of charity, which might help him with a conference which he was preparing on the subject.

The hardest test of humility is a sudden test, and amidst the unexpected strains that a long life in religion put on Father Sullivan's virtue, it remained wonderfully unwarped. I cannot recollect any very heroic example, but there were many minor ones. Thus a fellow-Jesuit recalls hearing Father Sullivan harshly rebuked for some mistake by a man years his junior. "I'm always putting my foot in it," was his only remark.

A Sister of Charity recalled how she heard a naïve but telling tribute paid to Father Sullivan's humility by a young Jesuit scholastic. He was comparing Father Sullivan with another holy man, and said that the difference between them was, in his opinion, that if you gave Father Sullivan a kick, he would really enjoy it, but that he would not be so sure of its effect on the other good Father.

Once, indeed, it is recalled that he let a touch of the old Adam appear. A certain Father had been treated with scant courtesy by the Reverend Mother of a convent which he visited, and, on his return home, mentioned the matter to Father Sullivan, who was his Superior. "You were quite right to stand up to her," said Father John. "That woman humiliated me before all her nuns." But even in this case, the Father who recalled the incident thought that Father John was more concerned to soothe his subject's outraged feelings than to relieve his own.

The Preface to this biography made mention of the difficulties encountered in writing it, and, at the close, the comparative poverty of the matter collected may again be emphasized. Yet this very defect may be regarded as a virtue, in the sense that it reflects the life recorded, in which talent and ability were lavished on obscure work, without a thought of recognition, much less of record.

As has already been noticed, only two writings of Father Sullivan ever found their way into print. One of them, the Preface to the *Life of John Haughton Steele*, has already been drawn on. The second is the Preface to the *Life of Mary Aikenhead*. There is a passage in it which may well close this final chapter, so fittingly does it apply to the writer's own life.

" . . . Wordsworth long ago told us in his *Excursion*: 'Strongest minds are often those of whom the noisy world hears least.' The words apply to life in general. How much more true, therefore, will they be of those whose lives are hidden with Christ in God.

" 'Hid are the saints of God,' says Newman. Yet sometimes the veil that hides them is lifted, and we get a glimpse of the greatness which is at once natural and supernatural, which shows the co-operation of grace and nature working out an harmonious evolution of character that takes all captive in admiration, if not in love.' "

APPENDIX

FAVOURS AFTER DEATH

IN the following pages some account will be given of cures or other favours attributed to Father Sullivan's intercession since his death. No attempt has been made to draw up an exhaustive catalogue, which would hardly be of interest to the general reader. Whether such favours have been widespread or not cannot be established definitely. More probably they have been confined to a comparatively small circle, chiefly those who knew Father Sullivan personally. It is however quite certain that recourse to his intercession continues up to the present time.

In March 1933, only a month after the death of Father Sullivan, occurred the cure of Mrs. G. M. Ryan, of Dublin. Her account is as follows:

"I had been ill with heart trouble and pernicious anæmia, and was so bad on March 19th that I was anointed, the doctor having given up hope of my recovery. I happened to hear of a cure wrought through Rev. Father John Sullivan having visited a Mrs. X (the case of pernicious vomiting mentioned on page 140) shortly before he died. It impressed me deeply, and I had a firm belief that if I could get any little relic of his, I should be cured. Thank God, I was favoured with a loan of his sacred stole, and can confidently say that from the moment I received it, I began to regain my strength steadily, invoking his intercession by the following aspiration. 'Rev. Father Sullivan, intercede for me through the Blessed Virgin Mary and the Sacred Heart of Jesus, if it be God's holy will to cure me.'

In September 1940, the doctor who attended Mrs. Ryan made the following statement:

"I saw Mrs. G. M. Ryan last Friday. I remember attending her in 1933 when she was confined to bed with endocarditis and a very advanced form of anæmia. She is now in perfect health, and has a little son about six years of age. In my opinion, her present healthy state is very surprising, and may be accounted for by some supernatural agency."

In the year of Father Sullivan's death, Sister X., a member of a community in the south of Ireland, fell ill. A Dublin doctor examined her, and declared that an operation was necessary, or else a long rest of about a year, during which she would have to undergo severe medical treatment. She was sent back to the convent to rest for some weeks before the decision should be made as to which would be the better course. During this time she placed her case in the hands of Father John Sullivan, begging of him to secure her cure through Our Lady's intercession without operation or treatment. After some weeks, her condition was found to be so improved that neither operation nor treatment was necessary.

This nun also received a number of spiritual favours through Father Sullivan's intercession.

Another member of the same community had consulted Father Sullivan shortly before his death about a family matter which was causing grief and anxiety to many. At the time, things looked very hopeless, as everything had been done for the refractory member who was causing the trouble, but in vain. Father Sullivan's words on that occasion filled his penitent with a great sense of his trust in God, so after his death, she kept asking him daily to obtain from God some solution of the difficulty. She touched a relic of him when making this daily request. In short time, an answer came in a satisfactory and unexpected manner.

The two following experiences were related by a lady who had had a close friendship with Father Sullivan from the time that her sons went to school at Clongowes.

"Father Sullivan has interceded for me on many occasions, through Our Lady of Lourdes. It was two weeks after his death, in February 1933, that D—— (one of her sons) got a blow from a snowball in his ear. It was such a serious accident that he had to be kept in a darkened room, and the doctor gave it as his opinion that he would never hear again with that ear.

"I started a novena to Father Sullivan, and asked him to intercede with Our Lady of Lourdes that D—— would be cured. At the end of fourteen days, D—— surprised the doctor by telling him that he could hear in that ear. The doctor said that it was nothing short of a miracle. D—— was sent to a Dublin specialist who confirmed what the doctor said, and reported that the healing of the perforated ear was perfect.

"The second time that Father Sullivan came to my assistance was in July 1934 when my two youngest boys, with a little girl and their nurse, were involved in a serious accident whilst driving in a pony and trap. The pony backed over a cliff, and fell with the trap fourteen feet on to the rocks below. The children were unhurt, but the poor, dear, faithful nurse was unconscious and bleeding dreadfully from a deep wound in her head. When brought to hospital, she was partially unconscious for nine days, then went completely blind, and the doctors expected the end at any moment. I kept on the prayers to Father Sullivan and Our Lady, and that night, when we expected she would not live until morning, I placed the little picture of Father Sullivan on her head. The following morning she spoke, and said, 'I can see,' and after that she made great progress and was allowed to sit up and leave her bed.

"Then it was found that she could not walk, one foot being very swollen owing to the breaking of a bone by her fall. She could not put on a shoe, and she was greatly worried by the thought that she was going to give further trouble. It was the eve of the Assumption, and I gave her Father Sullivan's little picture and told her to ask Father Sullivan to intercede with Our Lady that her foot might be cured.

"Next morning, she awoke early, and placed the little picture on her leg and started the Rosary. She had said it fifteen times before she received Holy Communion. When Sister came to dress her after breakfast, she went for her shoe and it fitted as if nothing had ever happened to her foot. She told the Sister about the picture and the rosaries, and then to the astonishment of them both, she found she could walk.

"I can never forget Father Sullivan's help and assistance in all my many wants, and I never pass his grave when in Clongowes without paying a little visit."

The doctor consulted in the first of the cases just described wrote as follows:

"Mr. D—— X—— came under my care in 1933.

He had been hit by a snowball over the left side of the head, and sustained a concussion injury of the drumhead of the left ear. There was a perforation of the tympanic membrane, and pus issued from the middle ear through this aperture for two weeks. He then made a remarkable recovery from the injury, the aperture closed up, and all symptoms disappeared."

A nun in a convent in the south of Ireland attributed to Father Sullivan's intercession several favours, the earliest of which was granted in the year following his death.

She wrote as follows:

"I first had recourse to Father Sullivan's intercession about 1934. I was then teaching in a small town. When the time came for choosing candidates for the Child of Mary sodality, the mother of one of the children tried to force me to admit her child among the chosen band, though her conduct in school had been very undesirable. The matter became more and more disagreeable, and finally the mother openly attacked the other candidates on their leaving the parish church after Mass.

"My dilemma had reached a crisis when I turned to Father John Sullivan with something like the following prayer: 'I know nothing about you except that people say you were very holy on earth and that you have great power in Heaven. I am placing my whole trust in you now; get me out of this trouble.' Within two hours, in spite of driving wind and rain, the woman in question sent one of her children to me with a letter of humble apology.

"About six months later, I was seriously ill with duodenal ulceration, when I got a very complicated seizure, which seemed to deprive me of all life. My face became drawn, my eyes turned, and my whole appearance was corpse-like. I was paralysed and without feeling until a Sister attached a relic of Father Sullivan to me. I experienced a cold sensation and a feeling of returning life. Though I was anointed the following morning and was supposed to be dangerously ill, I felt confident that I was on the road to recovery. I now enjoy splendid health which I believe is due to Father Sullivan's intercession.

"In 1936, the marriage of one of our Orphanage girls proved to be unhappy. God did not bless her with children, and her husband was very dissatisfied. He ill-treated her and even showed violence towards her. This continued until 1939, when I gave her a relic of Father Sullivan. We made a novena to him, asking for the privilege of motherhood for her, if it were God's will. Our prayers were answered, and she has now a very happy home."

In 1935, the recovery of a little boy, Michael Kevin Spencer, of Ballymoney, Co. Wexford, was attributed to the application of a relic of Father Sullivan. The boy became delicate in October 1934, when only eighteen months old, and refused to take food. In March 1935 he was brought to St. Ultan's hospital, Dublin, but his case was thought hopeless. On his return home, he rallied somewhat, but early in June a heavy discharge began to come from his ears. He was removed to a Dublin hospital, where an operation for double mastoid was declared necessary. In view of his weakened condition, there seemed little hope for his recovery.

Those who saw the child at this time described him as a living skeleton. A friend of the family who had great faith in Father Sullivan's intercession procured a relic, which was affixed to his pillow. The operation took place, and to the surprise of the doctors he recovered steadily, and was able to leave the hospital in December 1935.

The above facts were given by his parents, whose statement concluded: "He is now (1940) six years and three months old, and attending school daily in perfect health. We firmly believe the relic of Father John Sullivan saved his life when the best medical skill despaired of him."

The following favours were recorded by the community of a convent in the south of Ireland, where Father Sullivan was well known:

"In 1934, Mr. X., the director of an important business firm, was stricken with a serious internal disease. His medical advisers thought that if the disease followed its normal course, the patient would not live six months, and a specialist decided that an operation would be useless.

"The invalid's family were shocked by the verdict. Apart from their natural grief at the loss of a relative in the prime of life, there was the further fact that he held a key position in the family business and that his guidance could ill be dispensed with.

"A Sister of Mercy advised a member of the family to pray to Father Sullivan to intercede for the patient. Novenas were offered and the invalid carried on his person a relic of Father Sullivan.

"Contrary to general expectations, the disease remained stationary and inactive for more than six years. Mr. X., while still somewhat of an invalid, was able to attend satisfactorily to his business. At the time of writing, he is still alive and has had ample time to make arrangements for the continued success of the family business.

"In 1937, Mrs. Y. had a serious operation, and was dying of septic poisoning, when a neighbour sent us an urgent request for prayers. The poor patient was the mother of three young children, so we had no hesitation about asking for the necessary miracle. We sent the little relic of Father Sullivan, and started a novena, begging his intercession. The moment the relic was applied Mrs. Y., who had not slept for ten nights and days, fell into a natural, quiet sleep, from which she awoke four hours later, feeling that death had passed her by. From that hour, the improvement continued, until a short time later she was as well as ever.

"Mrs. Y., her husband and all her neighbours attribute her recovery to the intercession of Father Sullivan, for she had been given up by both doctors and priest."

In the same year, 1937, Father Sullivan's intercession was asked for the sister of one of the community, who wrote as follows:

"About May 1937, my sister became alarmingly ill. When removed to a nursing home, she grew worse daily. Treatment proved useless, so the doctors decided to operate, though they regarded her case as almost hopeless.

"Then we remembered Father Sullivan, procured a little relic and applied it, begging him to obtain through our Blessed Lady from the Sacred Heart the grant of our petition—which was the success of the operation. We promised in return a novena of Masses in thanksgiving for the graces bestowed on Father Sullivan, and publication of the favour with a view to his Beatification. A number of us joined in a novena, begging his intercession.

"At once the patient began to improve, and in one week was able to leave the nursing home, cured without operation. In a short time she was able to resume her household duties, and for over three years now she has led a normal active life, and has had no return of the illness.

"We have no hesitation in attributing her recovery to the intercession of Father Sullivan."

Again in 1937 a relic of Father Sullivan was sent by a member of the community to a gentleman living in another town in the south of Ireland. In 1940, he wrote as follows:

"Reply to your letter *re* my serious illness and recovery now nearly three years ago, I have no doubt whatever that my cure was due to the relic you then sent, together with the prayers of the community and those of the Poor Clares here beside us.

"There was very little hope for me at the time, on the part either of doctors or priests, and I personally think the change caused some surprise. The rapid recovery was also wonderful. I was lying up for six weeks when I was allowed to sit up for half an hour, a longer period next day, and on the third day I could walk round the room. Before a week was up, I was taken out for a drive. I felt so recovered that I drove the car home, and in a few more days I was back in the shop. I have had no trouble since, and the last X-ray examination showed that there was no sign at all of any previous ulceration."

Another cure recorded by the nuns of the same convent was that of Mr. Z., in 1939. An operation for gallstones was urgently needed, but, owing to the patient's weak condition, it could not be performed. Prayers to Father Sullivan and the application of a relic brought relief. Mr. Z's recovery was steady from that day, and when he was examined later, no trace of gallstones could be found.

In the summer of 1936, the community of a well-known convent were holding an important celebration. After the religious ceremonies in the morning, the afternoon was to be devoted to outdoor entertainments. At about 2 p.m., heavy rain came on, and there were all the signs of a very wet afternoon. The good nuns were in despair. A priest who was one of their guests, suggested to one of them, who had known Father Sullivan well, to seek his intercession. He handed her a small picture and relic of Father Sullivan. She asked what prayers she should say, and, as the matter was urgent, the priest suggested something very short, such as an Our Father and three Hail Marys. The nun took the picture in her hand and said the suggested prayers. She had hardly finished when it was observed that the rain had ceased. Within a few minutes, the sun shone out, and a perfect summer's afternoon followed, enabling the whole programme to be carried out successfully.

The cure from fits of Herbert Hickey, a little boy living at Balgaddy, Clondalkin, Co. Dublin, occurred in 1937. The child was then nearly two years of age, having been born on November 14th, 1935. On the first Saturday in August he got a fit for the first time. There seemed to be no particular reason for it, as he had cut all his teeth, and there was no question of convulsions. He remained unconscious for some hours, and was taken to the Richmond Hospital at midnight. He was kept there for three weeks and X-rayed very thoroughly. It was thought at first that his head might be abnormal, or that he might have rickets. Neither proved to be the case, and he was discharged from hospital as being free from fits. In about a week's time he had another very bad fit, and was brought first to the Meath Hospital and then back to the Richmond. The house-surgeon there began to think that the fits must be epileptic. He questioned the mother as to whether there was epilepsy in either her family or that of her husband, but there was none. The doctor then told Mrs. Hickey that all that could be done was to protect the child if he got further fits.

Some short time before, Mr. Hickey had been purchasing fowl in the vicinity of Clongowes, and met a woman living out on the bog who told him that her child had suffered from fits, and had been blessed by Father Sullivan and cured. She told him that Father Sullivan was since dead, but that he could get a relic of him in Clongowes. Accordingly, the day after the child had been sent home from the Richmond Hospital, his father and mother drove him down to Clongowes. They were in a state of great anxiety on the way, watching him carefully lest he should get another fit and injure himself. On their arrival, one of the priests got a relic for them. They kept it constantly on the child, night and day, enclosed in a small leather case. Since that day he never had another fit, and grew strong and healthy. The account of his cure was given by his parents in August 1940, just three years after it had taken place.

In the early winter of 1939, Father Sullivan's intercession was sought on behalf of a young married woman by the nuns of a convent where he had been a lifelong friend. Mrs. S—— had had an operation for acute appendicitis, after which complications set in, and she became unconscious for some days with a temperature of 106 degrees. During this time, a friend of hers rang up one of the nuns to ask for prayers. This nun immediately sent a relic of Father Sullivan, and an improvement showed itself at once. Next day the nun put up a notice asking the nuns for prayers, and saying: "Perhaps Father John Sullivan would obtain the miracle, if asked." From that on, the patient rallied, left hospital early in February, and made a complete recovery.

Early in May 1940, Mrs. Hurley, of Hospital, Co. Limerick, was admitted to St. Vincent's Hospital, Dublin, in a condition requiring a serious operation if her life was to be saved. However, she was found to be so weak that an operation was out of the question. She grew steadily worse, and was not able to take even a drink of water without vomiting. One night she was comatose, and, in the opinion of both the nun in charge of the ward, and of the assistant matron, was dying. Another patient in the hospital had with her the Vow Crucifix of Father Sullivan, which has been mentioned in the Life. It was given to Mrs. Hurley on three successive nights, and she was told to ask Father Sullivan to cure her.

The improvement was remarkable. She asked for drinks and solids, and took both with no ill effects. Her condition improved daily, and in a short time a successful operation was performed. The patient recovered completely, and returned home in July.

In October 1940, Mrs. E. Maguire, of Clonkeen, Carbury, Co. Kildare, wrote as follows:

"About fourteen months ago, my husband was in the Adelaide Hospital, Dublin, suffering from an ulcer in his right eye. He had to remain six weeks, and get treatment from the surgeon sometimes twice daily. He was regarded as lucky to recover in that time, as his case was a serious one, the ulcer being of an unusual type.

"In August of this year while we were on holidays, the eye became very sore, painful and swollen. The third day it was so bad that it caused us great anxiety. I remembered that I had a relic of Father Sullivan with me. I applied the relic to my husband's eye, and prayed to Father Sullivan to obtain his cure. Thank God, the next morning the eye was completely cured. All the inflammation and swelling were gone, there was no pain, and though my husband drove home over a hundred miles that evening, he never once or since then had any return of eye trouble."

INDEX

Acropolis, 45
Adelaide Hospital, Dublin, 276
Aikenhead, Mary, Life and Work of, 200
Aikenhead, Mother Mary, 126
Alexandra, Queen, 42
Aloysius, Sister, Mount Sackville, Dublin, 151, 152
Alps, 161
Angel Gabriel, 203, 205, 206, 209
Angelus, Father, O.M. Cap., Church Street, 69
Anglican Church, 115
Anima Christi, 251
Annascaul, Co. Kerry, 113
Anne, St., 132
Annunciation, 203
Ardee, Convent of Mercy, 29
Arden, Lord, 10
Armagh, Sacred Heart Convent, 161, 164
Armstrong, Serjeant, 13, 16
Assumption, 267
Athens, 55
Athy, Convent of Mercy, 172
Augustine, St., 64, 66, 79, 81, 102, 105, 116, 230
Avonmore, Viscount, 19

Baggot Street, Convent of Mercy, 182
Baily, Robert, 16
Baily, Robert Francis, 16
Balkan tours, 162
Ballsbridge, 257
Ballsbridge, Poor Clare Colettines, 191
Ballyjamesduff, Poor Clare Convent, 167 sqq.
Ballymore-Eustace, 138, 154
Barry, Father Thomas, 7 sqq.
Basso Hibernicon, 10
Beecher, Rev. Nicholas, of Ballygibbin, 10
Benedict, St., 143
Berkeley Gold Medal, 45
Bernard, St., 227
Berry, Henry, 7
Berry, Dr. Parsons, 2
Bethlehem, 103
Bibliographie der Buchbindereiliteratur, 18
Blagden, Jessica, 50
Blair, Abbot Sir Hunter, O.S.B., 46
Blandyke Papers, 200
Blessed Sacrament, 87, 92, 135, 156, 157, 159, 165, 166, 168, 170, 172, 203, 212, 214, 236
Bodkin, Dr. Thomas, 47
Book of Kells, 18
Bowen, Henry, of Kildorrery, 33, 34
Bradshaw, Letitia (Sister M. Emilian, Irish Sisters of Charity), 207
Brennan, Mrs., Dublin, 132, 145
Brereton, Mary, 4
Brickfield Lane, Night Refuge, 71
Brigid, Sister, Mount Sackville, Dublin, 151
Brigid, St., 144
Brindisi, 55
Browne, Father Michael, S.J., 77 sqq., 82, 94, 115, 215
Browne, W. T. M., Naas, 122
Buck Whaley, Memoirs of, 18

Burke-Savage, Rev. Roland, S.J., 104
Bury, 38
Butler, Sir William, 102
Butt, Isaac, 13
Byrne, William, 155, 162
Byron, 7

Callan, Mother Leontia, Poor Clare Convent, Ballyjamesduff, 67
Calvary, 166, 215
Camm, Dom Bede, O.S.B., 30
Capuchin Fathers, Kilkenny, 74
Capuchin Friary, Church Street, Dublin, 69
Carlow, 43, 73 sq., 125
Carlow, Poor Clare Colettines, 74
Carrigaline river, 10
Castle Hyde, near Fermoy, 9
Castleisland, Presentation Convent, 169, 170, 187
Castlemagner, 10
Catholic Church, 40, 47, 63, 69, 147, 207, 209, 215, 223, 225, 230, 254, 255, 259
Chamberlain, Agnes Gertrude, Mother General, Irish Sister of Charity, 70 sq.
Charity, 212, 213
Children of Mary, 268
Christian, Jonathan, 13
Christmas, 62, 110, 134, 142, 167, 168, 222
Clane, 128, 135
Clane, Presentation Convent, 153, 161, 183, 234, 247
Clare, St., 223
Clarendon Street, Dublin, 71
Cleggan, near Clifden, Galway, 114
Clongowes Wood College, 22, 24, 48, 64, 66, 68, 76, 93, 94, 96, 97 sqq., 103, 104, 107, 109, 112, 114, 117 sqq., 123 sqq., 127, 128, 130, 133, 135 sqq., 138, 139, 142, 144, 148 sqq., 157, 160, 161, 169, 170, 183, 193, 196, 198, 231, 235, 246, 247, 248, 251, 252, 258, 266, 267, 274
Clongowes Wood College Museum, 29
Clongowes Wood College, People's Church, 100, 118, 119, 124, 136, 158, 159, 252, 261
College Historical Society, 12
Columban, Father, O.Cist., Mount St. Joseph's, Roscrea, 184, 185
Commons, Journal of 1747, 18
Confession, 62, 107, 166, 173
Connolly, Martin, 155
Coonan, Thomas, Kilclough, Straffan, 150, 151
Cook Father, S.J., 115
Cork, 2, 5, 10, 43, 51, 59, 60
Cork Examiner, 16
Cork Historical and Archæological Society, Journal of, 2
Cotter, Rev. G. S., 10
Cotter, Rev. John Rogerson, 8, 10
Cotter, Rev. Joseph Rogerson, 10
Cotter, Sir James Laurence, 10
Coughlan, Anthony, Sallins, 127, 128
Court-na-Farraga, Killiney, 31
Crashaw's Poems, 200
Cribbin, John, 157
Cribbin, Thomas, 113
Croker, Richard, 49
Cruise, Mrs., Monkstown, 126
Cullen, Dr. Matthew, Bishop of Kildare and Leighlin, 252
Cullen, Father James, S.J., 68, 69
Curé d'Ars, 195
Curran, John Philpot, 12

D'Alton, Father Joseph, S.J., 118 sq.
Daly, Father James, S.J., 94
Darlington, Father Joseph, S.J., 25
David Copperfield, 230
Debes, Sister Crescentienne, St. Joseph's, Mount Sackville, Dublin, 151, 152
Delphine de St. Paul, Sister, Little Sisters of the Poor, Kilmainham, 196
Devane, Father R. S., S.J., 242

Devenish, 28
Devenish, Island of, 26, 29, 31
de Vere, Aubrey, 111
Dickens, 230
Dictionary of National Biography, 9, 11, 13
Dilemma of John Haughton Steele, 25, 200
Disciples of our Lord, 223, 224
Divina Commedia, 18
Divine Office, 209
Domigan, Mrs., Dunshane, Brannoxtown, 135, 136, 145
Donegal, 113
Dominicans, 227
Donnybrook, Royal Hospital, 91, 93
Dorset Street, Dublin, 35
Dowse, Chief Baron, 13, 19, 52
Dublin, 1, 6, 9, 12, 20, 21, 31, 32, 41, 42, 47, 48, 52, 53, 55, 58, 59, 60, 63, 68, 69, 70, 74, 90, 91, 96, 115, 127, 135, 139, 140, 154, 155, 190, 192, 242, 243, 248, 266, 269, 273, 275, 276
Dublin Review, 45
Duff, Frank, Founder of Legion of Mary, 242
Dunne, Rev. Mother, Sacred Heart Convent, Armagh, 20 21
Dyer, Mrs., Sutton, 129, 145

Eccles Street, Dublin, 12, 13, 20, 21, 36
Edward VII, King, 42
Elizabeth, St., 203 sqq.
Emmaus, 223, 224
Enniskillen, 24
Erne, Lough, 26, 27, 29
Erne, Lord, 99
Euphrosiné du Sacré Cœur, Sister, Little Sisters of the Poor, Kilmainham, 197
Eve, 221, 228
Everard (or Ilard), Father John, 4
Exham, Constance, 31, 32
Exham, John, 31, 32
Exham, William, Q.C., 31
Extreme Unction, 248

Fair, Rev. Eric, D.D., University College, Galway, 98, 99
Farm Street, London, 63
Farmer, Edward, 13
Fenians, 14
Fidelis, Father, O.M. Cap., Church Street, 69, 74
Finlay, Father Peter, S.J., 137
Finlay, Father Tom, S.J., 47
Finn, Bernard, of Naas, 136, 146
Firhouse, Tallaght, Carmelite Monastery, 92, 169
Fishamble Street Theatre, Dublin, 13
Fitzgerald, Mary, 6
Fitzpatrick, P. V., 119
Fitzpatrick, W. J., F.S.A., 7, 119
Fitzwilliam Place, Dublin, 9, 21, 31, 51, 52, 72
France, 23, 52, 53, 56, 57, 59, 60, 67, 227
Francesca, Sister Mary, Children's Hospital, Cappagh, 70
Francis, St., Third Order of, 59
Franciscan Order, 69, 70, 142
Fullam, Mrs. Laurence, 134, 135, 145

Gallen, Ferbane, Priory, 195, 196
Galway, 112
Garry, Kitty, 133, 134
Garvey, John, D.L., Bray, 259
Gavin, Father Michael, S.J., 63
Gaynor, Mother Mary John, 70
Gerrard, Capt. Edward, Royal Artillery, 116
Gladstone, 14, 15, 31
Glencairn, 49, 50, 57
Glencar, Kerry, 60
Glories of Mary, 106
Gortnacross, 5
Grace, 217
Greece, 43 sqq., 47, 55, 59, 100, 102, 104
Greek, 24, 43, 51, 100, 105, 229, 241
Guinness's Brewery, 72, 240
Gull Island, 27
Gwynn, Stephen, *Reminiscences of a Literary Man*, 49

Hail Mary, 141, 202, 273
Hampton, Drumcondra, Carmelite Monastery, 182, 183
Harcourt Street, Dublin, 31
Harold's Cross, Hospice for the Dying, 69, 91, 191
Haughton, Rev. Samuel, S.F. T.C.D., 29
Healy, Father, of Bray, 49
Healy, Maurice, K.C., 51
Heaven, 217
Hell, 79, 214
Henry, Denis, K.C., 57
Hermathena, 38
Hickey, Herbert, Balgaddy, Clondalkin, 273, 274
Highgate Hospital, London, 47
Hingston, Rev. James, LL.D., Vicar of Cloyne, 8
Historical and Topographical Notes on Buttevant, Castletownroche, Doneraile, Mallow, by Col. Grove White, 5
Hodder river, 86, 90
Hogan, Rev. E., S.J., 26
Holy Communion, 66, 87, 148, 155, 209, 246, 250, 267
Holy Ghost, 170, 186, 187, 205, 207, 209, 210, 214, 217 sqq., 221, 225, 226, 229
Hooks, Jeremiah, Naas, 121
Humility, 216, 219
Hurley, Mrs., Hospital, Limerick, 275

Ightermurragh, 10
Ignatius Loyola, St., 72, 85, 143, 167, 174, 223
Ignatius Loyola, St., *Spiritual Exercises*, 77
Invincibles, 15, 49, 51
Irish Monthly, 30

Jackson, Arthur Stanley, Q.C., 12
Jephson, Hon. Col., 3
Jephson Norreys, Sir Denham, 6
Jervis Street Hospital, Dublin, 132
Job, 208
John Berchmans, St., 80
John Chrysostom, St., 105
John of the Cross, St., 72
John Baptist, St., 208, 209, 211
John, St., Evangl., 188, 212, 213, 226, 233
Joseph, Mother Stanislaus, Mercy Convent, Baggot Street, 72
Joseph, Sister Mary, Sisters of Charity, Donnybrook, 191
Joseph, Sister Mary, Mount Sackville, 151, 152
Joseph, St., 214, 220
Judas, 215, 227

Kane, Capt., R.N., 'of the *Calliope*,' 49
Kell, Ann, 5
Kell, Mary, 5
Kell, Pedder, 5
Kell, Randal (jun.), 4 sqq.
Kell, Randal (sen.), 4, 5
Kell, Robert Philpot, 5
Kell, William, 5
Kelly, Father Edward, S., J., 68
Kelly, Father Tom, S. J., 68
Kelly, Father William, S. J., 68, 69
Kenney, Father Peter, S.J., 153
Keogh, Justice, 49, 50
Kilmainham, Little Sisters of the Poor, 22, 196
King's Inns, 41
Kottabos, 37

Lancashire, 88, 89
Latin, 24, 81, 86, 88, 99, 101, 105, 229, 237
Lavallière, Eve, 232
Le Havre, 52
Lincoln's Inn, 42
Linus, Sister Mary, 69 sqq.
Litany of the Holy Name, 251
Livy, 95, 96
Lloyd, Desmond, 260
Lloyd, Mrs. Wilmot, 31
Lohort Castle, 10
London, 11, 42, 47, 55, 58
Longworth, Theresa, 19, 20
Louis of France, St., 227
Lower Leeson Street, Sacred Heart Convent, 17, 175 sqq.

Luke, St., 203, 209, 211, 212, 213, 216, 220, 221, 223, 224, 226, 228, 229
Lynch, Anne, 6
Lynch, Canon J. F., 5
Lynch, John (jun.), 6
Lynch, John (sen.), 5 sq.
Lynch, Miss, 36
Lynch, Robert, 6
Lynch, William, 6
Lysaght, Ned, 3

Macedonia, 43
Madden, D. Owen, 7
Madden, Dr. R. R., 7
Magdalen, 46
Magi, 222
Magnificat, 209, 223
Maguire, John Francis, 16, 38
Maguire, E., Clonkeen, Carbury, Co. Kildare, 276
Mahaffy, Dr. J. P., 38, 45
Maher, Father Michael, S.J., 87
Malachy, Brother, O. Cist., Mount St. Joseph's, Roscrea, 187
Mallow, 1 sqq., 7, 9, 11, 12, 14, 16, 43
Mapother, Dr., 47
Margoliouth, Professor D. S., 39 sq.
Mark, St., 214
Martha, St., 227
Martin, Father, General of the Society of Jesus, 37
Mary Magdalen, St., 102, 212, 213, 226, 227, 233
Mass, 62, 67, 86, 91 sq., 106, 113, 114, 119, 124 sqq., 128 sqq., 137, 148, 149, 153, 154, 166, 169, 170, 172, 178, 183, 188, 189, 193, 211, 223, 228, 235, 247, 248, 252, 256, 268, 271
Mathew, Father, Apostle of Temperance, 16
Mathew, Lord Justice, 43, 75
Matthew, St., 214
Maturin, Dr., 36
Maturin, Father, 36
Mayne, Robert, Solicitor, 13
Maynooth, 28, 123
Merrion Square, Dublin, 52, 54, 59
Messiah, The, 13
Messias, 205
Midleton, Cork, 12, 36, 52
Milltown Park, Dublin, 37, 52, 69, 84, 90, 91, 93
Minch, Capt. Sidney B., 100
Mitchelstown, Cork, Presentation Convent, 177 sqq.
Modernism, 37
Molaise, St., 31
Molony, Sir Thomas, Vice-Chancellor, Dublin University, 41, 42
Monica, St., 66, 81, 105, 175, 230
Mooney, Sister Mary Ursula, 71
Moore, Thomas, 9 sqq.
Moore, Thomas, Journal and Correspondence of, 9
Morley, 15
Mount Anville, Dublin, Sacred Heart Convent, 144, 159, 172 sqq., 190
Mount Athos, Monastery of, 44, 51
Mountjoy Square, Dublin, 21
Muratorian fragment, 95
Murphy, Judge James, Q.C., 49, 50, 51, 57, 63
Murphy, Mrs., postmistress, Ballymore-Eustace, 138, 139
Murphy, Mrs., 49, 58
Murphy, Rt. Hon. Edward Sullivan, Lord Justice, 50
Museum, National, Dublin, 17, 18
McCann, James, 74
McCann, Mrs., 74
McConnell, Father James P., S.J., 115
McDermott, Archdeacon, 158, 159
McDonagh, Francis, 13
McSwinney, R. F., 43

Naas, 43, 122, 136
Naish, John, Lord Chancellor of Ireland, 13
National University, 34, 60
Nazareth, 218, 220, 233
Nevin, John, Betaghstown, 152
Newman, Cardinal, 102, 106, 263
Nolan, Father Patrick, S.J., 85

O'Brien, R. Barry, *Dublin Castle and the Irish People*, 15
O'Brien, Judge William, P.C., 36, 43, 51, 52, 59, 67, 73 sq.
O'Brien, Sister Mary Joseph Stanislaus, 72 sqq.
O'Brien, William, M.P., 43
O'Connell, Daniel, 118, 119
O'Connell, Maurice, 118
O'Connell, Morgan, 118
O'Connor, Dr. Charles, of Celbridge, 124, 148
O'Doherty, John, 28
O'Hagan, Lord, 13
O'Kiely, Mrs. Esther, 60
Old Munster Circuit, 51
Oliver, Father, O.Cist., Mount St. Joseph's, Roscrea, 185 sqq.
O'Neill, Eliza, 20, 130
O'Neill, Father George, S.J., 14
Onomasticon Goedelicum, 26
Orby, 49
O'Riordan, Jack, 64
O'Riordan, Mrs., 66
O'Sullivan, Father Charles, P.P., Adrigole, 187, 188
Otis-Cox, Miss Carrie, 52
Otis-Cox, Mrs. John, 67
Our Lady, 100, 106, 127, 138, 143, 165, 197, 203, 204, 205 sqq., 213 sq., 218, 220, 225, 229, 265, 266 sq., 271
Our Father, 141, 201, 211, 273
Our Lord, 65, 103, 106, 110, 165, 167, 173, 176, 187, 188, 195, 203, 204, 208, 211 sqq., 231 sqq., 237, 260
Oxford, 45, 46, 117

Paley, 39
Palles, Chief Baron, 13, 14
Palmer, Professor, 34, 38
Park, Virginia, 67
Parnell, 15
Passion, 81, 105, 172, 176
Patrick, St., 175, 223
Paul, St., 102, 117, 186, 223
Pedder, Belcher, 5
Perfection, 221
Perry, A. W., 44, 48
Peter, Father, O.M. Cap., Church Street, 69
Peter, St., 188, 211, 213, 226
Pettit, Canon, Dublin, 182 sq.
Philpot, Elizabeth, 4 sqq.
Philpot, Robert, 4, 5
Pike Card Case, 59
Pioneer Total Abstinence Association, 68
Pius IX, Pope, 46
Pius X, Pope, *Lamentabili*, 37
Portora, Royal School, 24 sqq.
Poverty, 222
Power, Emily, 129, 130
Prayer, 222 sq.
Protestant Church, 25, 79
Protestantism, 82, 259
Pue's Occurrences, 2
Purbrick, Father, Provincial Society of Jesus, 38
Purser, Dr. Louis Claude, vi, 30
Purser, Professor, 33, 38

Raglan Road, Dublin, 9
Rahan College, 76
Rakes of Mallow, 4, 14
Rathangan, Convent of Mercy, 171, 172
Rathfarnham Castle, Dublin, 72, 103, 127, 155, 161, 183, 190, 192, 200, 234 sqq., 257
Rathfarnham, Loreto Abbey, 243
Reform Club, 43, 47
Rice, Archdeacon, 177, 178
Richmond Hospital, Dublin, 274
Robertson Commission, 34
Robinson, Dr. John, M.O., Johnstown, 131
Roche, Father George R., S.J., 98, 251 sqq.
Rochestown, Cork, 69
Rome, 46, 47, 59, 96, 99, 101
Ronan, Stephen, K.C., 57
Rosary, 64, 131, 225, 267
Roscrea, Cistercian Abbey, 184 sqq.
Roscrea, Sacred Heart Convent, 144
Rourke, John, Sallins, 128
Royal Dublin Society, 2

Royal Meath Militia, 7
Royal University, Dublin, 91
Russell, Lord, of Killowen, 222
Russell, Rt. Hon. Lord John, M.P., 9
Ryan, Mrs. G. M., Dublin, 264, 265

Sacred Heart, 81, 117, 226, 235, 265
Salonika, 54
Sandymount, 56
Sayce, *Empires of the East*, 38
Shakespeare, 52
Sheehan, Canon, 14
Shelley, 96
Simmonscourt, Dublin, Poor Clare Colettines, 200
Sin, 228
Sisters of Charity, Hospice, Harold's Cross, 69
Sisters of Charity, Mount St. Anne's, Milltown, 92
Sisters of Charity, St. Mary's Hospital, Cappagh, 243
Sisters of Mercy, Brickfield Lane, 71
Sisters of Mercy, Elphin, 158
Skibbereen, Cork, Convent of Mercy, 182
Smythe, Hon. Eliza Maria, 6
Smyth, Mrs. W., Clongowes Wood College, 155, 246
Society of Jesus, English Province, 36, 84, 87, 115
Society of Jesus, Irish Province, 21, 30, 37, 52, 60, 67, 68, 71, 75, 76, 84, 87, 117, 161, 162, 164, 167, 184, 185, 199, 230, 237, 255, 261
Sophocles, 96
Souls, Holy, 166
Spencer, Lord, 15
Spencer, Michael Kevin, Ballymoney, Wexford, 269
Stack, Rev. Canon C. M., Carrickmacross, 25
St. Aloysius College, S.J., Sydney, 69
Stanislaus Joseph, Rev. Mother, Convent of Mercy, Baggot Street, 21, 23
Stanislaus, St., 76
Stations of the Cross, 107, 166, 202, 215
Steele, Dr. William, 25, 27 sqq.
Steele, Frederick, 29
Steele, John Haughton, 25, 26, 28 sqq., 64, 66, 99, 262
Steele, Rev. William B., 25
St. Francis Xavier's, Upper Gardiner Street, 68, 137, 261
St. George's Church, George's Place, Dublin, 20
St. Macartan's Seminary, Monaghan, 28
St. Moritz, 44
Stonyhurst College, 84 sqq., 200
St. Peter's, Rome, 256
Strangford, Lionel, 5th Viscount, 7
St. Stanislaus College, Tullamore, *see* Tullabeg
Students' Magazine, 34
Studies, 14
St. Ultan's Hospital, Dublin, 269
St. Vincent's Hospital, Dublin, 156, 248, 275
Sullivan, Anne, 5, 12
Sullivan, Anne, her daughter, 12
Sullivan, Annie, 17, 23, 58
Sullivan, Charlotte, 52
Sullivan, Sir Edward, Lord Chancellor of Ireland, 1, 6, 7, 9, 10, 12 sqq., 35, 42, 44, 49, 51, 58, 99; birth, 12; enters Trinity College, 12; called to Bar, 12; rise to Lord Chancellorship, 13; election to Parliament, 14; political influence, 15; break with Gladstone, 15; marries Elizabeth Baily, 16; Yelverton case, 19; death, 42
Sullivan, Sir Edward, *Stray Shots*, 15
Sullivan, Sir Edward, 2nd baronet, authority on bookbinding, 17 sq.; schoolfellow of Oscar Wilde, 45; godfather of Mr. Justice Murphy, 50, 75

Sullivan, Edward, 1, 5, 6, 7, 9, 10, 12
Sullivan, Elizabeth, 17
Sullivan, James (jun.), 12
Sullivan, James (sen.), 6 sq., 8, 9
Sullivan, James, M.D., 6
Sullivan, Father John, S.J., birth, 20; childhood, 21 sqq.; school-days at Portora, 24 sqq.; meets Gladstone, 31; drowning of his brother, Robert, 31; enters Trinity College, 33; connection with Tyrrell family, 33 sqq.; article in *Hermathena*, 39 sq.; called to Bar, 42; death of his father, 42; travels, 43 sqq.; with Dr. Mahaffy in Greece, 45 sqq.; friendship with family of Judge Murphy, 49 sqq.; with Judge William O'Brien, 51; reminiscences of Miss Otis-Cox, 52 sqq.; of Mrs. O'Kiely, 60 sqq.; received into Church, 63; influence of his mother in conversion, 65; friendship with Jesuit Fathers, 68 sq.; with Sisters of Charity and Mercy, 69 sq.; enters novitiate of Society of Jesus, 75; testimonies of fellow-novices, 77 sqq.; takes first Vows, 82; philosophy at Stonyhurst, 84 sqq.; theology at Milltown Park, 90; ordained, 92; master at Clongowes, 94; testimonies of former pupils, 98 sqq.; on vacations, 112 sqq.; tertianship at Tullabeg, 114 sqq.; work in People's Church at Clongowes, 118 sqq.; testimony of doctors, 145 sqq.; spiritual favours, 148 sqq.; episode at Clane convent, 153 sqq.; ascetical practices, 156 sqq. retreats: Armagh, 164 sqq.; Waterford, 166; Ballyjamesduff, 167 sqq.; Firhouse, 169; Castleisland, 169 sq.; Swinford, 171; Rathangan, 171 sq.; Athy, 172; Mt. Anville, Dundrum, 172 sqq.; Mitchelstown, 177; Roscrea, Cistercian Abbey, 184 sqq. Indifference to food, 181 sqq.; his confidence in direction, 189 sqq.; teachings, 199 sqq. (see headings in text); impressions of retreat to novices, 228 sqq.; Rector of Rathfarnham Castle, 234 sqq.; kindness to juniors, 238 sq.; interest in Retreat House, 242; illness, 247; death, 252; characteristics, 253 sqq.; his contempt of self, 260; favours attributed to his intercession after death, 264 sqq.
Sullivan, Lady, wife of Lord Chancellor, 20, 21, 23, 60, 130
Sullivan, Lady, wife of Sir William, 54
Sullivan, Mary, 6
Sullivan, Robert, 18, 31, 32
Sullivan, Sir William, R.M., 19, 21, 31, 48, 53, 59, 67, 161, 249, 250, 251, 255 sq., 260; career, 18; baptized surreptitiously, 21; at Father John's deathbed, 249; affection for Father John, 260
Sullivan, William, Solicitor, 12
Surflen, John, 5
Swilly, Lough, 113
Swinford, Convent of Mercy, 171

Taranto, 96
Tears, Holy, 165
Temple Street, Children's Hospital, 239
Teresa, St., 72, 167, 204, 219, 223
Thecla, Mother, Irish Sisters of Charity, 156, 250 sq.
Thom's Directory, 13
Tomkin, Father Nicholas J., S.J., 123
Tractarian School, 36
Tranquilla, Rathmines, Carmel of the Nativity, 182
Tricoupis, M., Prime Minister of Greece, 43, 55
Trinity College, Dublin, 12, 25, 26, 27, 29, 30, 33 sqq., 39, 41, 44, 45, 48, 54, 260
Tullabeg, 72 sq., 76, 82, 87, 91, 114 sqq., 201, 229, 259

Twiss, Dr. Henry Fitzpatrick (formerly Berry), 2, 5 sqq., 12, 14
Tyrrell, Father George, 35 sqq.
Tyrrell, Professor, 33 sqq., 37 sqq., 45
Tyrrell, Willie, 35

Undercliffe, Killiney, 31
University Church, St. Stephen's Green, 151
Ursuline Convent, Cork, 62
Ursuline Convent, Waterford, 166 sq.

Wales, Prince of, 42
Wales, Princess of, 42
Walsh, Archbishop, 92
Walsh, Margaret, Kilmurray, Enfield, 131
Wilde, Oscar, 45 sqq.
Wicklow, Dominican Convent, 202
Williams, Mrs., 126
Wilson, Herbert, K.C., vi, 44, 48
Wordsworth, 262

Xavier, St. Francis, 223

Yacovides, Demetrius, 53 sq.
Yelverton, Barry, 12
Yelverton trial, 19, 20

Zachaeus, 237
Zachary, 203 sqq., 208 sqq.